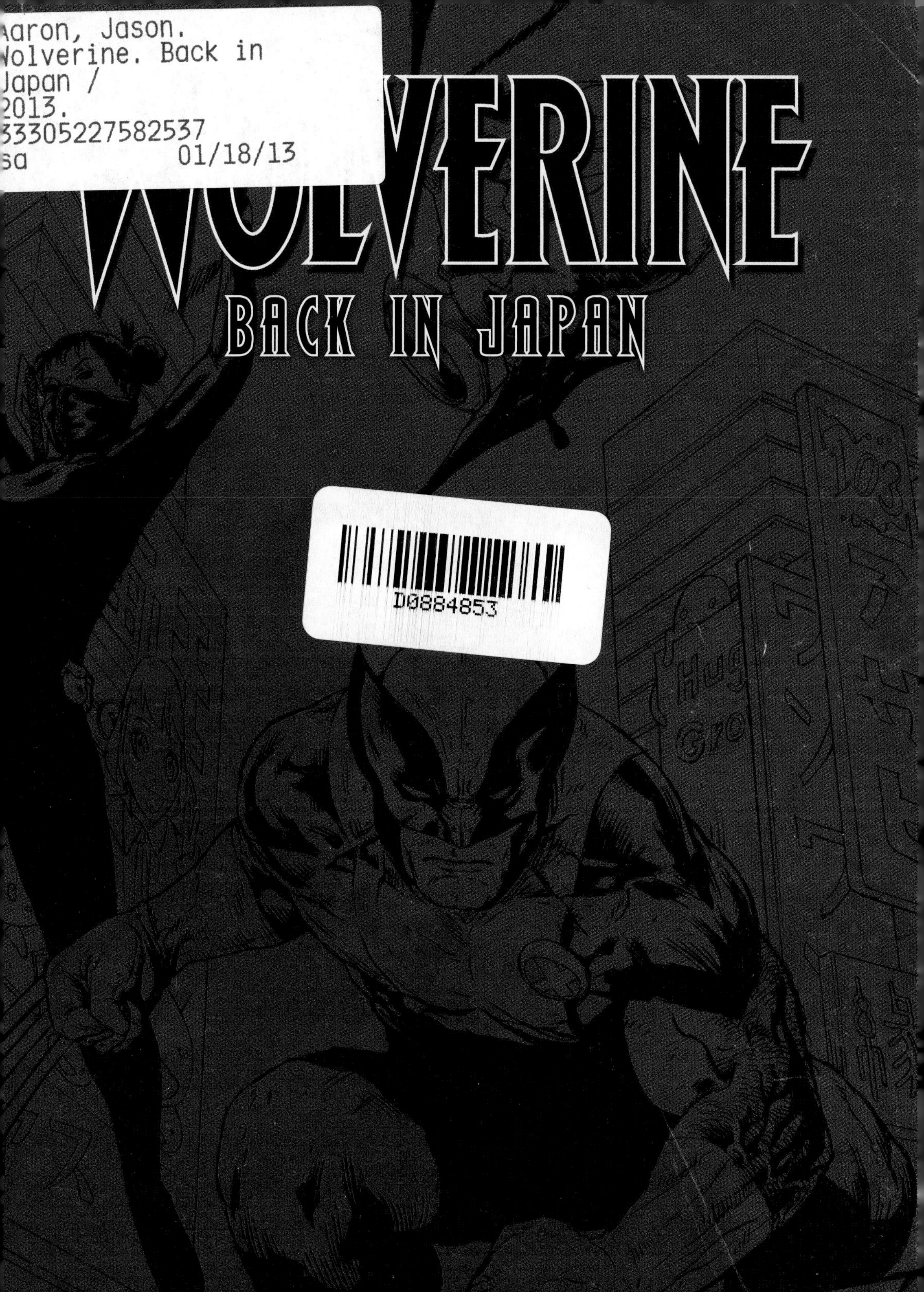
WOLVERINE
BACK IN JAPAN

VERINE: BACK IN JAPAN. Contains material originally published in magazine form as WOLVERINE #300-304. First printing 2012. Hardcover ISBN# 978-0-7851-6143-1. Softcover ISBN# 978-0--6144-8. Published by MARVEL WORLDWIDE, INC., a subsidiary of MARVEL ENTERTAINMENT, LLC. OFFICE OF PUBLICATION: 135 West 50th Street, New York, NY 10020. Hardcover: $24.99 per copy in the U.S. and $27.99 in Canada (GST #R127032852). Softcover: $19.99 per copy in the U.S. and $21.99 in Canada (GST #R127032852). dian Agreement #40668537. **Printed in the U.S.A.** ALAN FINE, EVP - Office of the President, Marvel Worldwide, Inc. and EVP & CMO Marvel Characters B.V.; DAN BUCKLEY, Publisher & President - Print, Animation gital Divisions; JOE QUESADA, Chief Creative Officer; TOM BREVOORT, SVP of Publishing; DAVID BOGART, SVP of Operations & Procurement, Publishing; RUWAN JAYATILLEKE, SVP & Associate sher, Publishing; C.B. CEBULSKI, SVP of Creator & Content Development; DAVID GABRIEL, SVP of Publishing Sales & Circulation; MICHAEL PASCIULLO, SVP of Brand Planning & Communications; 'KEEFE, VP of Operations & Logistics; DAN CARR, Executive Director of Publishing Technology; SUSAN CRESPI, Editorial Operations Manager; ALEX MORALES, Publishing Operations Manager; STAN Chairman Emeritus. For information regarding advertising in Marvel Comics or on Marvel.com, please contact John Dokes, SVP Integrated Sales and Marketing, at jdokes@marvel.com. For Marvel cription inquiries, please call 800-217-9158. **Manufactured between 5/7/2012 and 6/4/2012 (hardcover), and 5/7/2012 and 12/3/2012 (softcover), by R.R. DONNELLEY, INC., SALEM, VA, USA.**

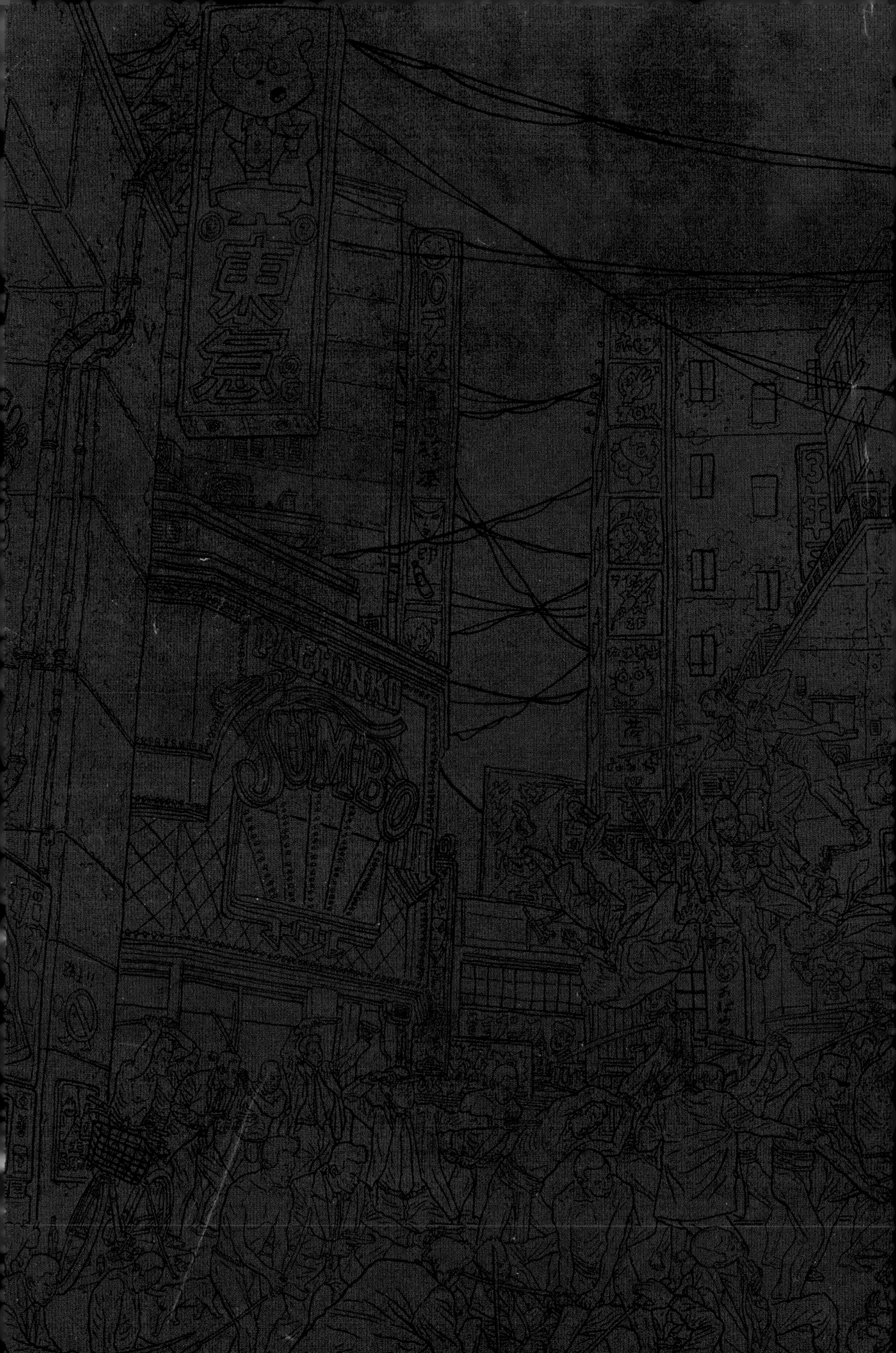
PACHINKO
JUMBO

Collection Editor JENNIFER GRÜNWALD • Assistant Editors ALEX STARBUCK & NELSON RIBEIRO
Editor, Special Projects MARK D. BEAZLEY • Senior Editor, Special Projects JEFF YOUNGQUIST
Senior Vice President of Sales DAVID GABRIEL • SVP of Brand Planning & Communications MICHAEL PASCIULLO
Book Design JEFF POWELL

Editor in Chief AXEL ALONSO • Chief Creative Officer JOE QUESADA
Publisher DAN BUCKLEY • Executive Producer ALAN FINE

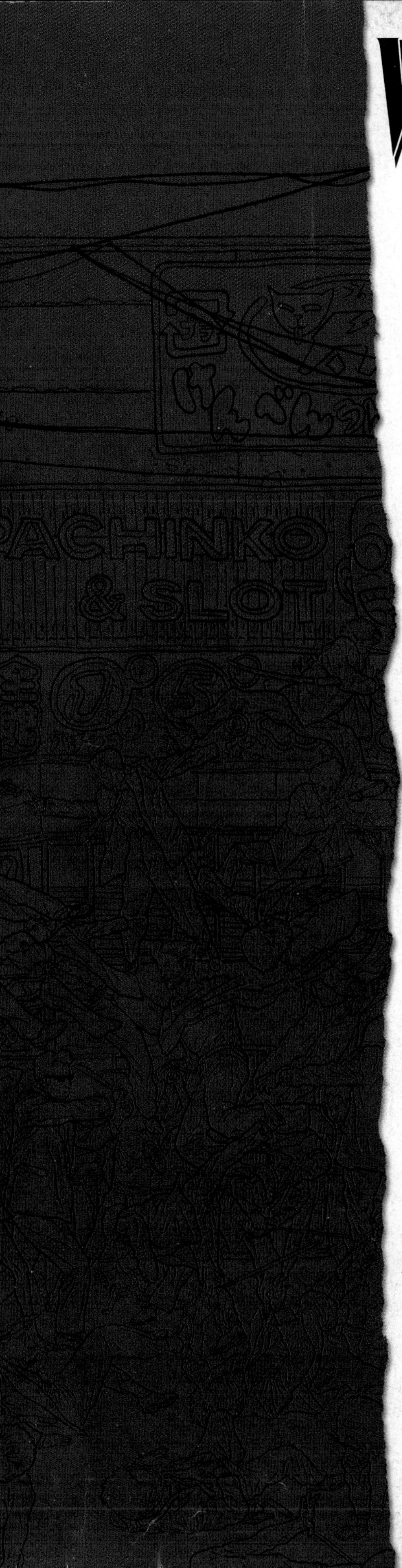

WOLVERINE BACK IN JAPAN

WRITER **JASON AARON**

#300

ART, CHAPTERS 1, 4 & 7
ADAM KUBERT WITH **PAUL MOUNTS**
ART, CHAPTERS 2 & 5
RON GARNEY WITH **JASON KEITH**
ART, CHAPTERS 3 & 6
STEVE SANDERS WITH **SOTOCOLOR**
LETTERER **VC'S CORY PETIT**
COVER ART **ADAM KUBERT** & **LAURA MARTIN**

#301

ART, CHAPTERS 8, 11 & 12
BILLY TAN WITH **JASON KEITH**
ART, CHAPTERS 9 & 10
STEVE SANDERS WITH **SOTOCOLOR**
LETTERER **VC'S CORY PETIT**
COVER ART **OLIVIER COIPEL** & **JUSTIN PONSOR**

#302

ART, CHAPTERS 13, 15 & 16
BILLY TAN WITH **JASON KEITH**
ART, CHAPTERS 14 & 16
STEVE SANDERS WITH **SOTOCOLOR**
LETTERER **VC'S CLAYTON COWLES**
COVER ART **ART ADAMS** & **PETER STEIGERWALD**

#303

ART, CHAPTERS 17 & 20
BILLY TAN WITH **MATT MILLA** &
RACHELLE ROSENBERG
ART, CHAPTERS 18 & 19
STEVEN SANDERS WITH **CHRIS SOTOMAYOR**
ART, CHAPTER 19
PACO DIAZ WITH **JIM CHARALAMPIDIS**
LETTERER **VC'S CHRIS ELIOPOULOS**
COVER ART **BRANDON PETERSON**

#304

ART **STEVE DILLON, RON GARNEY** &
PAUL PELLETIER WITH **DAVE MEIKIS,**
MIKE PERKINS, JEFTE PALO, DANIEL ACUÑA,
STEVE SANDERS & **RENATO GUEDES**
COLOR ART **MATTHEW WILSON,**
MATT MILLA, RAIN BEREDO,
ANDY TROY & **CHRIS SOTOMAYOR**
LETTERER **VC'S CORY PETIT**
COVER ART **DALE KEOWN** & **JASON KEITH**

ASSISTANT EDITORS **JODY LEHEUP,**
SEBASTIAN GIRNER & **JAKE THOMAS**
EDITOR **JEANINE SCHAEFER** GROUP EDITOR **NICK LOWE**

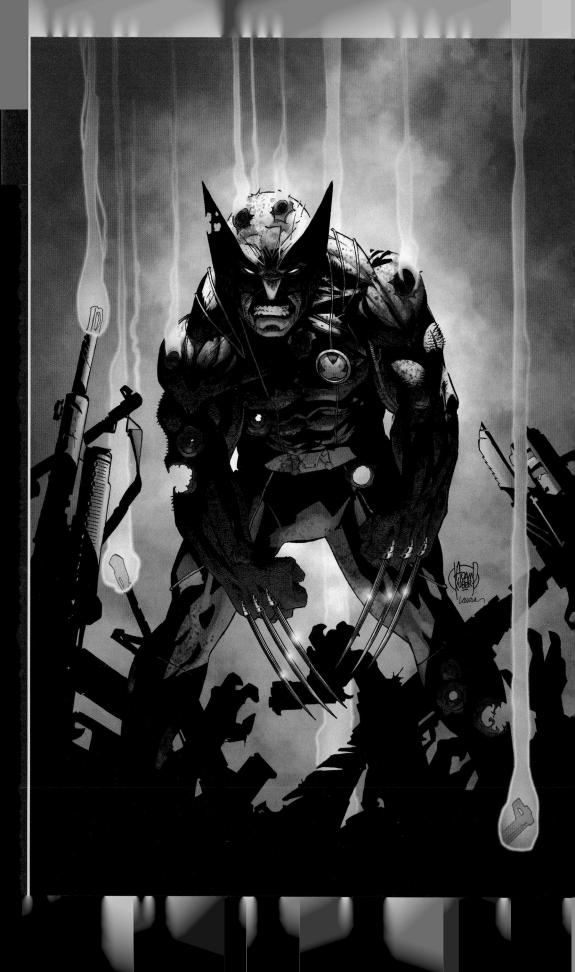

Many years ago, a secret government organization abducted the man called Logan, a mutant possessing razor-sharp bone claws and the ability to heal from any wound. In their attempt to create the perfect living weapon, the organization bonded the unbreakable metal Adamantium to his skeleton. The process was excruciating and by the end, there was little left of the man known as Logan. He had become...

WOLVERINE

PREVIOUSLY...

In his long life, Wolverine has grown to love the country of Japan like a second home. Years ago, it was there that he came across a dying mother with her daughter and promised the woman he would raise the child. Wolverine adopted Amiko Kobayashi but his life as an X-Man keeps him from spending much time with his daughter.

Now, trouble is brewing in the streets of Tokyo, and Wolverine is convinced that someone is trying to incite a mob war between the Hand ninja sect and the Yakuza. He must return to Japan to set things right.

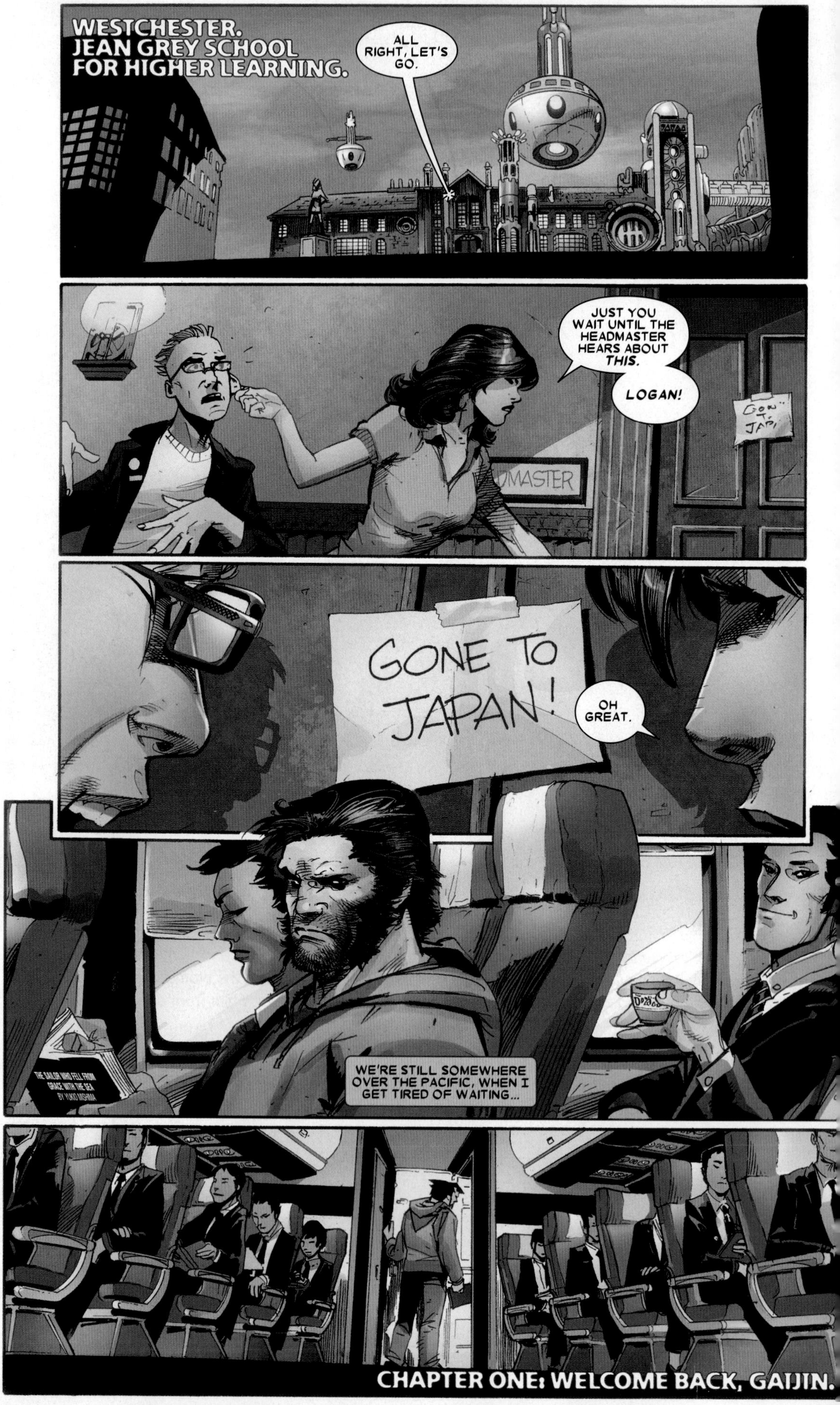
WESTCHESTER. JEAN GREY SCHOOL FOR HIGHER LEARNING.
ALL RIGHT, LET'S GO.
JUST YOU WAIT UNTIL THE HEADMASTER HEARS ABOUT *THIS.*
LOGAN!
GONE TO JAPAN!
OH GREAT.
THE SAILOR WHO FELL FROM GRACE WITH THE SEA BY YUKIO MISHIMA
WE'RE STILL SOMEWHERE OVER THE PACIFIC, WHEN I GET TIRED OF WAITING...
CHAPTER ONE: WELCOME BACK, GAIJIN.

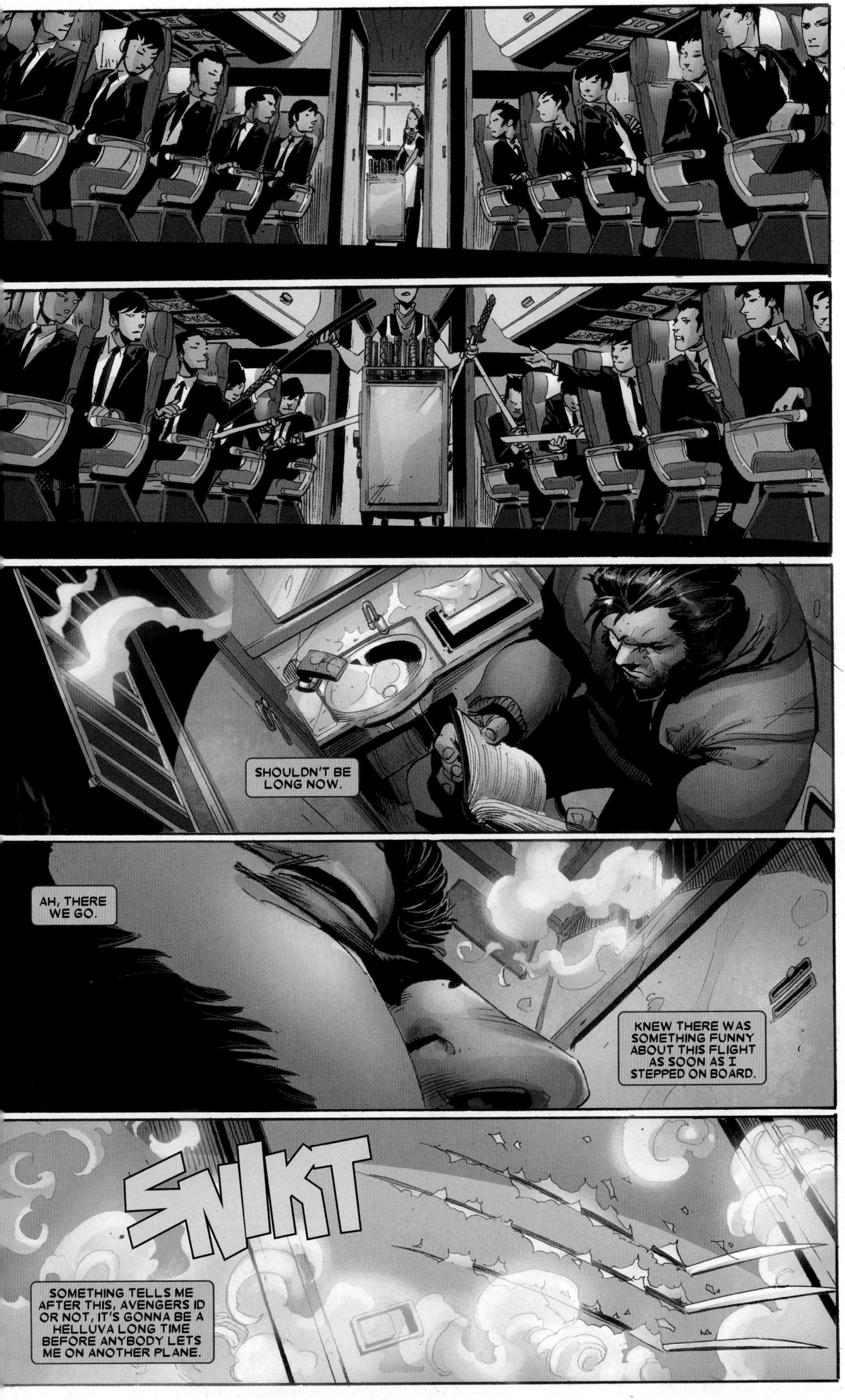
SHOULDN'T BE LONG NOW.
AH, THERE WE GO.
KNEW THERE WAS SOMETHING FUNNY ABOUT THIS FLIGHT AS SOON AS I STEPPED ON BOARD.
SNIKT
SOMETHING TELLS ME AFTER THIS, AVENGERS ID OR NOT, IT'S GONNA BE A HELLUVA LONG TIME BEFORE ANYBODY LETS ME ON ANOTHER PLANE.

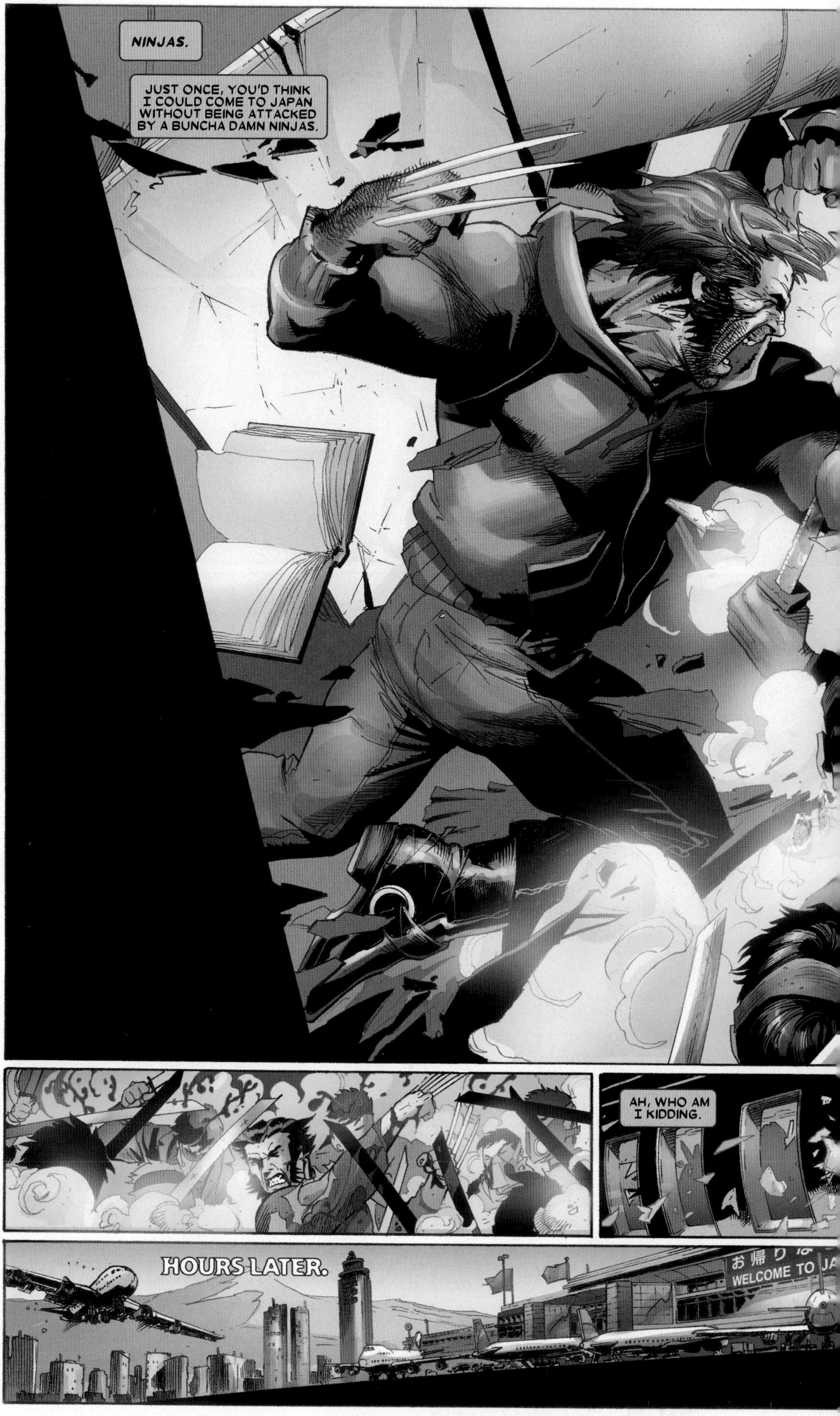
NINJAS.
JUST ONCE, YOU'D THINK I COULD COME TO JAPAN WITHOUT BEING ATTACKED BY A BUNCHA DAMN NINJAS.
AH, WHO AM I KIDDING.
HOURS LATER.

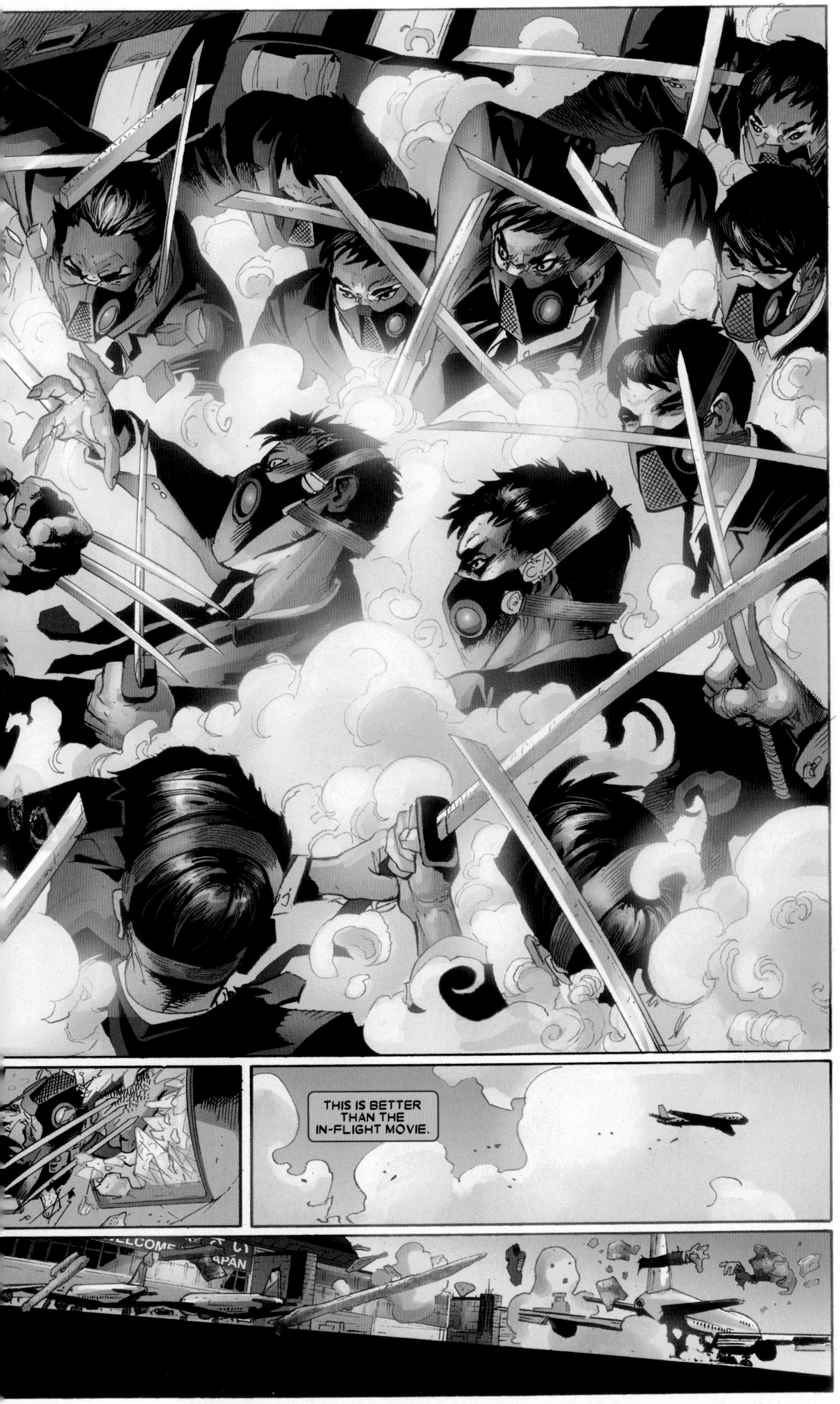
THIS IS BETTER THAN THE IN-FLIGHT MOVIE.

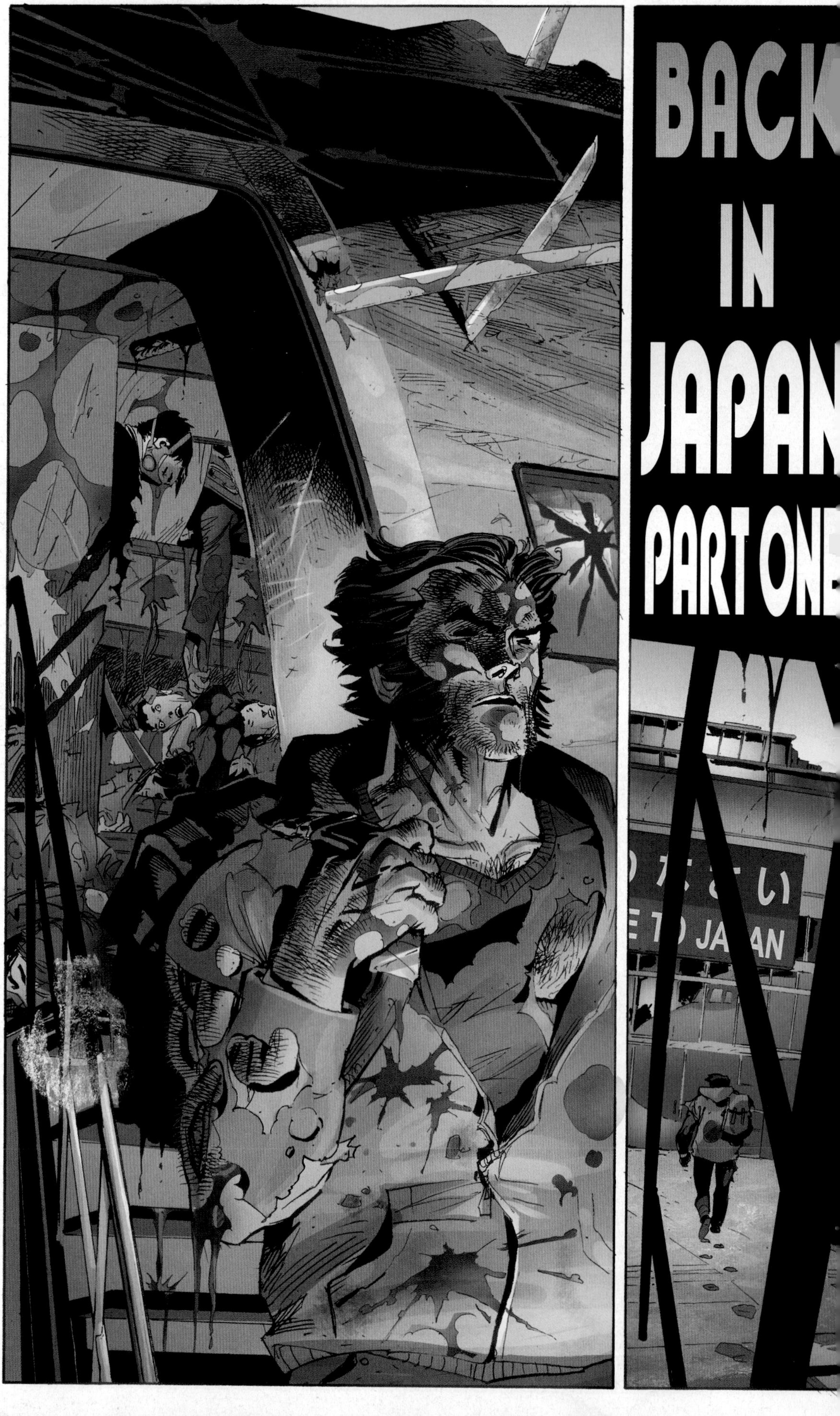
BACK
IN
JAPAN
PART ONE

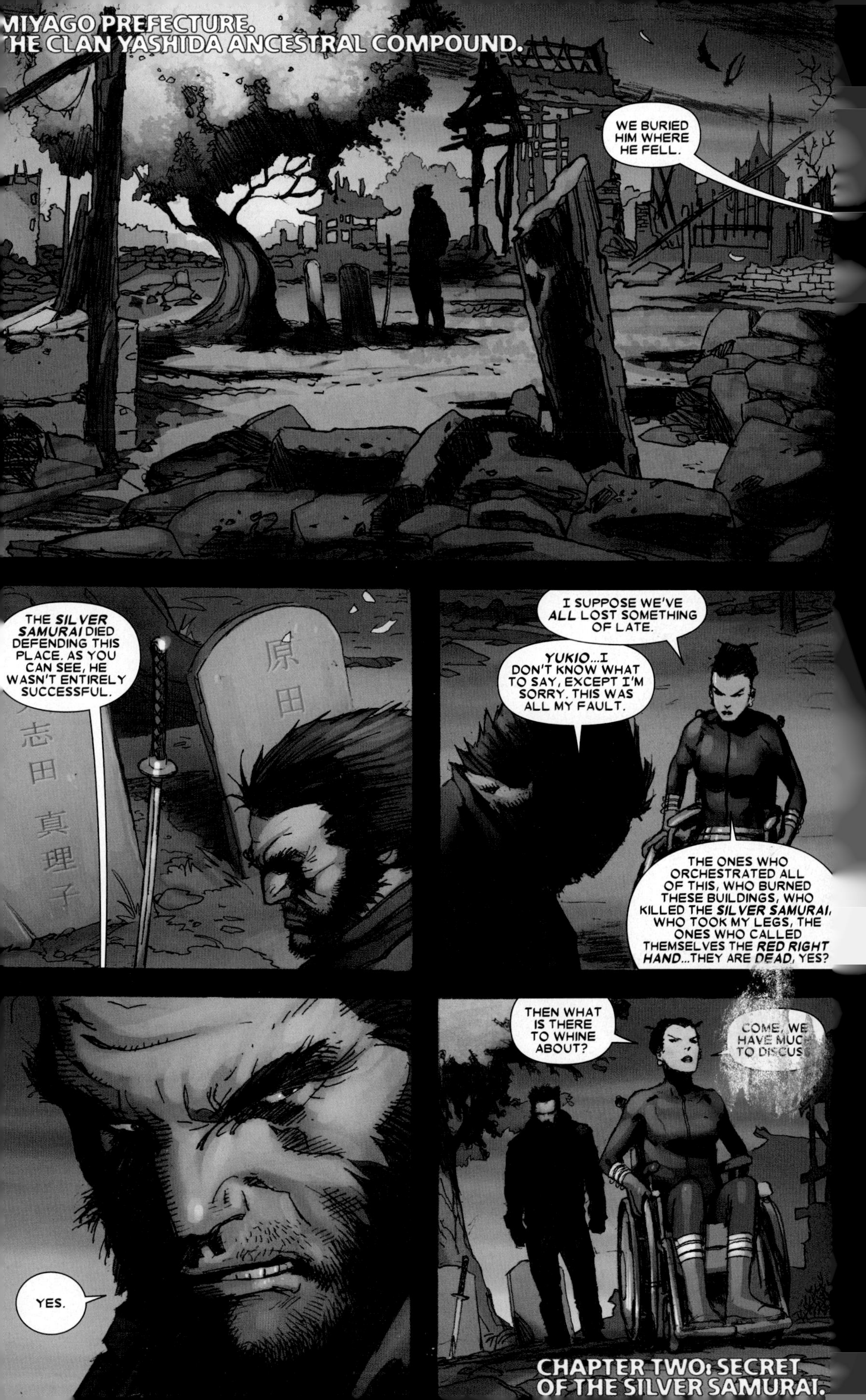
MIYAGO PREFECTURE.
HE CLAN YASHIDA ANCESTRAL COMPOUND.
WE BURIED HIM WHERE HE FELL.
THE SILVER SAMURAI DIED DEFENDING THIS PLACE. AS YOU CAN SEE, HE WASN'T ENTIRELY SUCCESSFUL.
原田
志田 真理子
I SUPPOSE WE'VE ALL LOST SOMETHING OF LATE.
YUKIO...I DON'T KNOW WHAT TO SAY, EXCEPT I'M SORRY. THIS WAS ALL MY FAULT.
THE ONES WHO ORCHESTRATED ALL OF THIS, WHO BURNED THESE BUILDINGS, WHO KILLED THE SILVER SAMURAI, WHO TOOK MY LEGS, THE ONES WHO CALLED THEMSELVES THE RED RIGHT HAND...THEY ARE DEAD, YES?
YES.
THEN WHAT IS THERE TO WHINE ABOUT?
COME, WE HAVE MUCH TO DISCUS
CHAPTER TWO: SECRET OF THE SILVER SAMURAI.

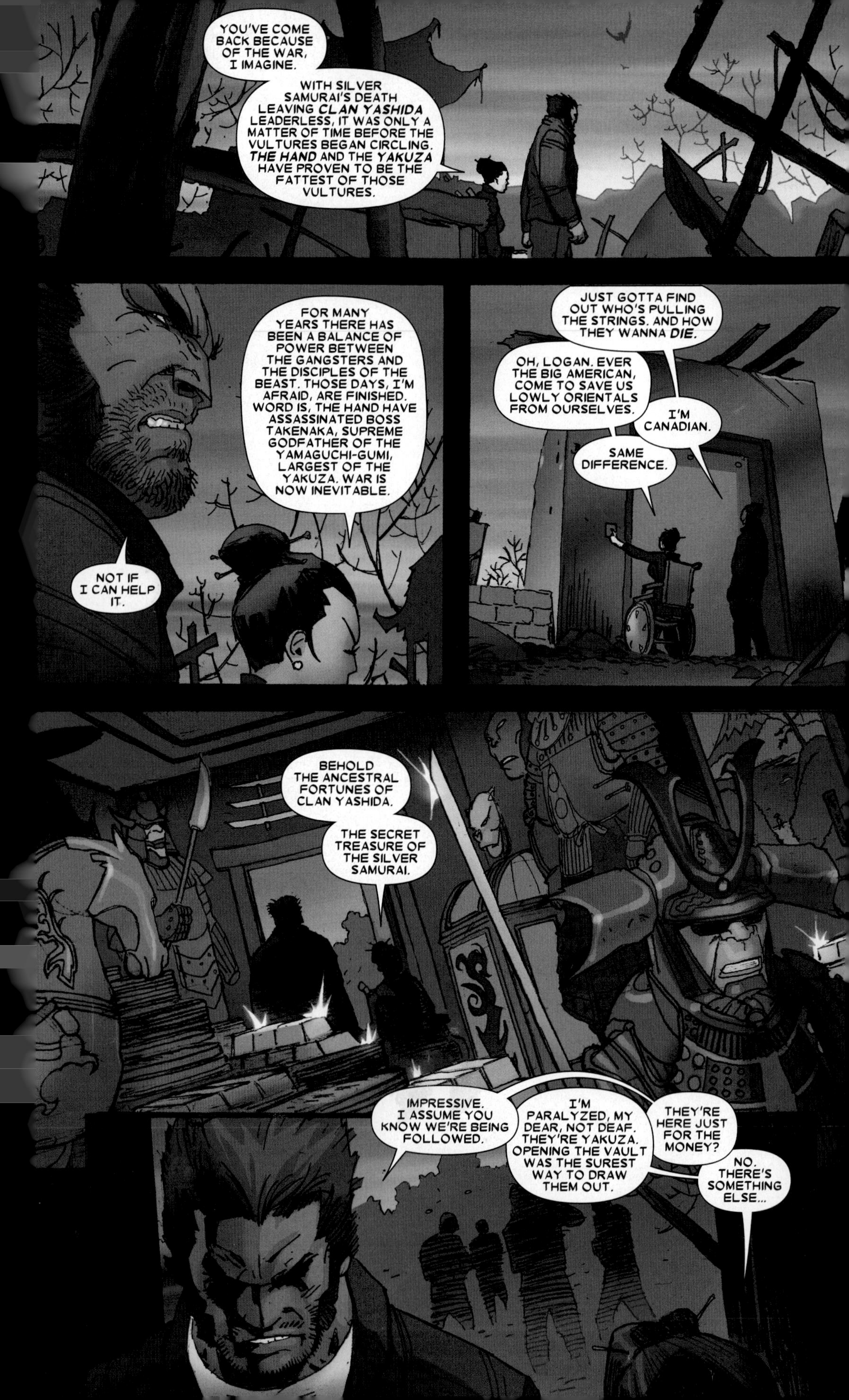
YOU'VE COME BACK BECAUSE OF THE WAR, I IMAGINE.
WITH SILVER SAMURAI'S DEATH LEAVING CLAN YASHIDA LEADERLESS, IT WAS ONLY A MATTER OF TIME BEFORE THE VULTURES BEGAN CIRCLING. THE HAND AND THE YAKUZA HAVE PROVEN TO BE THE FATTEST OF THOSE VULTURES.
FOR MANY YEARS THERE HAS BEEN A BALANCE OF POWER BETWEEN THE GANGSTERS AND THE DISCIPLES OF THE BEAST. THOSE DAYS, I'M AFRAID, ARE FINISHED. WORD IS, THE HAND HAVE ASSASSINATED BOSS TAKENAKA, SUPREME GODFATHER OF THE YAMAGUCHI-GUMI, LARGEST OF THE YAKUZA. WAR IS NOW INEVITABLE.
NOT IF I CAN HELP IT.
JUST GOTTA FIND OUT WHO'S PULLING THE STRINGS. AND HOW THEY WANNA DIE.
OH, LOGAN. EVER THE BIG AMERICAN, COME TO SAVE US LOWLY ORIENTALS FROM OURSELVES.
I'M CANADIAN.
SAME DIFFERENCE.
BEHOLD THE ANCESTRAL FORTUNES OF CLAN YASHIDA.
THE SECRET TREASURE OF THE SILVER SAMURAI.
IMPRESSIVE. I ASSUME YOU KNOW WE'RE BEING FOLLOWED.
I'M PARALYZED, MY DEAR, NOT DEAF. THEY'RE YAKUZA. OPENING THE VAULT WAS THE SUREST WAY TO DRAW THEM OUT.
THEY'RE HERE JUST FOR THE MONEY?
NO. THERE'S SOMETHING ELSE...

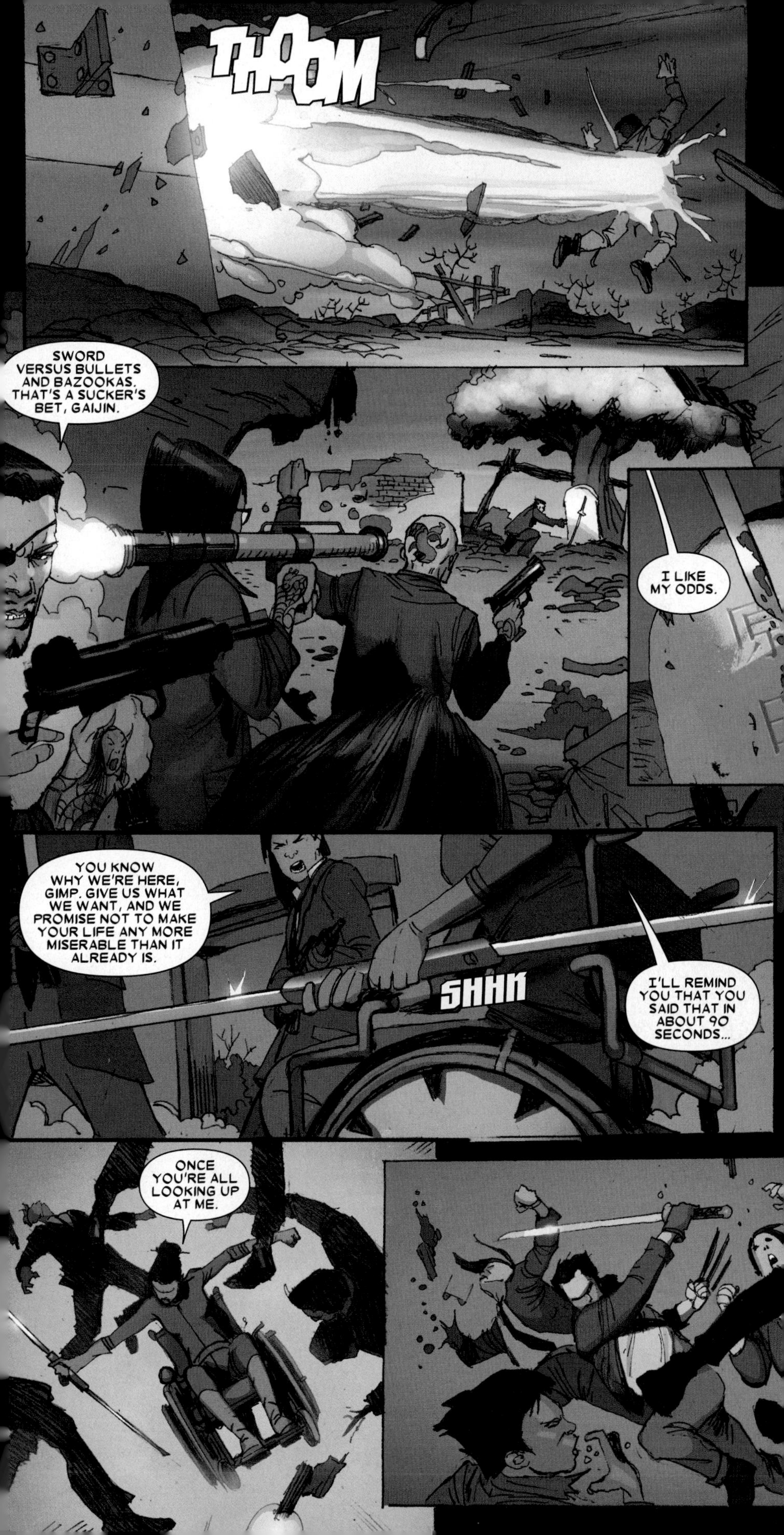
THOOOM
SWORD VERSUS BULLETS AND BAZOOKAS. THAT'S A SUCKER'S BET, GAIJIN.
I LIKE MY ODDS.
YOU KNOW WHY WE'RE HERE, GIMP. GIVE US WHAT WE WANT, AND WE PROMISE NOT TO MAKE YOUR LIFE ANY MORE MISERABLE THAN IT ALREADY IS.
SHHK
I'LL REMIND YOU THAT YOU SAID THAT IN ABOUT 90 SECONDS...
ONCE YOU'RE ALL LOOKING UP AT ME.

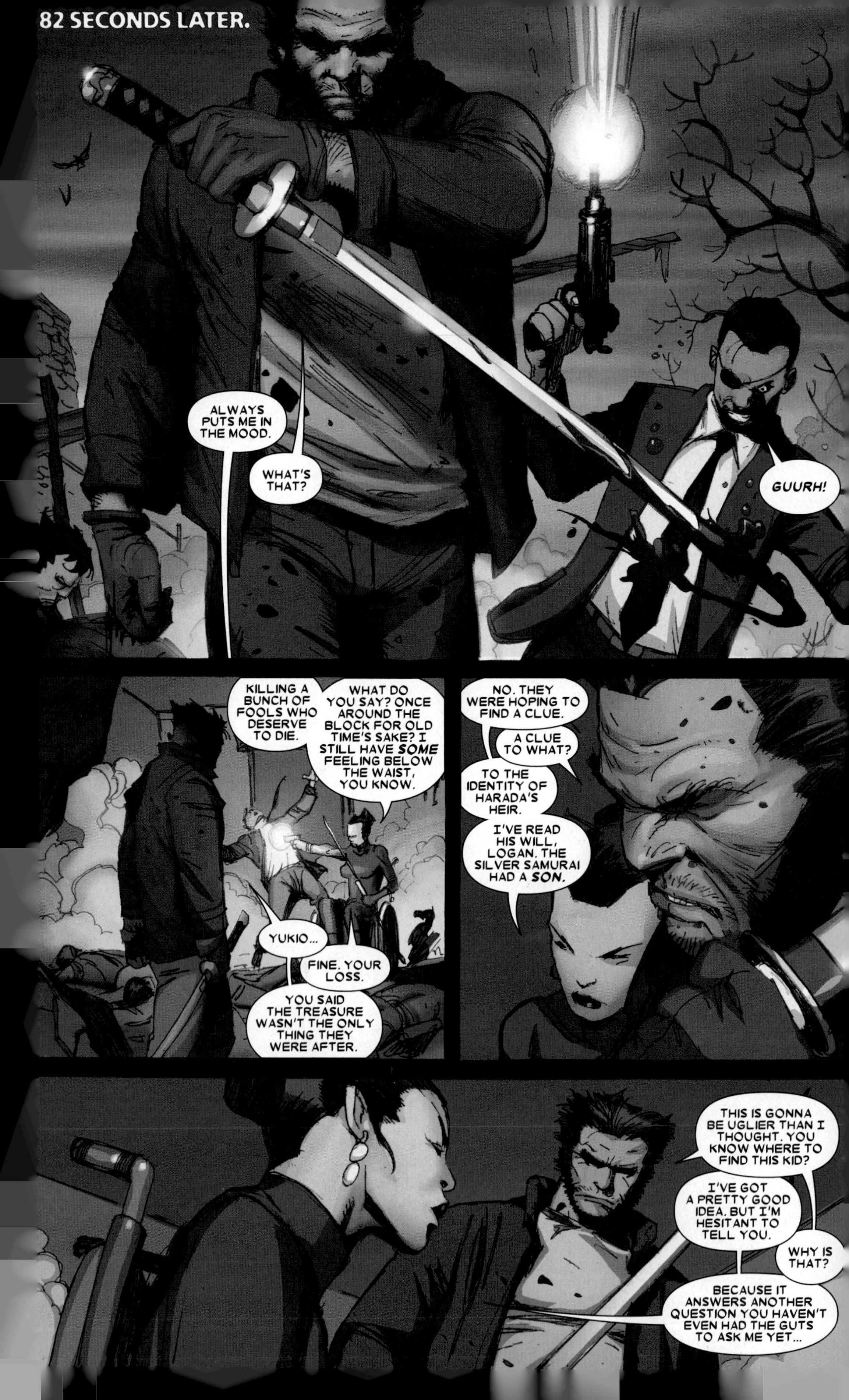
82 SECONDS LATER.
ALWAYS PUTS ME IN THE MOOD.
WHAT'S THAT?
GUURH!
KILLING A BUNCH OF FOOLS WHO DESERVE TO DIE.
WHAT DO YOU SAY? ONCE AROUND THE BLOCK FOR OLD TIME'S SAKE? I STILL HAVE SOME FEELING BELOW THE WAIST, YOU KNOW.
YUKIO...
FINE. YOUR LOSS.
YOU SAID THE TREASURE WASN'T THE ONLY THING THEY WERE AFTER.
NO. THEY WERE HOPING TO FIND A CLUE.
A CLUE TO WHAT?
TO THE IDENTITY OF HARADA'S HEIR.
I'VE READ HIS WILL, LOGAN. THE SILVER SAMURAI HAD A SON.
THIS IS GONNA BE UGLIER THAN I THOUGHT. YOU KNOW WHERE TO FIND THIS KID?
I'VE GOT A PRETTY GOOD IDEA. BUT I'M HESITANT TO TELL YOU.
WHY IS THAT?
BECAUSE IT ANSWERS ANOTHER QUESTION YOU HAVEN'T EVEN HAD THE GUTS TO ASK ME YET...

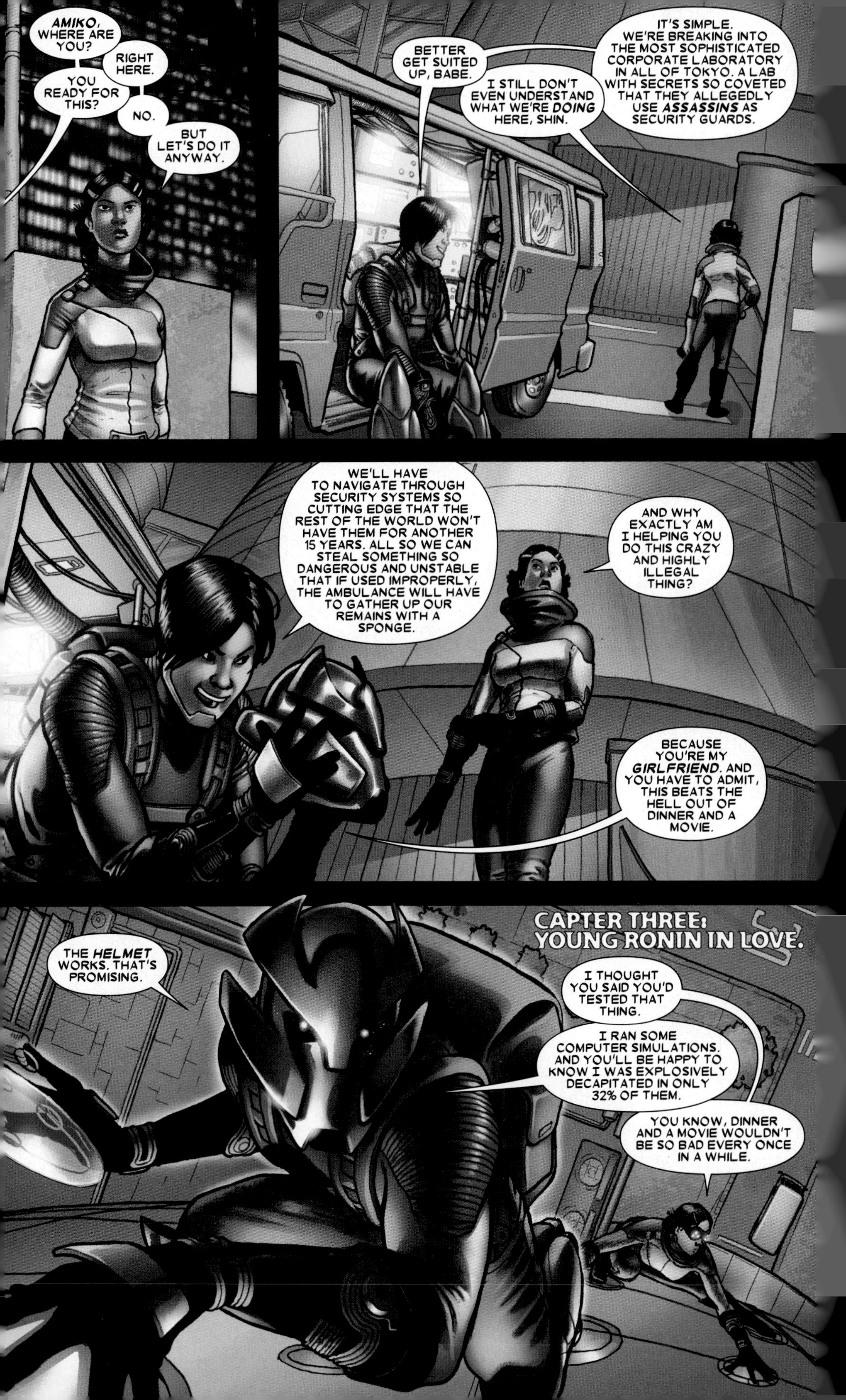
AMIKO, WHERE ARE YOU?
RIGHT HERE.
YOU READY FOR THIS?
NO.
BUT LET'S DO IT ANYWAY.
BETTER GET SUITED UP, BABE.
I STILL DON'T EVEN UNDERSTAND WHAT WE'RE DOING HERE, SHIN.
IT'S SIMPLE. WE'RE BREAKING INTO THE MOST SOPHISTICATED CORPORATE LABORATORY IN ALL OF TOKYO. A LAB WITH SECRETS SO COVETED THAT THEY ALLEGEDLY USE ASSASSINS AS SECURITY GUARDS.
WE'LL HAVE TO NAVIGATE THROUGH SECURITY SYSTEMS SO CUTTING EDGE THAT THE REST OF THE WORLD WON'T HAVE THEM FOR ANOTHER 15 YEARS. ALL SO WE CAN STEAL SOMETHING SO DANGEROUS AND UNSTABLE THAT IF USED IMPROPERLY, THE AMBULANCE WILL HAVE TO GATHER UP OUR REMAINS WITH A SPONGE.
AND WHY EXACTLY AM I HELPING YOU DO THIS CRAZY AND HIGHLY ILLEGAL THING?
BECAUSE YOU'RE MY GIRLFRIEND. AND YOU HAVE TO ADMIT, THIS BEATS THE HELL OUT OF DINNER AND A MOVIE.
CAPTER THREE: YOUNG RONIN IN LOVE.
THE HELMET WORKS. THAT'S PROMISING.
I THOUGHT YOU SAID YOU'D TESTED THAT THING.
I RAN SOME COMPUTER SIMULATIONS. AND YOU'LL BE HAPPY TO KNOW I WAS EXPLOSIVELY DECAPITATED IN ONLY 32% OF THEM.
YOU KNOW, DINNER AND A MOVIE WOULDN'T BE SO BAD EVERY ONCE IN A WHILE.

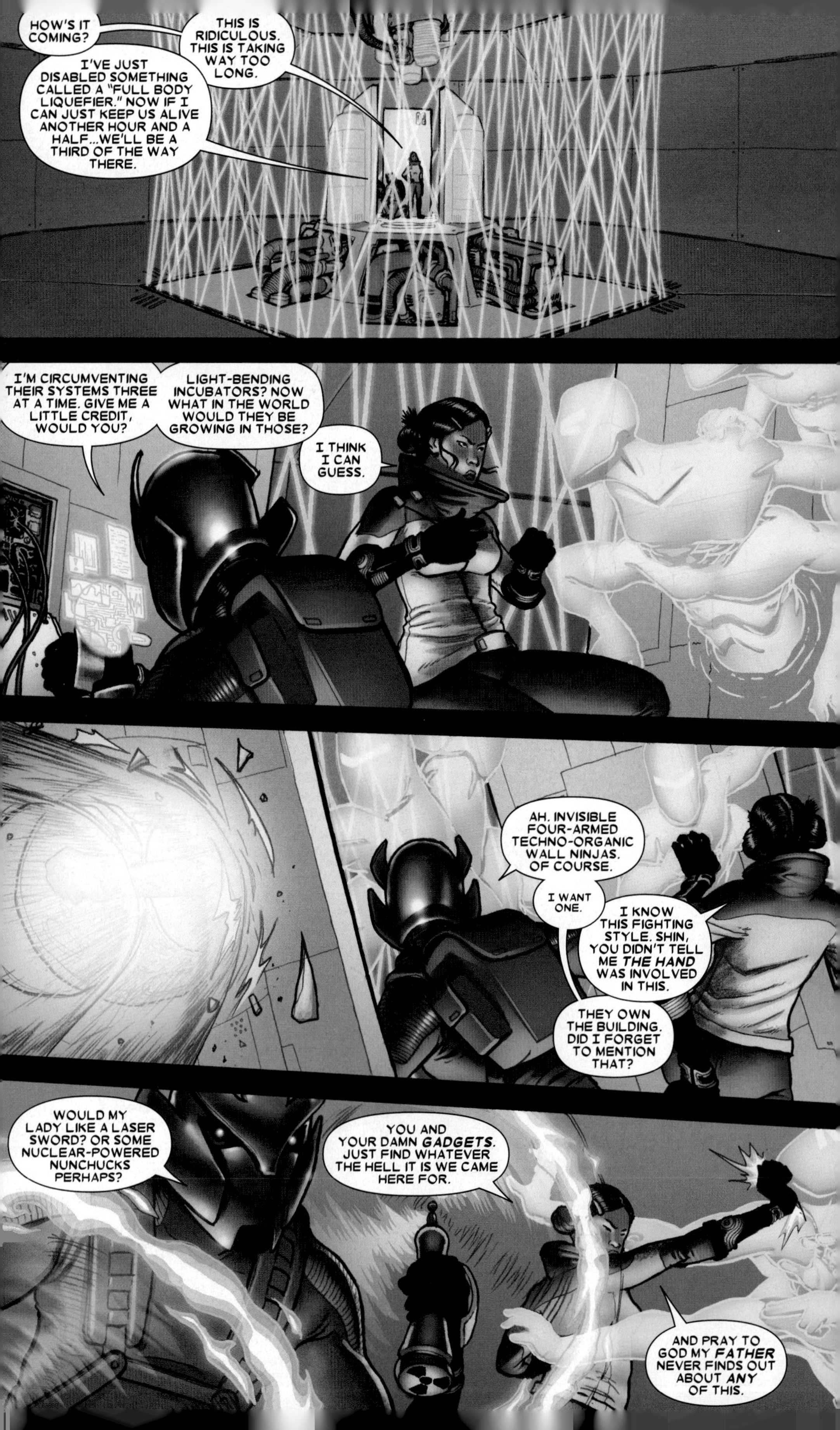

HOW'S IT COMING?
THIS IS RIDICULOUS. THIS IS TAKING WAY TOO LONG.
I'VE JUST DISABLED SOMETHING CALLED A "FULL BODY LIQUEFIER." NOW IF I CAN JUST KEEP US ALIVE ANOTHER HOUR AND A HALF...WE'LL BE A THIRD OF THE WAY THERE.
I'M CIRCUMVENTING THEIR SYSTEMS THREE AT A TIME. GIVE ME A LITTLE CREDIT, WOULD YOU?
LIGHT-BENDING INCUBATORS? NOW WHAT IN THE WORLD WOULD THEY BE GROWING IN THOSE?
I THINK I CAN GUESS.
AH. INVISIBLE FOUR-ARMED TECHNO-ORGANIC WALL NINJAS. OF COURSE.
I WANT ONE.
I KNOW THIS FIGHTING STYLE. SHIN, YOU DIDN'T TELL ME *THE HAND* WAS INVOLVED IN THIS.
THEY OWN THE BUILDING. DID I FORGET TO MENTION THAT?
WOULD MY LADY LIKE A LASER SWORD? OR SOME NUCLEAR-POWERED NUNCHUCKS PERHAPS?
YOU AND YOUR DAMN **GADGETS**. JUST FIND WHATEVER THE HELL IT IS WE CAME HERE FOR.
AND PRAY TO GOD MY ***FATHER*** NEVER FINDS OUT ABOUT ***ANY*** OF THIS.

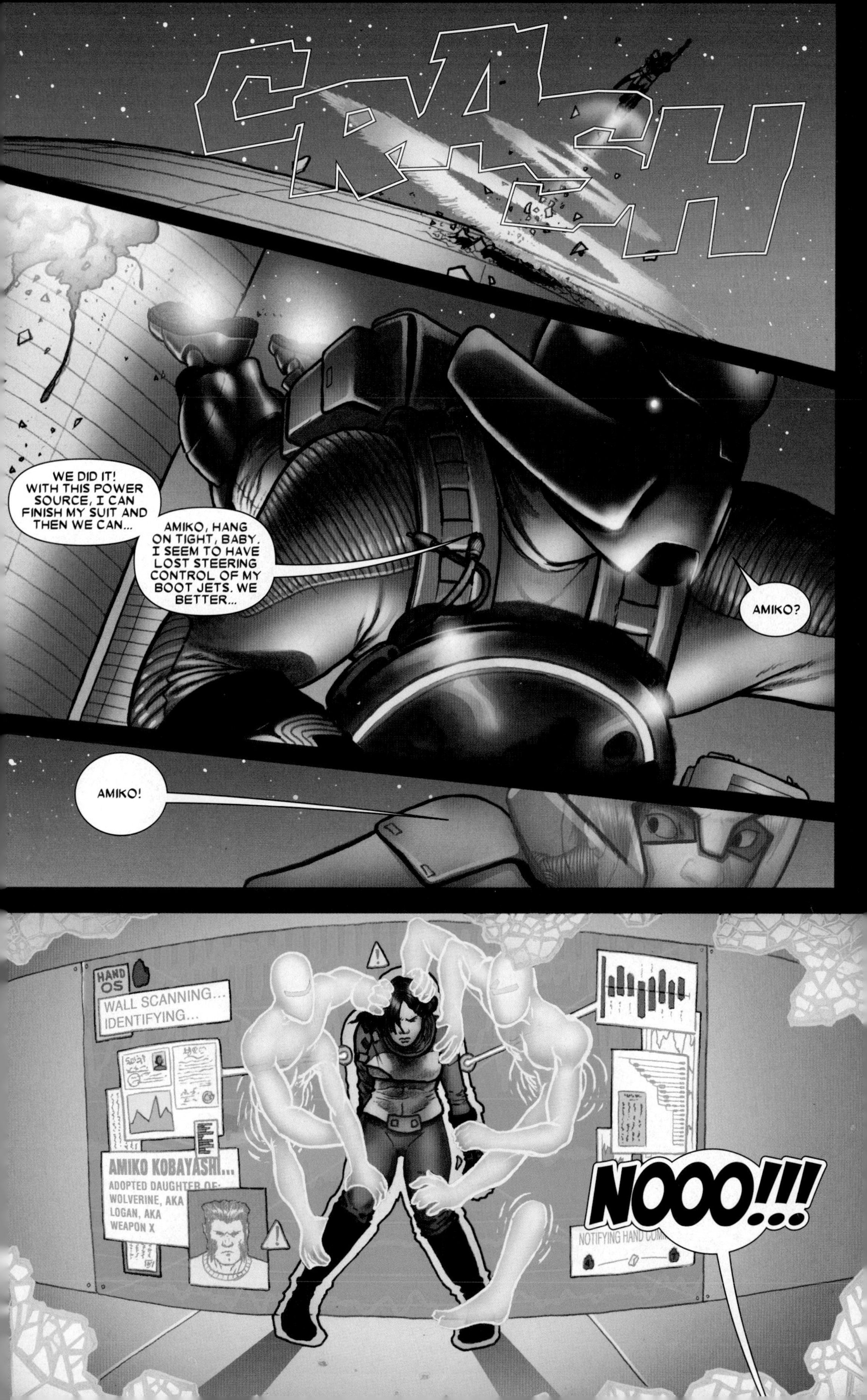
CRASH
WE DID IT! WITH THIS POWER SOURCE, I CAN FINISH MY SUIT AND THEN WE CAN...
AMIKO, HANG ON TIGHT, BABY. I SEEM TO HAVE LOST STEERING CONTROL OF MY BOOT JETS. WE BETTER...
AMIKO?
AMIKO!
HAND OS
WALL SCANNING...
IDENTIFYING...
AMIKO KOBAYASHI...
ADOPTED DAUGHTER OF:
WOLVERINE, AKA
LOGAN, AKA
WEAPON X
NOOO!!!

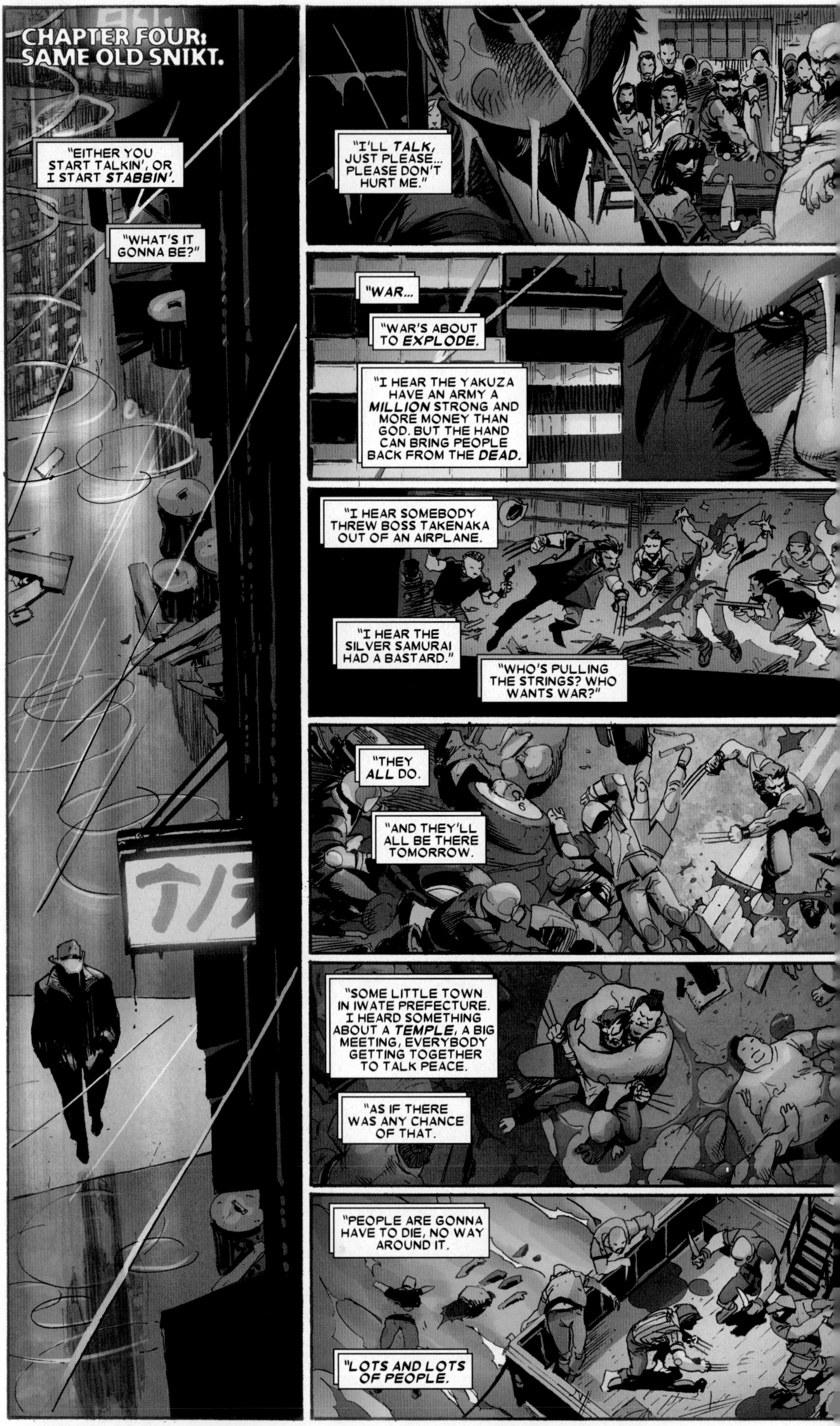
CHAPTER FOUR: SAME OLD SNIKT.
"EITHER YOU START TALKIN', OR I START STABBIN'.
"WHAT'S IT GONNA BE?"
"I'LL TALK, JUST PLEASE... PLEASE DON'T HURT ME."
"WAR...
"WAR'S ABOUT TO EXPLODE.
"I HEAR THE YAKUZA HAVE AN ARMY A MILLION STRONG AND MORE MONEY THAN GOD. BUT THE HAND CAN BRING PEOPLE BACK FROM THE DEAD.
"I HEAR SOMEBODY THREW BOSS TAKENAKA OUT OF AN AIRPLANE.
"I HEAR THE SILVER SAMURAI HAD A BASTARD."
"WHO'S PULLING THE STRINGS? WHO WANTS WAR?"
"THEY ALL DO.
"AND THEY'LL ALL BE THERE TOMORROW.
"SOME LITTLE TOWN IN IWATE PREFECTURE. I HEARD SOMETHING ABOUT A TEMPLE, A BIG MEETING, EVERYBODY GETTING TOGETHER TO TALK PEACE.
"AS IF THERE WAS ANY CHANCE OF THAT.
"PEOPLE ARE GONNA HAVE TO DIE, NO WAY AROUND IT.
"LOTS AND LOTS OF PEOPLE.

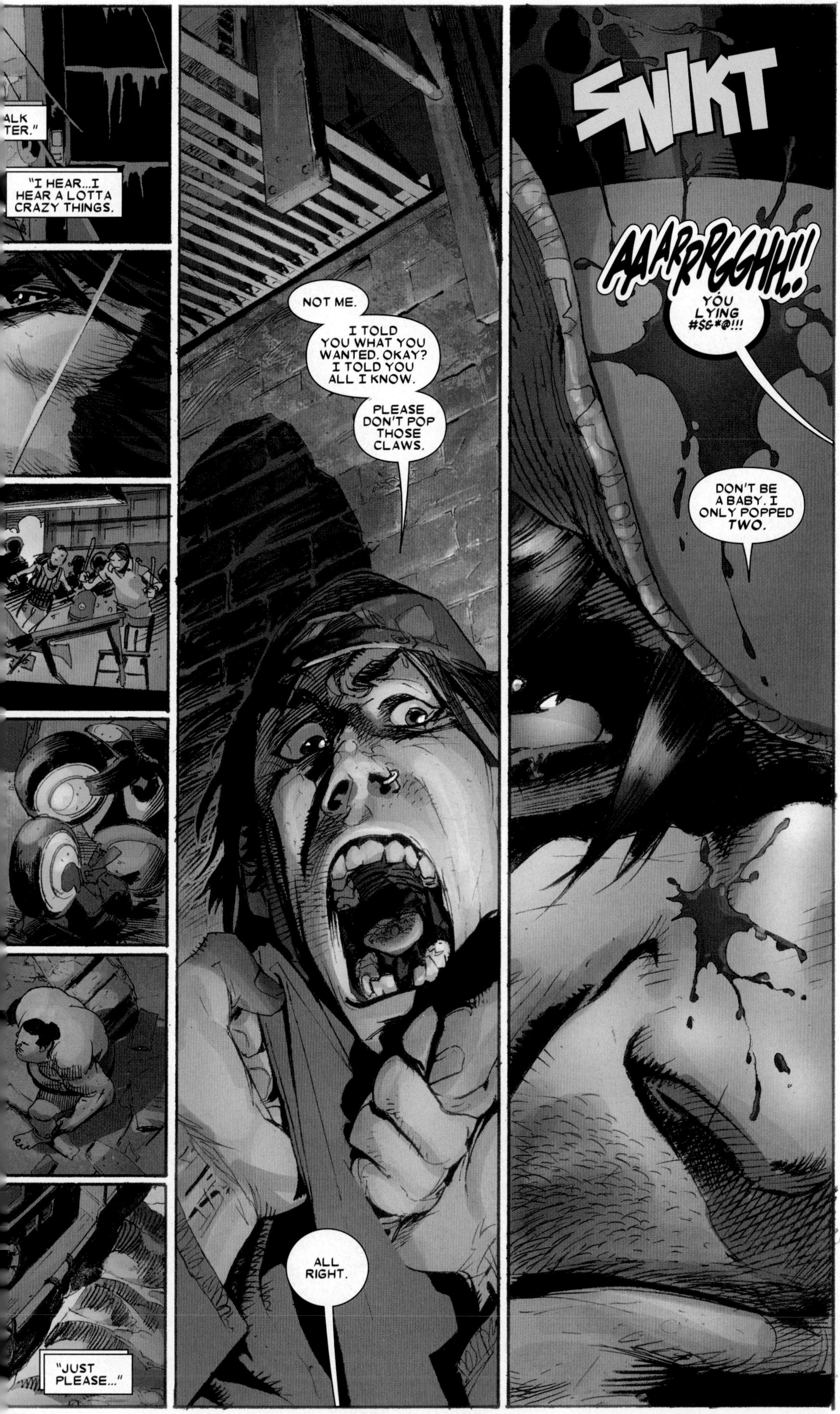

...ALK ...TER."
"I HEAR...I HEAR A LOTTA CRAZY THINGS.
"JUST PLEASE..."
NOT ME.
I TOLD YOU WHAT YOU WANTED. OKAY? I TOLD YOU ALL I KNOW.
PLEASE DON'T POP THOSE CLAWS.
ALL RIGHT.
SNIKT
AAARRRGGHH!!
YOU LYING #$&*@!!!
DON'T BE A BABY. I ONLY POPPED TWO.

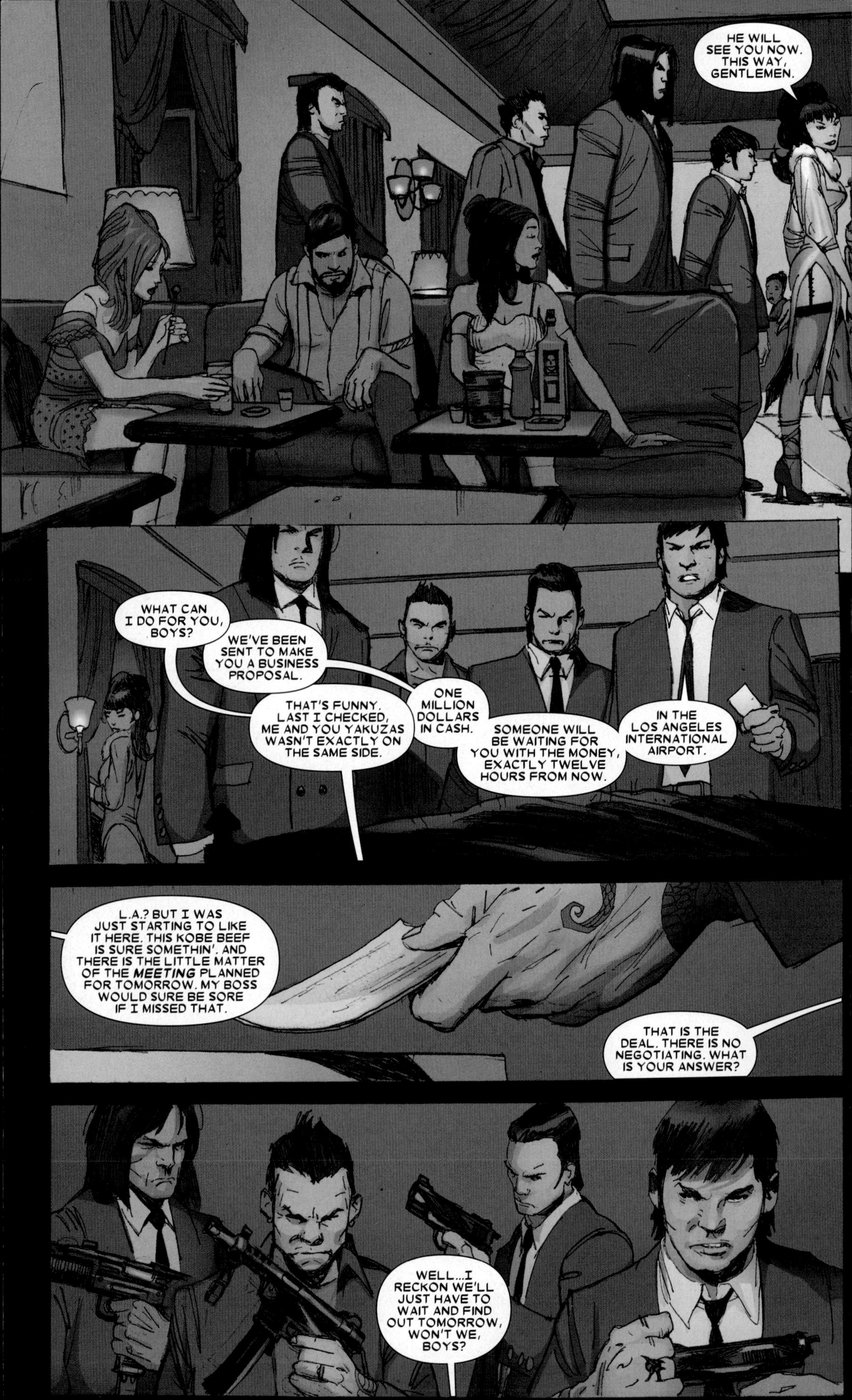
HE WILL SEE YOU NOW. THIS WAY, GENTLEMEN.
WHAT CAN I DO FOR YOU, BOYS?
WE'VE BEEN SENT TO MAKE YOU A BUSINESS PROPOSAL.
THAT'S FUNNY. LAST I CHECKED, ME AND YOU YAKUZAS WASN'T EXACTLY ON THE SAME SIDE.
ONE MILLION DOLLARS IN CASH.
SOMEONE WILL BE WAITING FOR YOU WITH THE MONEY, EXACTLY TWELVE HOURS FROM NOW.
IN THE LOS ANGELES INTERNATIONAL AIRPORT.
L.A.? BUT I WAS JUST STARTING TO LIKE IT HERE. THIS KOBE BEEF IS SURE SOMETHIN'. AND THERE IS THE LITTLE MATTER OF THE MEETING PLANNED FOR TOMORROW. MY BOSS WOULD SURE BE SORE IF I MISSED THAT.
THAT IS THE DEAL. THERE IS NO NEGOTIATING. WHAT IS YOUR ANSWER?
WELL...I RECKON WE'LL JUST HAVE TO WAIT AND FIND OUT TOMORROW, WON'T WE, BOYS?

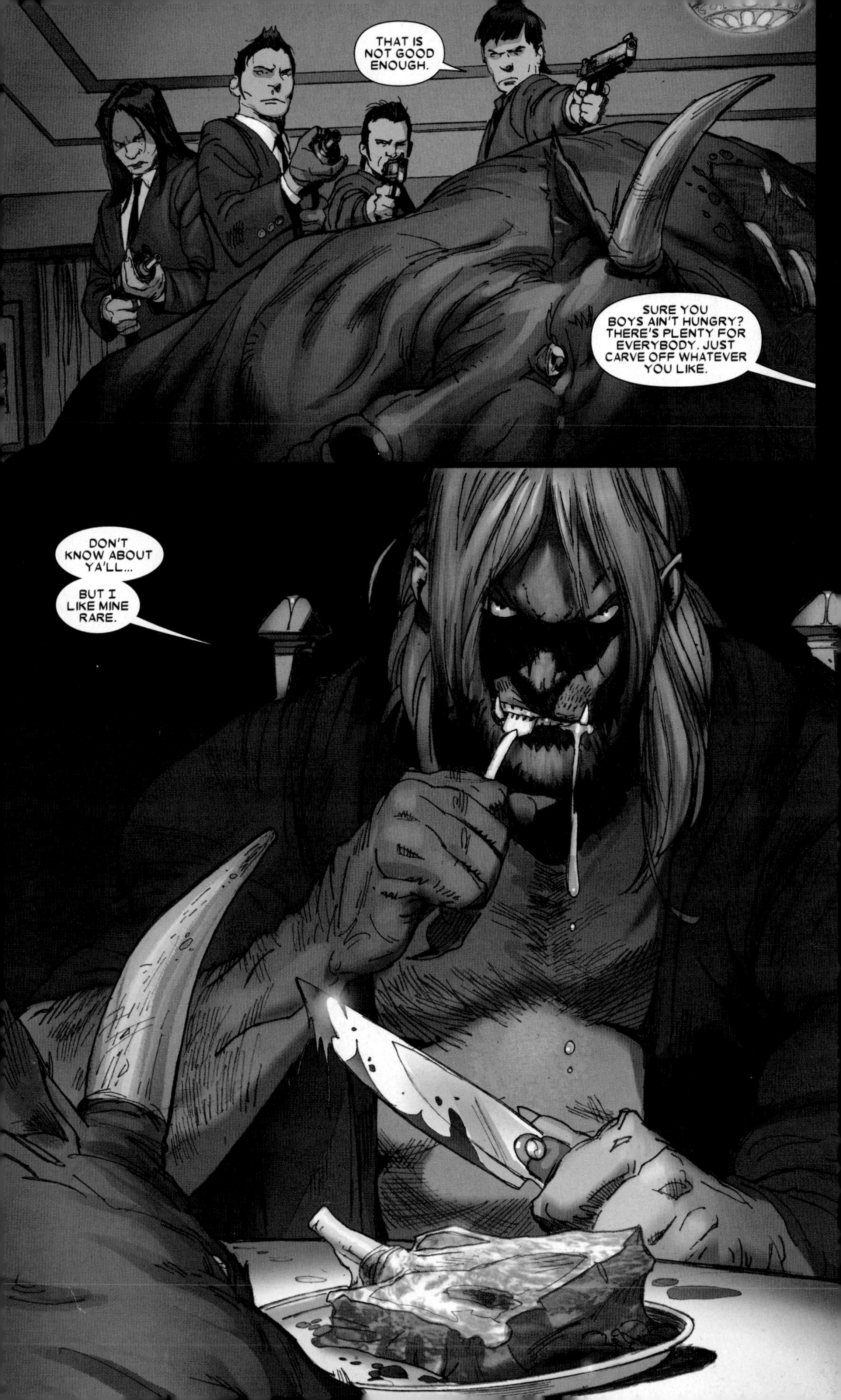
THAT IS NOT GOOD ENOUGH.
SURE YOU BOYS AIN'T HUNGRY? THERE'S PLENTY FOR EVERYBODY. JUST CARVE OFF WHATEVER YOU LIKE.
DON'T KNOW ABOUT YA'LL...
BUT I LIKE MINE RARE.

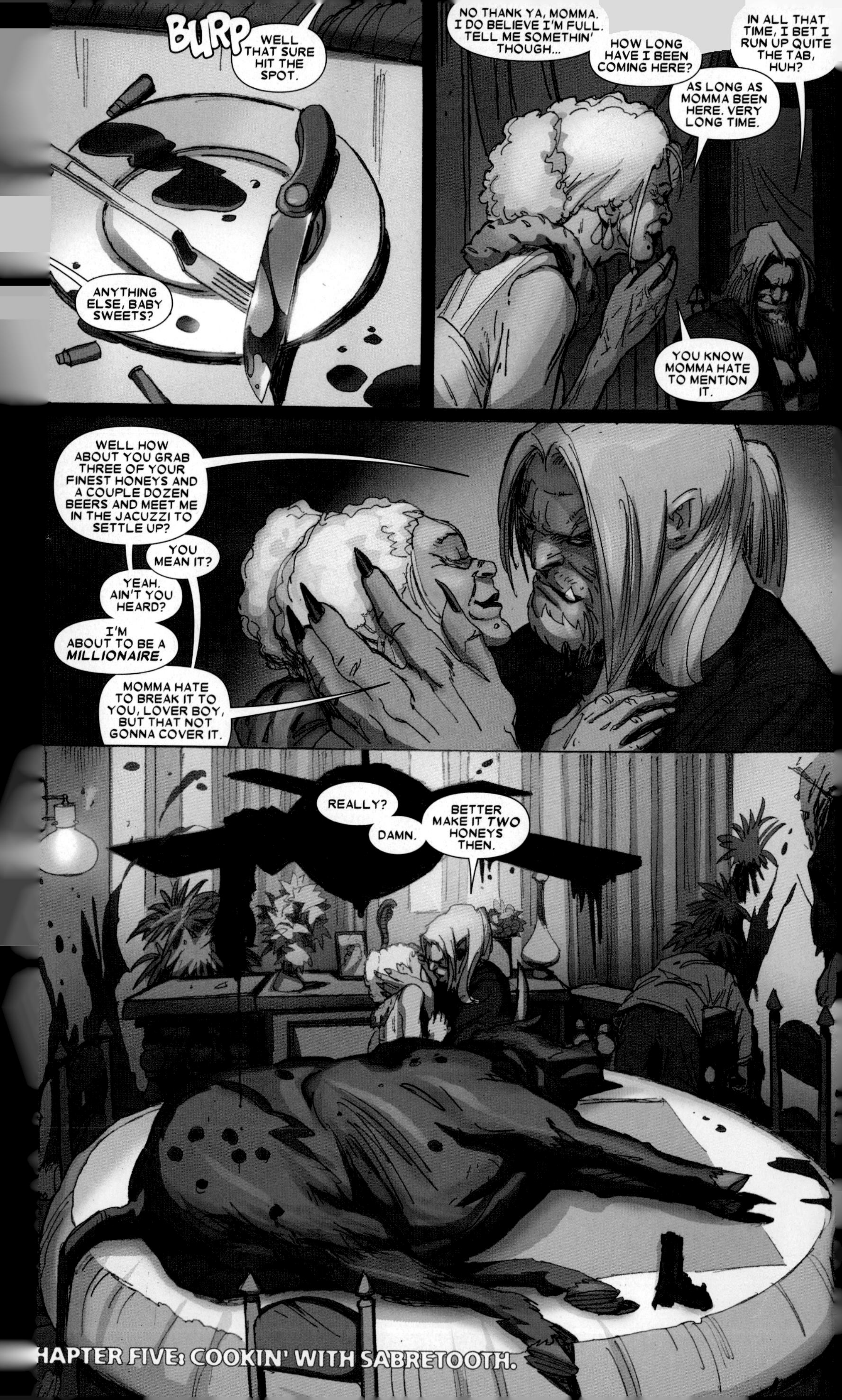
BURP
WELL THAT SURE HIT THE SPOT.
ANYTHING ELSE, BABY SWEETS?
NO THANK YA, MOMMA. I DO BELIEVE I'M FULL. TELL ME SOMETHIN' THOUGH...
HOW LONG HAVE I BEEN COMING HERE?
AS LONG AS MOMMA BEEN HERE. VERY LONG TIME.
IN ALL THAT TIME, I BET I RUN UP QUITE THE TAB, HUH?
YOU KNOW MOMMA HATE TO MENTION IT.
WELL HOW ABOUT YOU GRAB THREE OF YOUR FINEST HONEYS AND A COUPLE DOZEN BEERS AND MEET ME IN THE JACUZZI TO SETTLE UP?
YOU MEAN IT?
YEAH. AIN'T YOU HEARD?
I'M ABOUT TO BE A *MILLIONAIRE.*
MOMMA HATE TO BREAK IT TO YOU, LOVER BOY, BUT THAT NOT GONNA COVER IT.
REALLY?
DAMN.
BETTER MAKE IT *TWO* HONEYS THEN.
HAPTER FIVE: COOKIN' WITH SABRETOOTH.

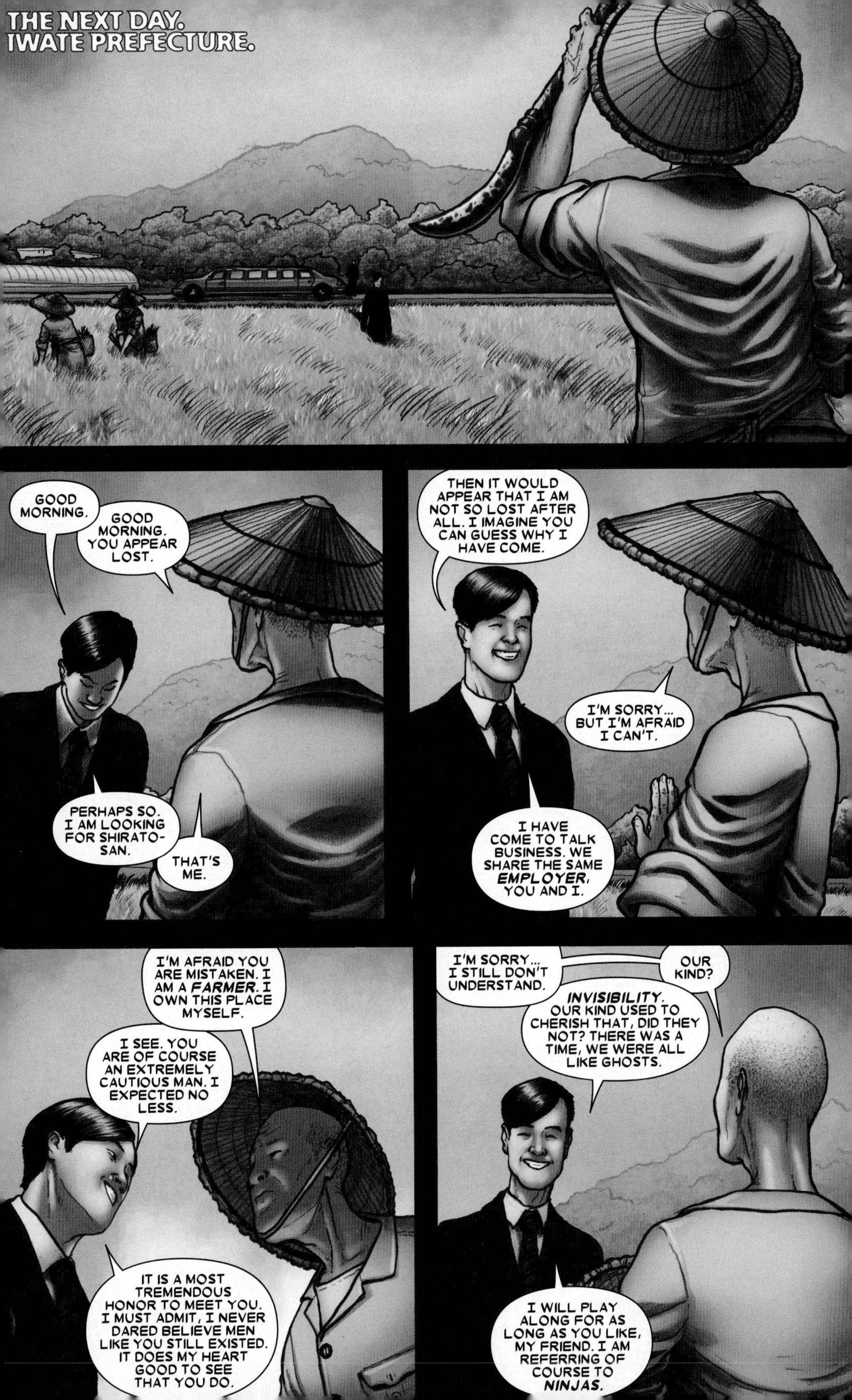
THE NEXT DAY. IWATE PREFECTURE.
GOOD MORNING.
GOOD MORNING. YOU APPEAR LOST.
PERHAPS SO. I AM LOOKING FOR SHIRATO-SAN.
THAT'S ME.
THEN IT WOULD APPEAR THAT I AM NOT SO LOST AFTER ALL. I IMAGINE YOU CAN GUESS WHY I HAVE COME.
I'M SORRY... BUT I'M AFRAID I CAN'T.
I HAVE COME TO TALK BUSINESS. WE SHARE THE SAME EMPLOYER, YOU AND I.
I'M AFRAID YOU ARE MISTAKEN. I AM A FARMER. I OWN THIS PLACE MYSELF.
I SEE. YOU ARE OF COURSE AN EXTREMELY CAUTIOUS MAN. I EXPECTED NO LESS.
IT IS A MOST TREMENDOUS HONOR TO MEET YOU. I MUST ADMIT, I NEVER DARED BELIEVE MEN LIKE YOU STILL EXISTED. IT DOES MY HEART GOOD TO SEE THAT YOU DO.
I'M SORRY... I STILL DON'T UNDERSTAND.
OUR KIND?
INVISIBILITY. OUR KIND USED TO CHERISH THAT, DID THEY NOT? THERE WAS A TIME, WE WERE ALL LIKE GHOSTS.
I WILL PLAY ALONG FOR AS LONG AS YOU LIKE, MY FRIEND. I AM REFERRING OF COURSE TO NINJAS.

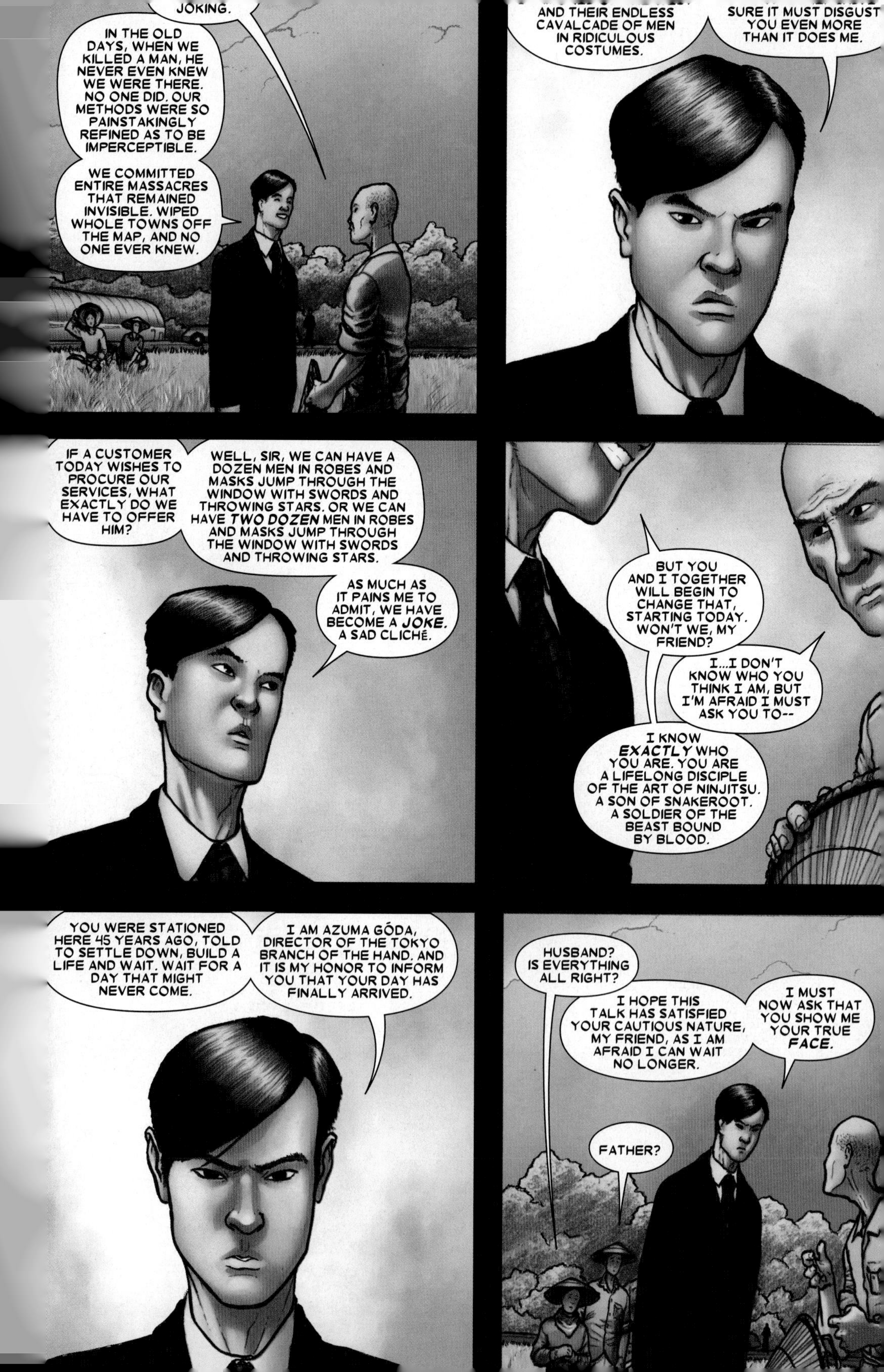

JOKING.
IN THE OLD DAYS, WHEN WE KILLED A MAN, HE NEVER EVEN KNEW WE WERE THERE. NO ONE DID. OUR METHODS WERE SO PAINSTAKINGLY REFINED AS TO BE IMPERCEPTIBLE.
WE COMMITTED ENTIRE MASSACRES THAT REMAINED INVISIBLE. WIPED WHOLE TOWNS OFF THE MAP, AND NO ONE EVER KNEW.
AND THEIR ENDLESS CAVALCADE OF MEN IN RIDICULOUS COSTUMES.
SURE IT MUST DISGUST YOU EVEN MORE THAN IT DOES ME.
IF A CUSTOMER TODAY WISHES TO PROCURE OUR SERVICES, WHAT EXACTLY DO WE HAVE TO OFFER HIM?
WELL, SIR, WE CAN HAVE A DOZEN MEN IN ROBES AND MASKS JUMP THROUGH THE WINDOW WITH SWORDS AND THROWING STARS. OR WE CAN HAVE *TWO DOZEN* MEN IN ROBES AND MASKS JUMP THROUGH THE WINDOW WITH SWORDS AND THROWING STARS.
AS MUCH AS IT PAINS ME TO ADMIT, WE HAVE BECOME A *JOKE.* A SAD CLICHÉ.
BUT YOU AND I TOGETHER WILL BEGIN TO CHANGE THAT, STARTING TODAY. WON'T WE, MY FRIEND?
I...I DON'T KNOW WHO YOU THINK I AM, BUT I'M AFRAID I MUST ASK YOU TO--
I KNOW *EXACTLY* WHO YOU ARE. YOU ARE A LIFELONG DISCIPLE OF THE ART OF NINJITSU. A SON OF SNAKEROOT. A SOLDIER OF THE BEAST BOUND BY BLOOD.
YOU WERE STATIONED HERE 45 YEARS AGO, TOLD TO SETTLE DOWN, BUILD A LIFE AND WAIT. WAIT FOR A DAY THAT MIGHT NEVER COME.
I AM AZUMA GÓDA, DIRECTOR OF THE TOKYO BRANCH OF THE HAND. AND IT IS MY HONOR TO INFORM YOU THAT YOUR DAY HAS FINALLY ARRIVED.
HUSBAND? IS EVERYTHING ALL RIGHT?
I HOPE THIS TALK HAS SATISFIED YOUR CAUTIOUS NATURE, MY FRIEND, AS I AM AFRAID I CAN WAIT NO LONGER.
I MUST NOW ASK THAT YOU SHOW ME YOUR TRUE *FACE.*
FATHER?

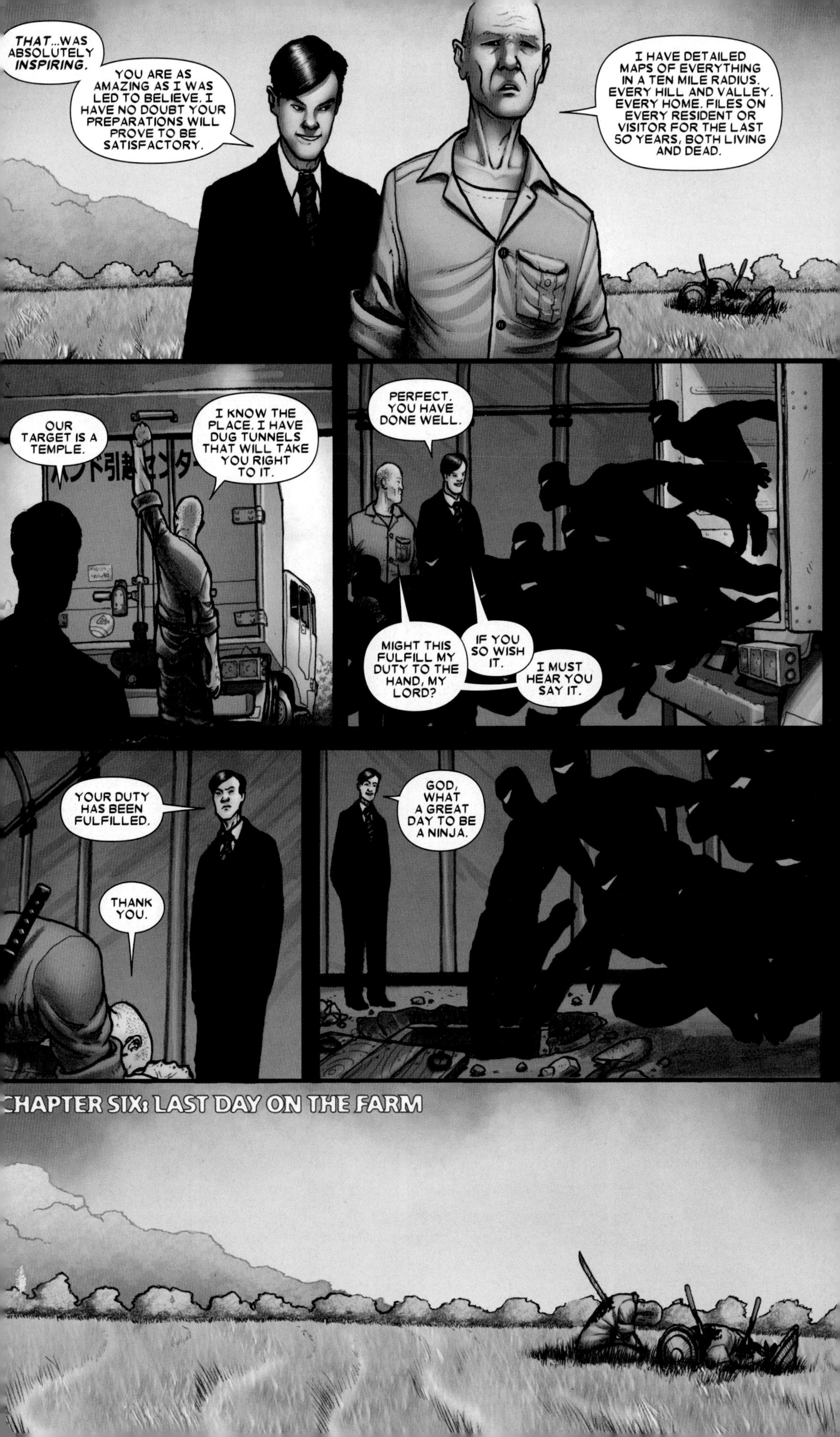
THAT...WAS ABSOLUTELY INSPIRING.
YOU ARE AS AMAZING AS I WAS LED TO BELIEVE. I HAVE NO DOUBT YOUR PREPARATIONS WILL PROVE TO BE SATISFACTORY.
I HAVE DETAILED MAPS OF EVERYTHING IN A TEN MILE RADIUS. EVERY HILL AND VALLEY. EVERY HOME. FILES ON EVERY RESIDENT OR VISITOR FOR THE LAST 50 YEARS, BOTH LIVING AND DEAD.
OUR TARGET IS A TEMPLE.
I KNOW THE PLACE. I HAVE DUG TUNNELS THAT WILL TAKE YOU RIGHT TO IT.
PERFECT. YOU HAVE DONE WELL.
MIGHT THIS FULFILL MY DUTY TO THE HAND, MY LORD?
IF YOU SO WISH IT.
I MUST HEAR YOU SAY IT.
YOUR DUTY HAS BEEN FULFILLED.
THANK YOU.
GOD, WHAT A GREAT DAY TO BE A NINJA.
CHAPTER SIX: LAST DAY ON THE FARM

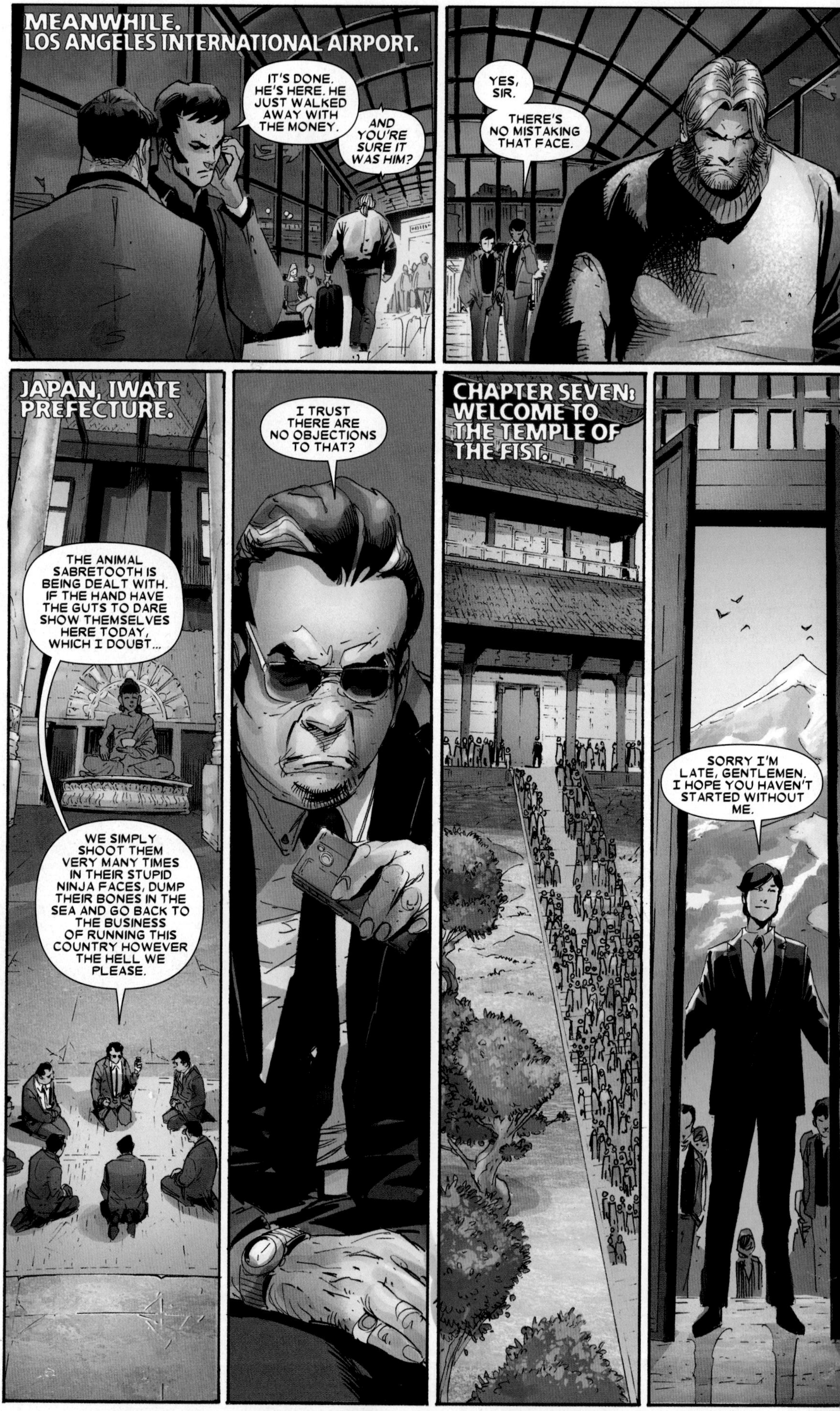
MEANWHILE. LOS ANGELES INTERNATIONAL AIRPORT.
IT'S DONE. HE'S HERE. HE JUST WALKED AWAY WITH THE MONEY.
AND YOU'RE SURE IT WAS HIM?
YES, SIR.
THERE'S NO MISTAKING THAT FACE.
JAPAN, IWATE PREFECTURE.
THE ANIMAL SABRETOOTH IS BEING DEALT WITH. IF THE HAND HAVE THE GUTS TO DARE SHOW THEMSELVES HERE TODAY, WHICH I DOUBT...
WE SIMPLY SHOOT THEM VERY MANY TIMES IN THEIR STUPID NINJA FACES, DUMP THEIR BONES IN THE SEA AND GO BACK TO THE BUSINESS OF RUNNING THIS COUNTRY HOWEVER THE HELL WE PLEASE.
I TRUST THERE ARE NO OBJECTIONS TO THAT?
CHAPTER SEVEN: WELCOME TO THE TEMPLE OF THE FIST.
SORRY I'M LATE, GENTLEMEN. I HOPE YOU HAVEN'T STARTED WITHOUT ME.

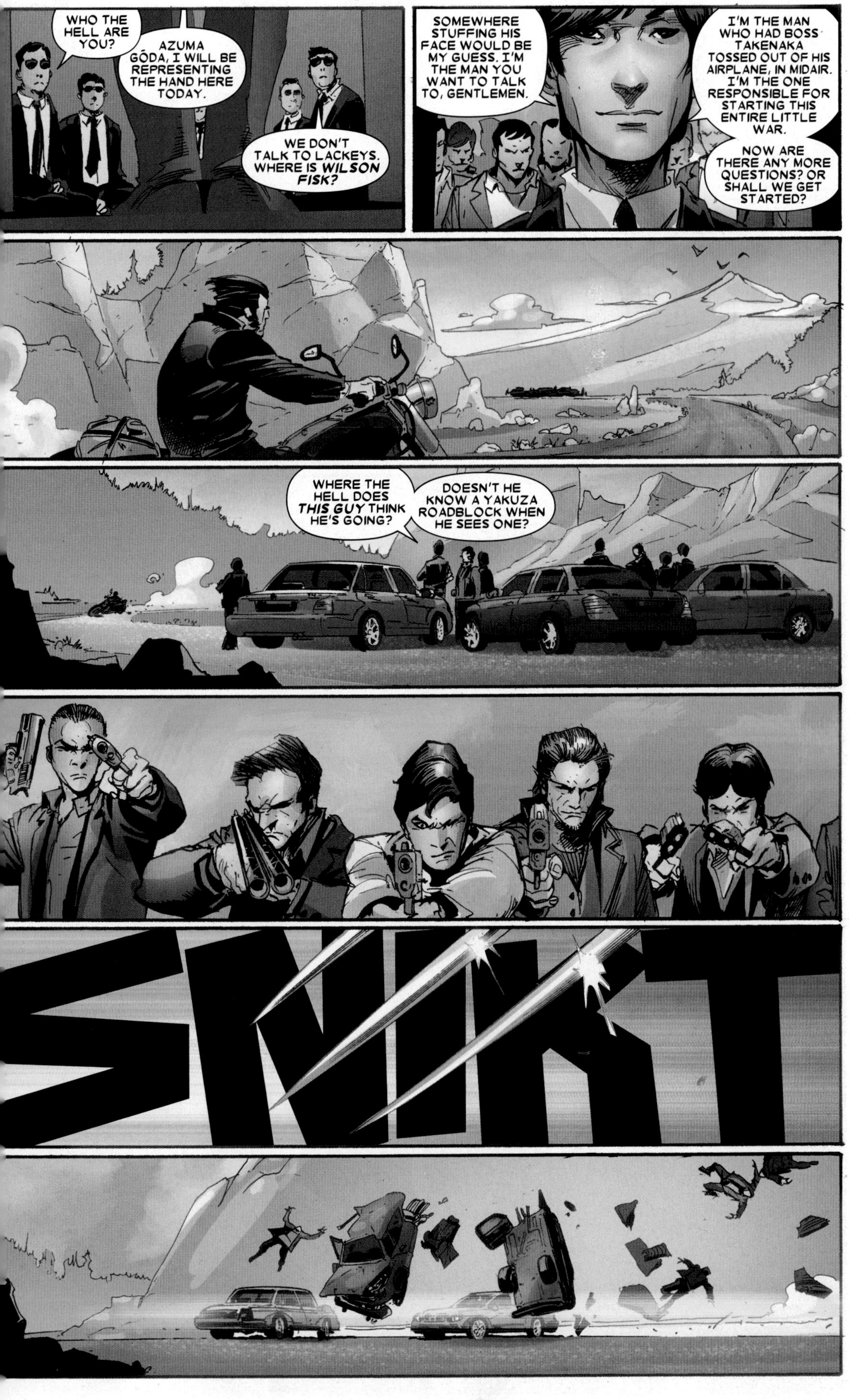
WHO THE HELL ARE YOU?
AZUMA GÓDA, I WILL BE REPRESENTING THE HAND HERE TODAY.
WE DON'T TALK TO LACKEYS. WHERE IS *WILSON FISK?*
SOMEWHERE STUFFING HIS FACE WOULD BE MY GUESS. I'M THE MAN YOU WANT TO TALK TO, GENTLEMEN.
I'M THE MAN WHO HAD BOSS TAKENAKA TOSSED OUT OF HIS AIRPLANE, IN MIDAIR. I'M THE ONE RESPONSIBLE FOR STARTING THIS ENTIRE LITTLE WAR.
NOW ARE THERE ANY MORE QUESTIONS? OR SHALL WE GET STARTED?
WHERE THE HELL DOES *THIS GUY* THINK HE'S GOING?
DOESN'T HE KNOW A YAKUZA ROADBLOCK WHEN HE SEES ONE?
SNIKT

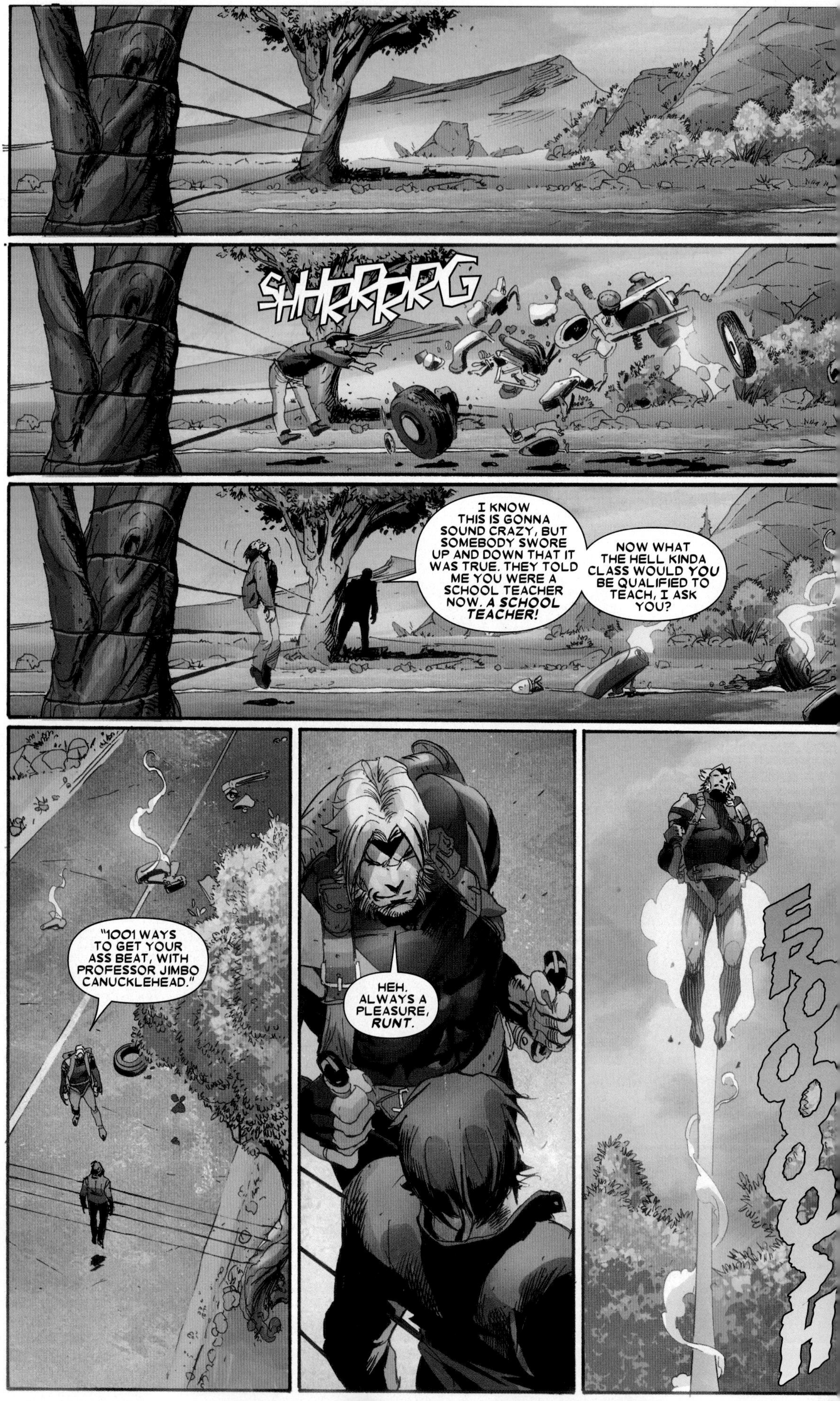
SHHRRRRG
I KNOW THIS IS GONNA SOUND CRAZY, BUT SOMEBODY SWORE UP AND DOWN THAT IT WAS TRUE. THEY TOLD ME YOU WERE A SCHOOL TEACHER NOW. *A SCHOOL TEACHER!*
NOW WHAT THE HELL KINDA CLASS WOULD *YOU* BE QUALIFIED TO TEACH, I ASK YOU?
"1001 WAYS TO GET YOUR ASS BEAT, WITH PROFESSOR JIMBO CANUCKLEHEAD."
HEH. ALWAYS A PLEASURE, *RUNT*.
FROOOOOSH

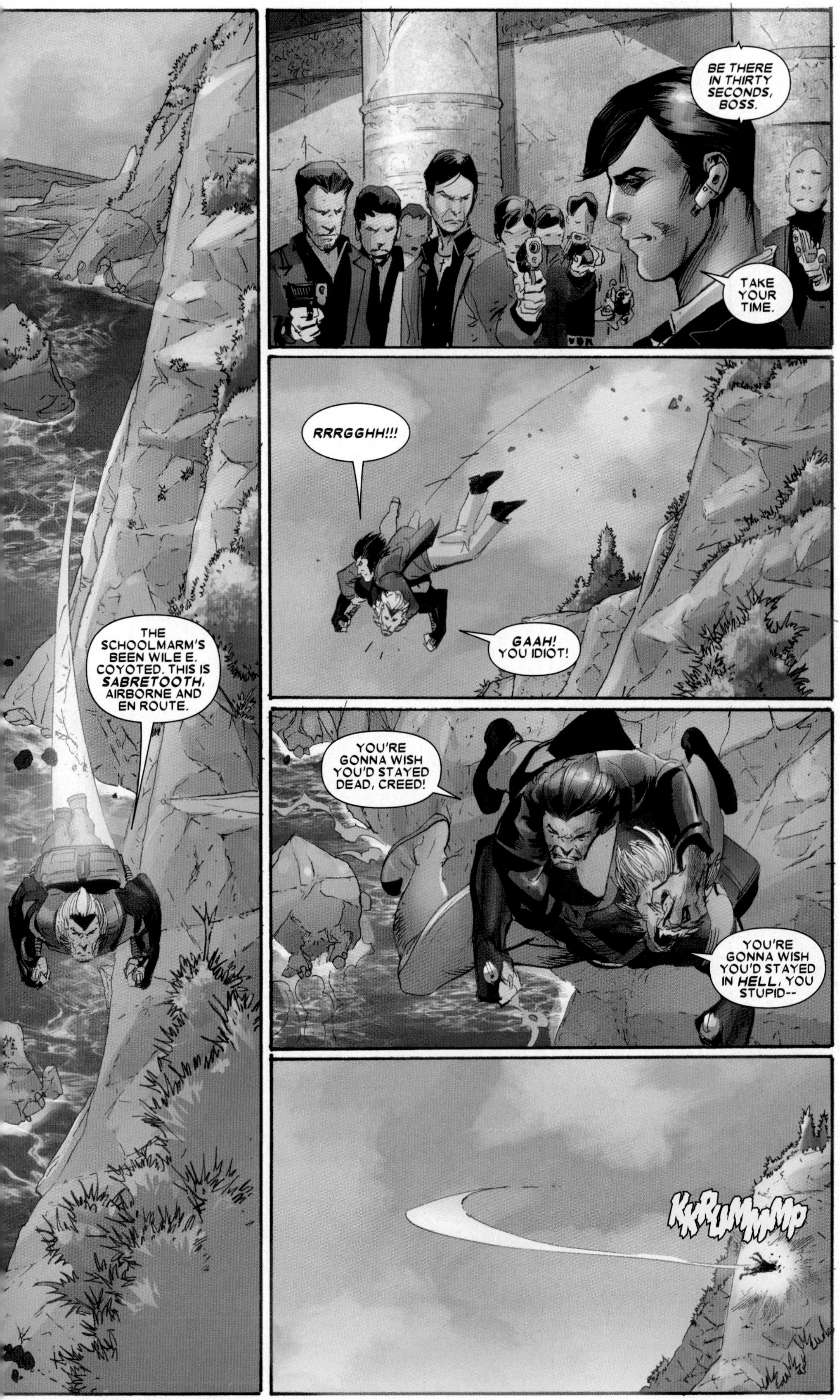
THE SCHOOLMARM'S BEEN WILE E. COYOTED. THIS IS SABRETOOTH, AIRBORNE AND EN ROUTE.
BE THERE IN THIRTY SECONDS, BOSS.
TAKE YOUR TIME.
RRRGGHH!!!
GAAH! YOU IDIOT!
YOU'RE GONNA WISH YOU'D STAYED DEAD, CREED!
YOU'RE GONNA WISH YOU'D STAYED IN HELL, YOU STUPID--
KKRUMMMMP

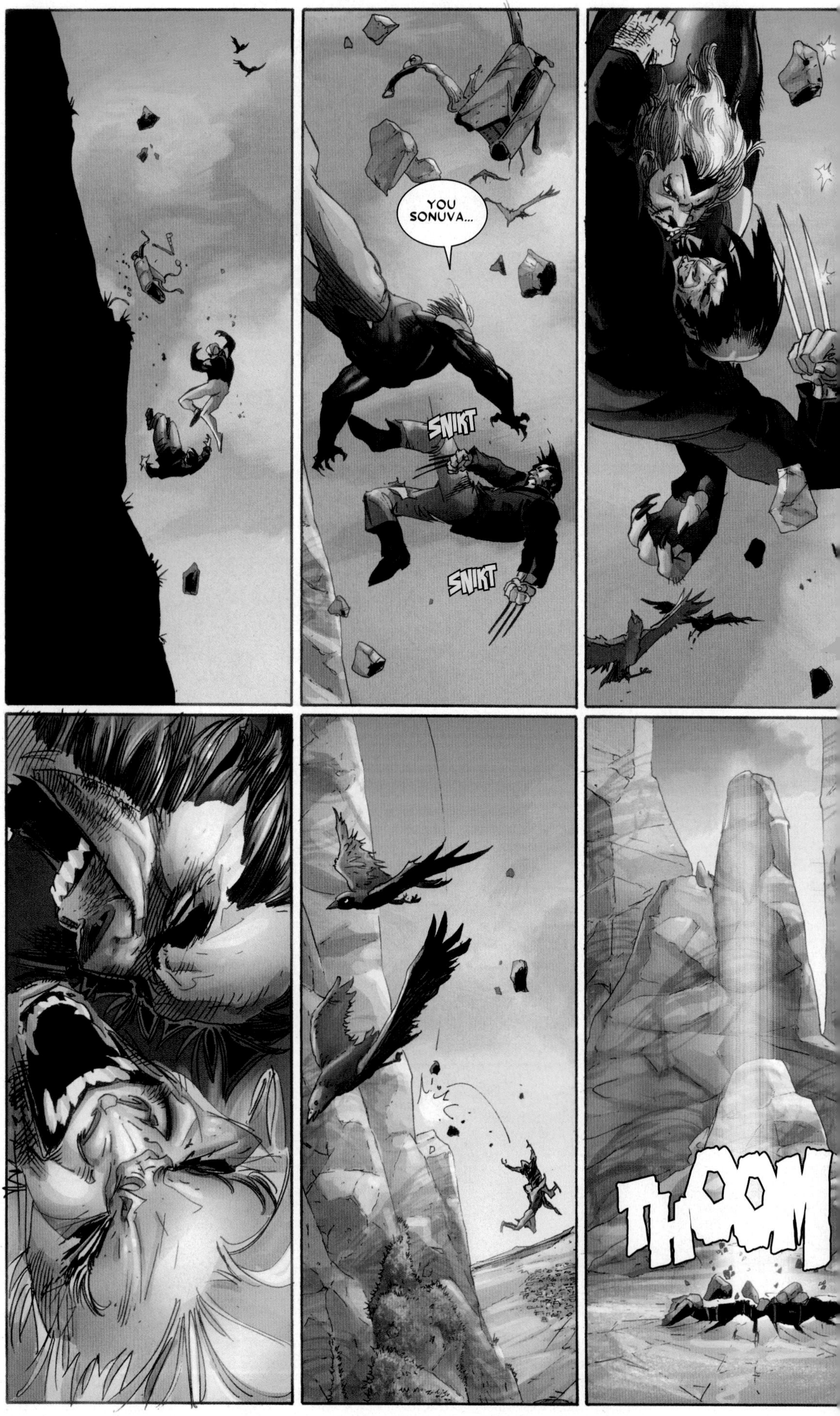
YOU SONUVA...
SNIKT
SNIKT
THOOM

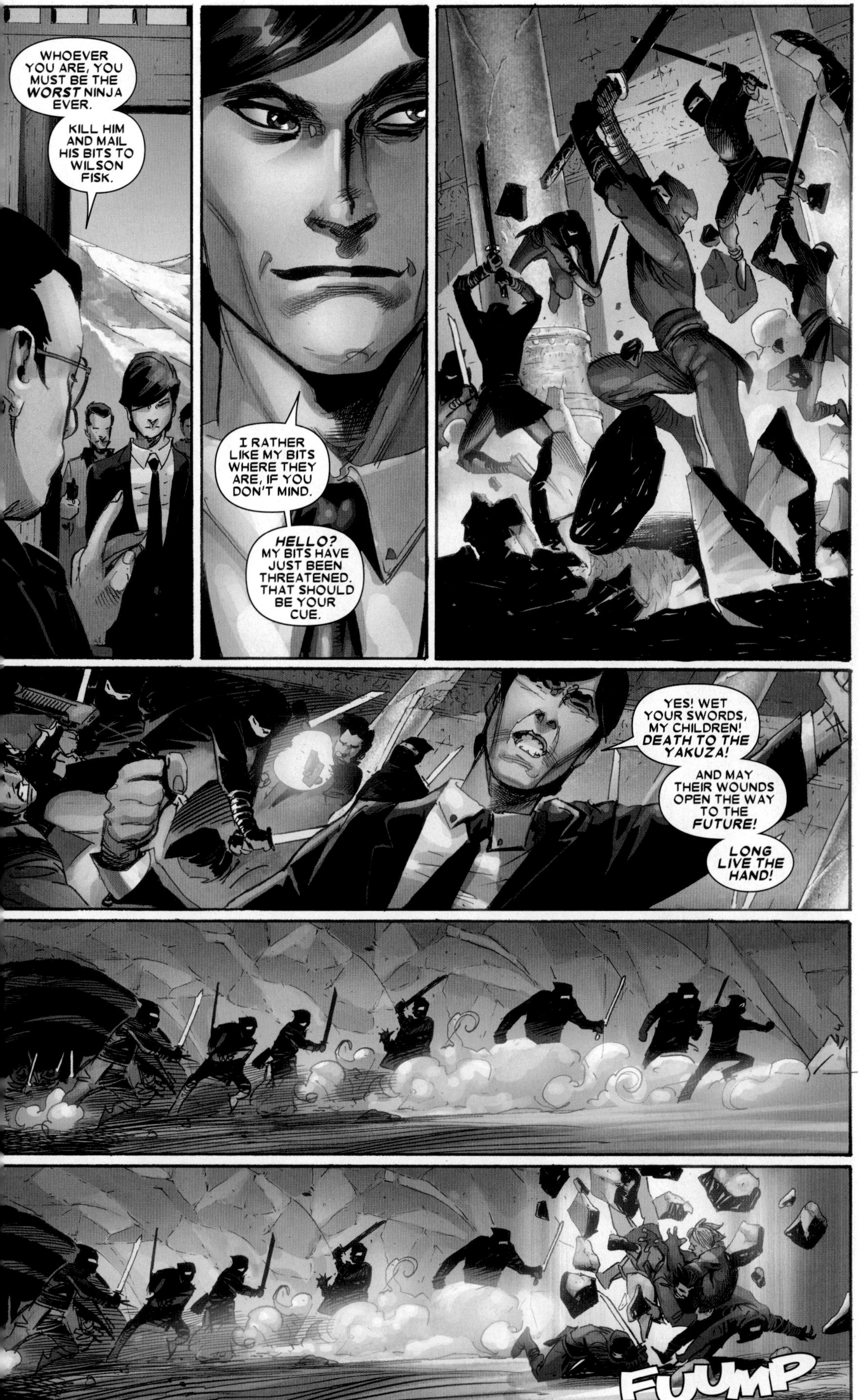

WHOEVER YOU ARE, YOU MUST BE THE WORST NINJA EVER.
KILL HIM AND MAIL HIS BITS TO WILSON FISK.
I RATHER LIKE MY BITS WHERE THEY ARE, IF YOU DON'T MIND.
HELLO? MY BITS HAVE JUST BEEN THREATENED. THAT SHOULD BE YOUR CUE.
YES! WET YOUR SWORDS, MY CHILDREN! DEATH TO THE YAKUZA!
AND MAY THEIR WOUNDS OPEN THE WAY TO THE FUTURE!
LONG LIVE THE HAND!
FUUMP

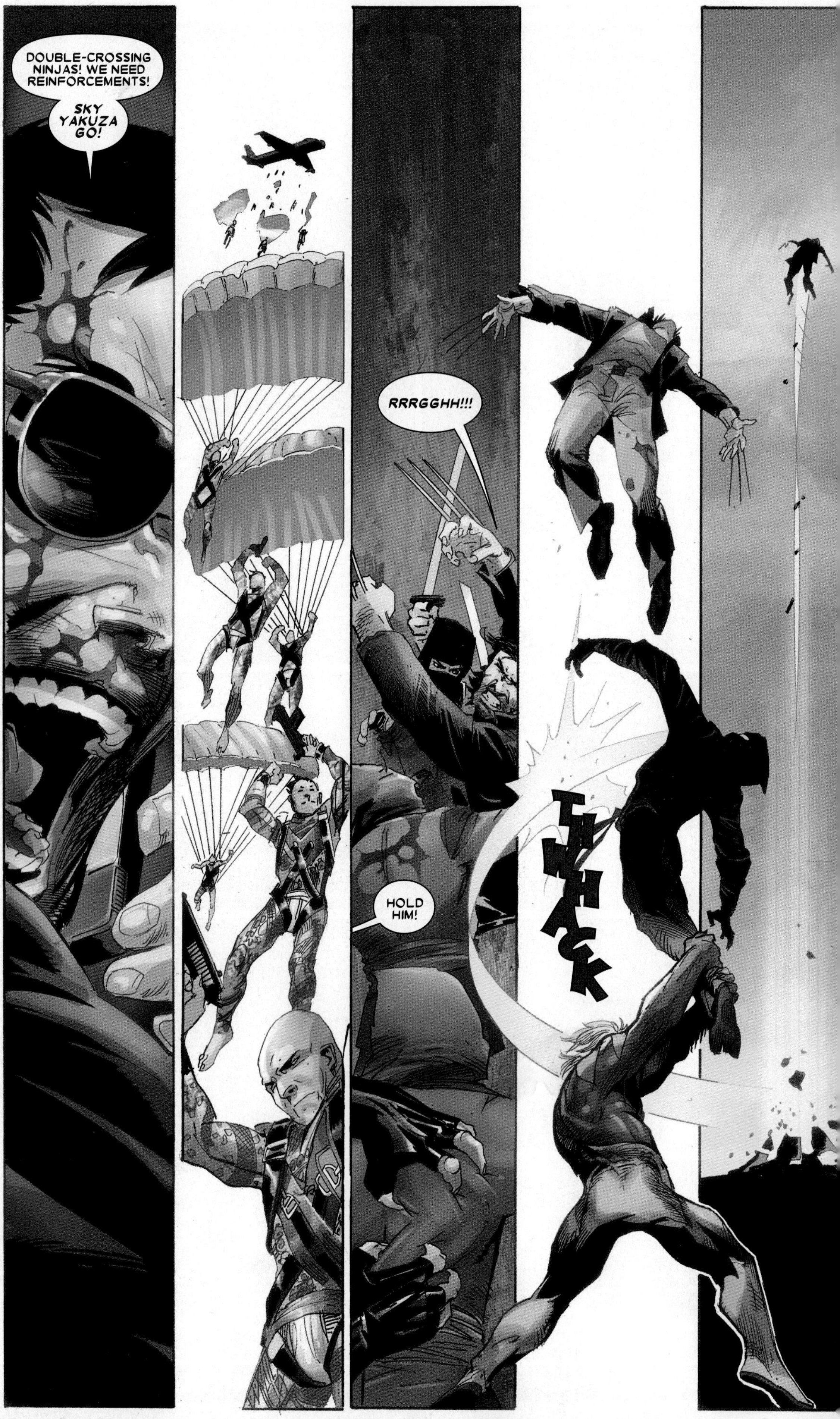
DOUBLE-CROSSING NINJAS! WE NEED REINFORCEMENTS!
SKY YAKUZA GO!
RRRGGHH!!!
HOLD HIM!
THWHACK

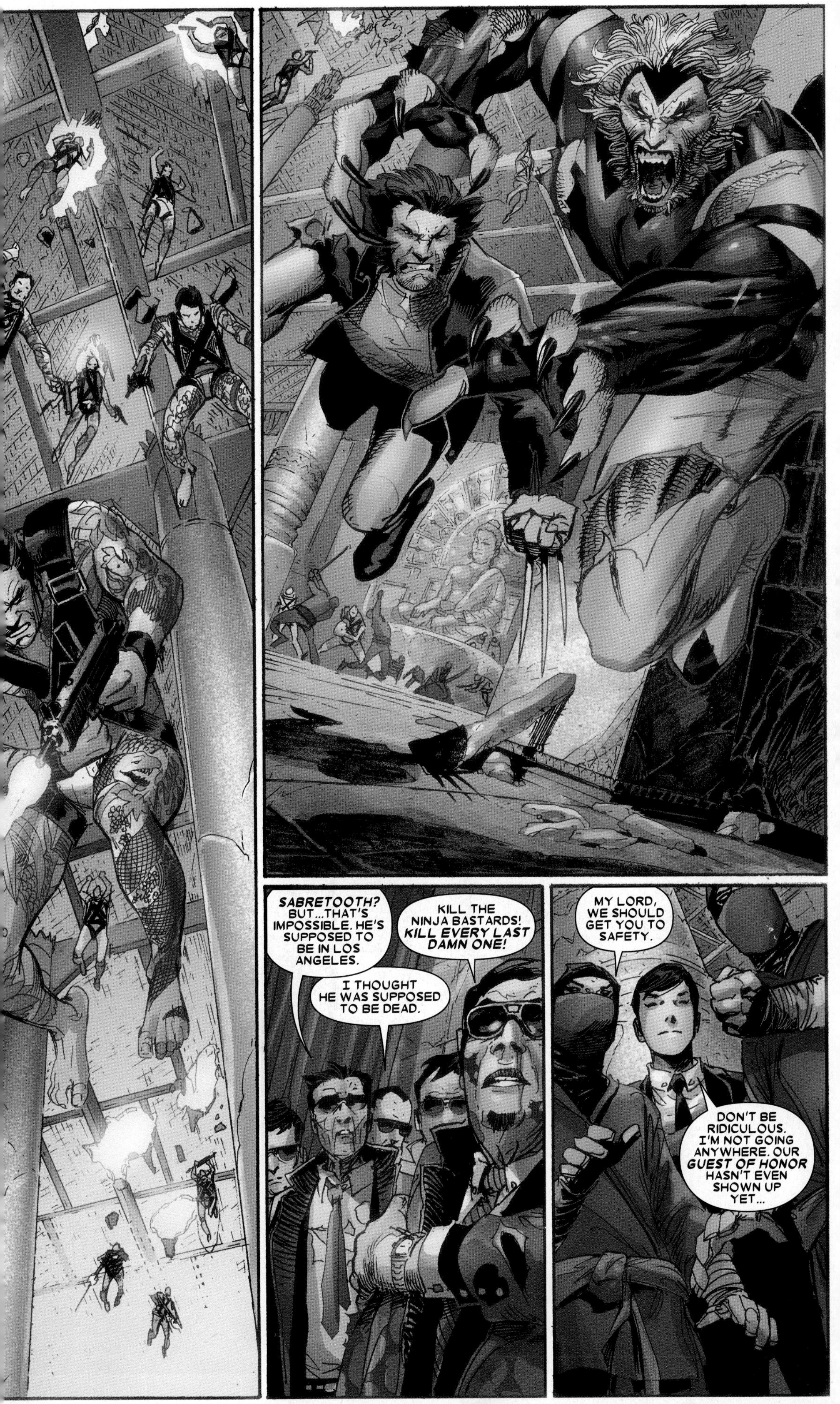
SABRETOOTH? BUT...THAT'S IMPOSSIBLE. HE'S SUPPOSED TO BE IN LOS ANGELES.
I THOUGHT HE WAS SUPPOSED TO BE DEAD.
KILL THE NINJA BASTARDS! KILL EVERY LAST DAMN ONE!
MY LORD, WE SHOULD GET YOU TO SAFETY.
DON'T BE RIDICULOUS. I'M NOT GOING ANYWHERE. OUR GUEST OF HONOR HASN'T EVEN SHOWN UP YET...

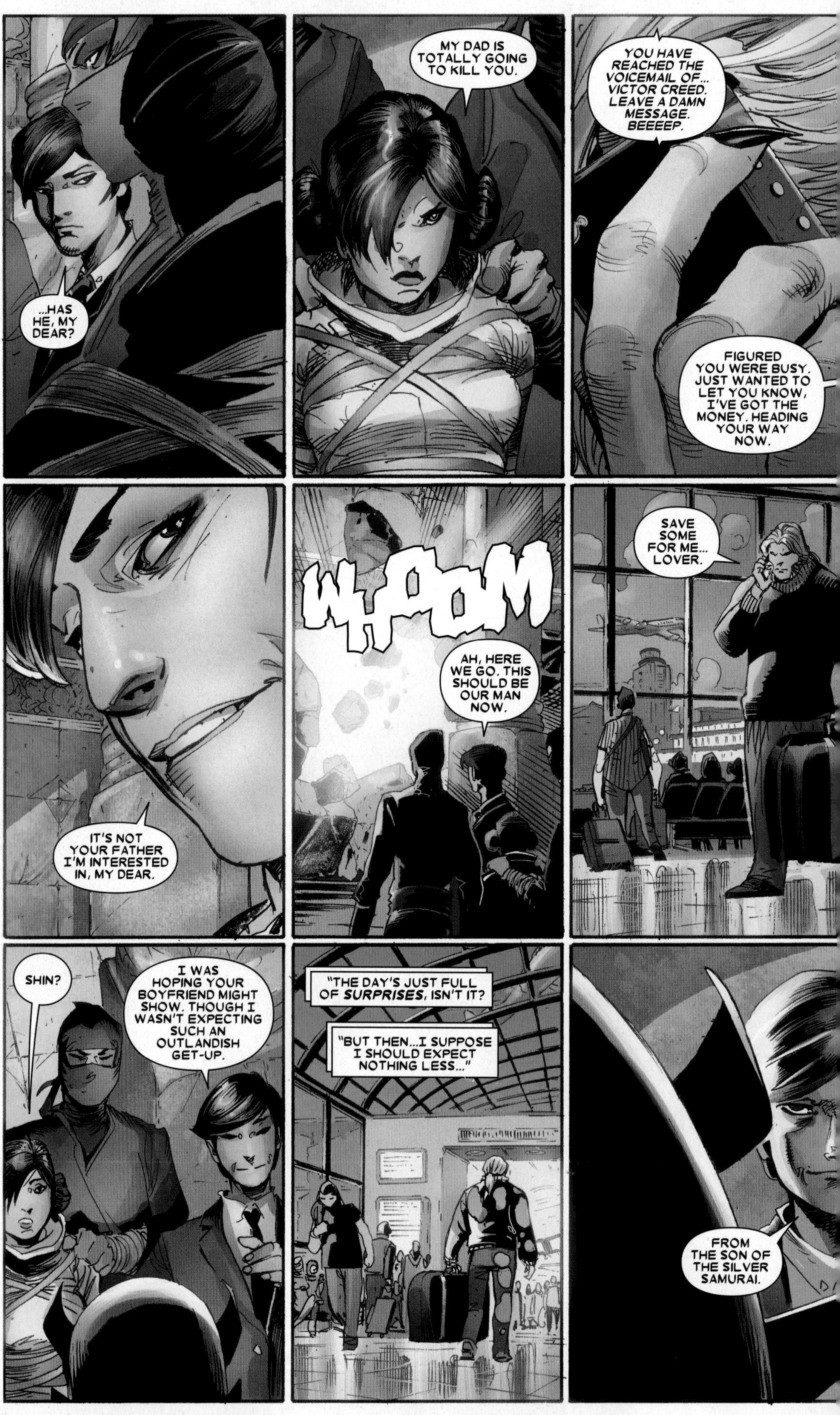
...HAS HE, MY DEAR?
MY DAD IS TOTALLY GOING TO KILL YOU.
YOU HAVE REACHED THE VOICEMAIL OF... VICTOR CREED. LEAVE A DAMN MESSAGE. BEEEEP.
FIGURED YOU WERE BUSY. JUST WANTED TO LET YOU KNOW, I'VE GOT THE MONEY. HEADING YOUR WAY NOW.
IT'S NOT YOUR FATHER I'M INTERESTED IN, MY DEAR.
WHOOM
AH, HERE WE GO. THIS SHOULD BE OUR MAN NOW.
SAVE SOME FOR ME... LOVER.
SHIN?
I WAS HOPING YOUR BOYFRIEND MIGHT SHOW. THOUGH I WASN'T EXPECTING SUCH AN OUTLANDISH GET-UP.
"THE DAY'S JUST FULL OF SURPRISES, ISN'T IT?
"BUT THEN...I SUPPOSE I SHOULD EXPECT NOTHING LESS..."
FROM THE SON OF THE SILVER SAMURAI.

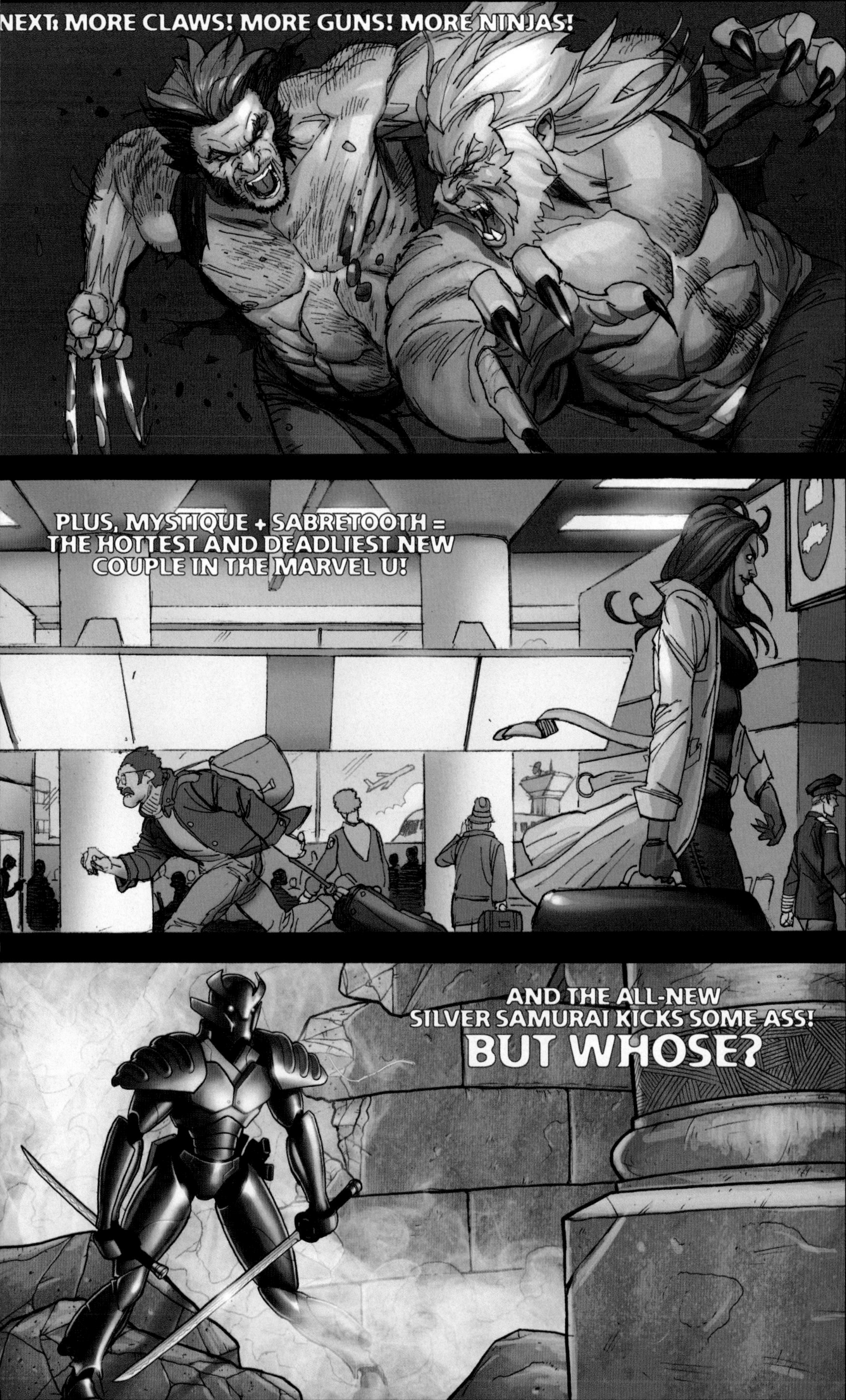
NEXT: MORE CLAWS! MORE GUNS! MORE NINJAS!
PLUS, MYSTIQUE + SABRETOOTH = THE HOTTEST AND DEADLIEST NEW COUPLE IN THE MARVEL U!
AND THE ALL-NEW SILVER SAMURAI KICKS SOME ASS!
BUT WHOSE?

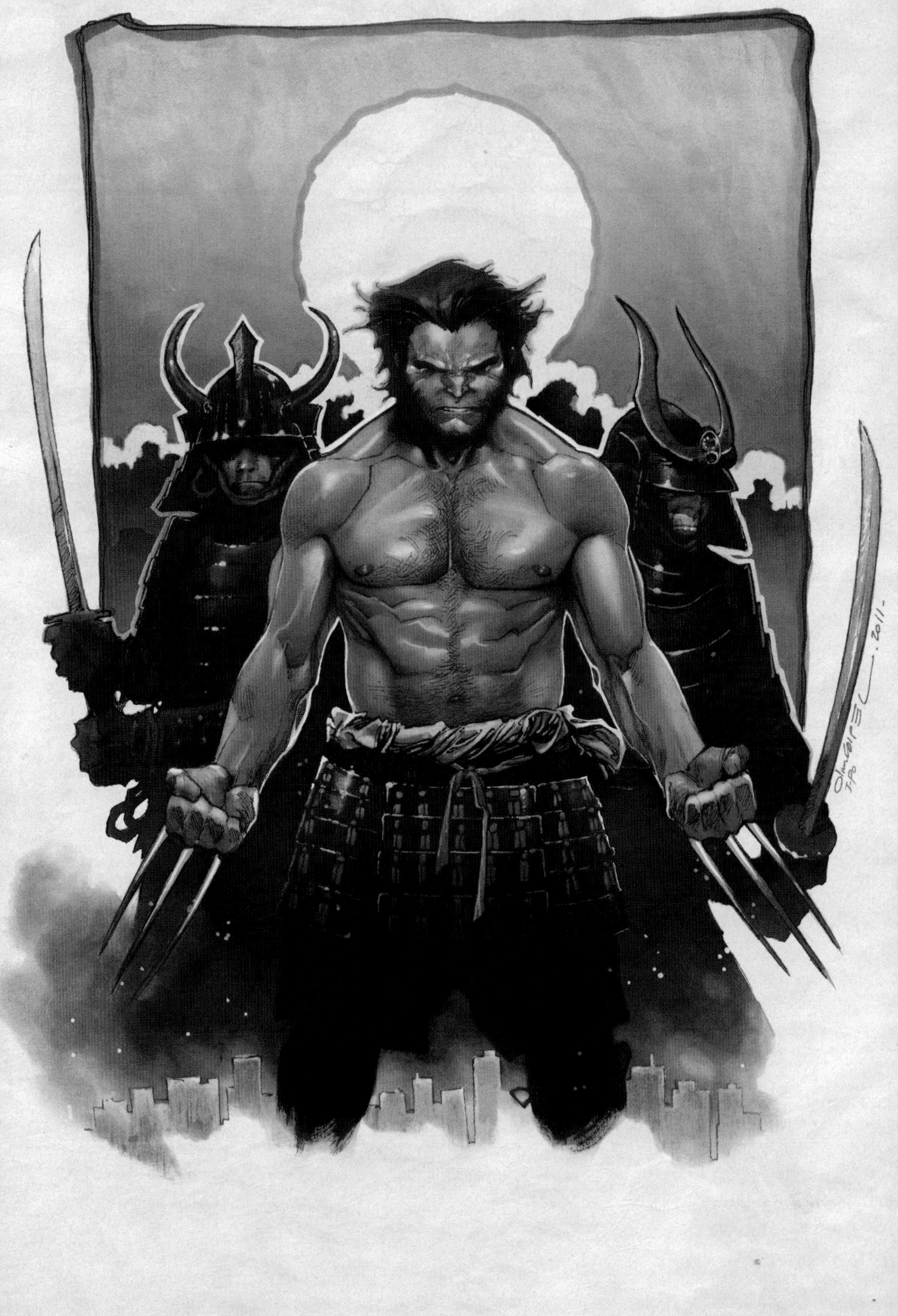

301

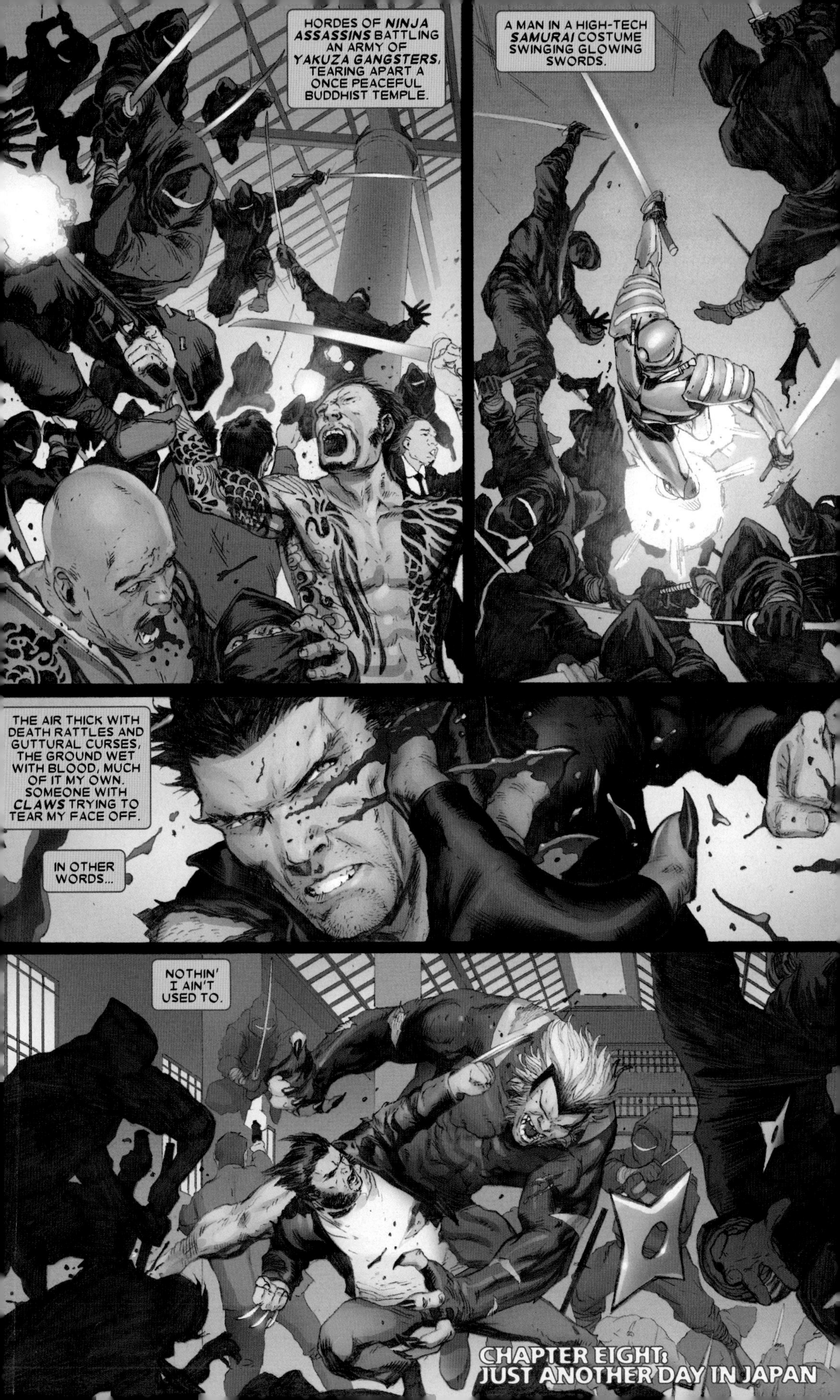

HORDES OF NINJA ASSASSINS BATTLING AN ARMY OF YAKUZA GANGSTERS, TEARING APART A ONCE PEACEFUL BUDDHIST TEMPLE.
A MAN IN A HIGH-TECH SAMURAI COSTUME SWINGING GLOWING SWORDS.
THE AIR THICK WITH DEATH RATTLES AND GUTTURAL CURSES, THE GROUND WET WITH BLOOD, MUCH OF IT MY OWN. SOMEONE WITH CLAWS TRYING TO TEAR MY FACE OFF.
IN OTHER WORDS...
NOTHIN' I AIN'T USED TO.
CHAPTER EIGHT:
JUST ANOTHER DAY IN JAPAN

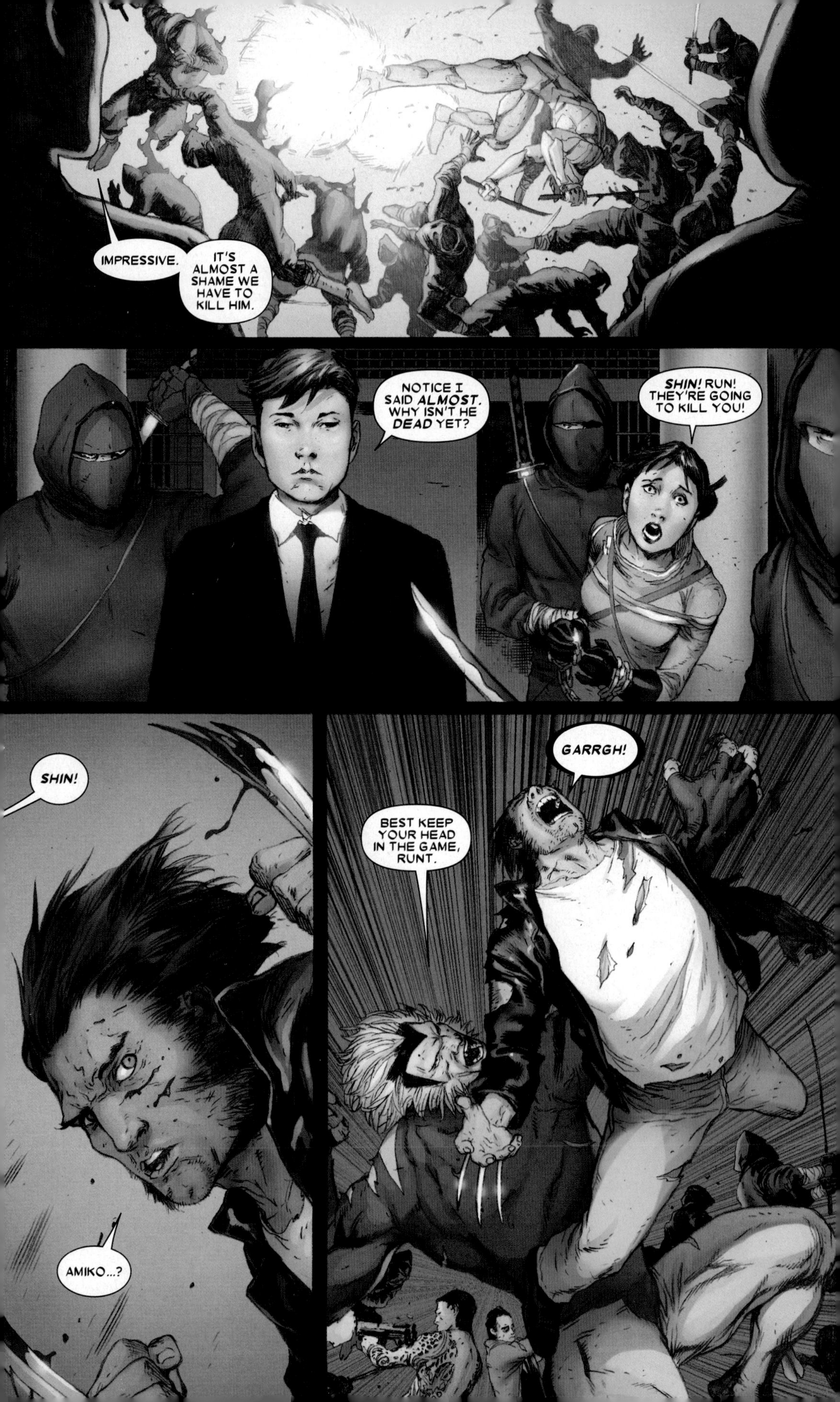
IMPRESSIVE.
IT'S ALMOST A SHAME WE HAVE TO KILL HIM.
NOTICE I SAID ALMOST. WHY ISN'T HE DEAD YET?
SHIN! RUN! THEY'RE GOING TO KILL YOU!
SHIN!
AMIKO...?
GARRGH!
BEST KEEP YOUR HEAD IN THE GAME, RUNT.

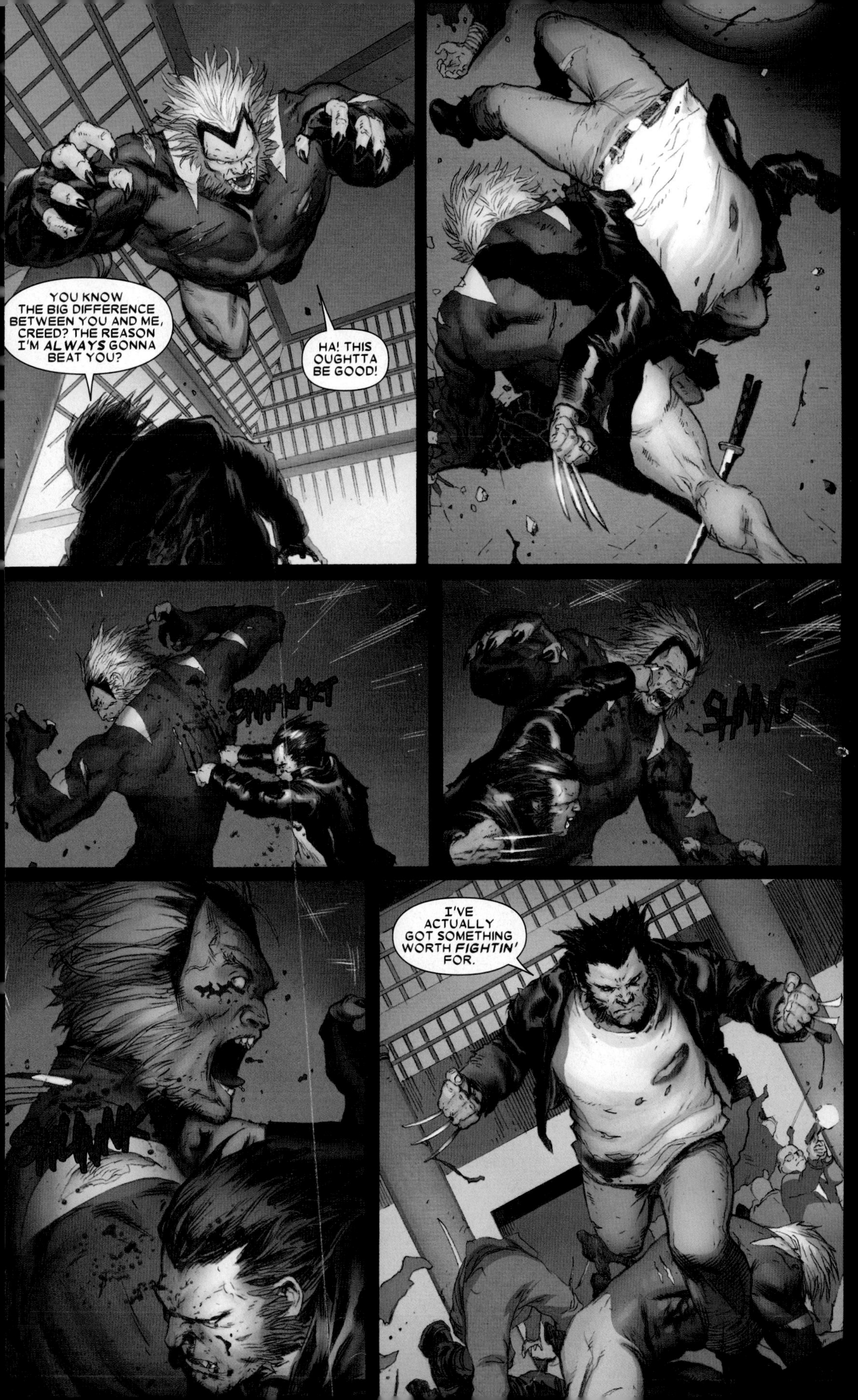
YOU KNOW THE BIG DIFFERENCE BETWEEN YOU AND ME, CREED? THE REASON I'M *ALWAYS* GONNA BEAT YOU?
HA! THIS OUGHTTA BE GOOD!
I'VE ACTUALLY GOT SOMETHING WORTH *FIGHTIN'* FOR.

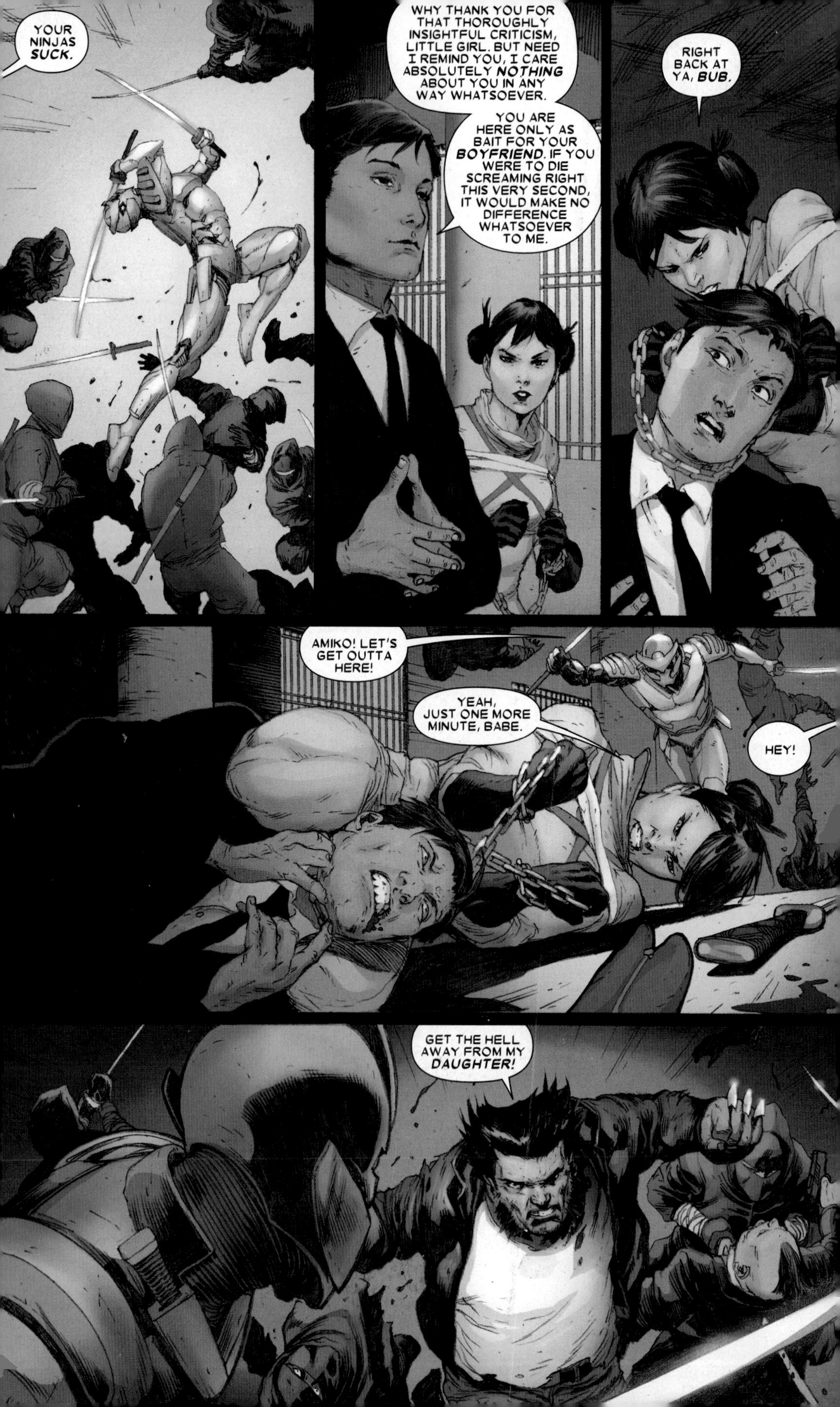
YOUR NINJAS *SUCK.*
WHY THANK YOU FOR THAT THOROUGHLY INSIGHTFUL CRITICISM, LITTLE GIRL. BUT NEED I REMIND YOU, I CARE ABSOLUTELY *NOTHING* ABOUT YOU IN ANY WAY WHATSOEVER.
YOU ARE HERE ONLY AS BAIT FOR YOUR *BOYFRIEND.* IF YOU WERE TO DIE SCREAMING RIGHT THIS VERY SECOND, IT WOULD MAKE NO DIFFERENCE WHATSOEVER TO ME.
RIGHT BACK AT YA, *BUB.*
AMIKO! LET'S GET OUTTA HERE!
YEAH, JUST ONE MORE MINUTE, BABE.
HEY!
GET THE HELL AWAY FROM MY *DAUGHTER!*

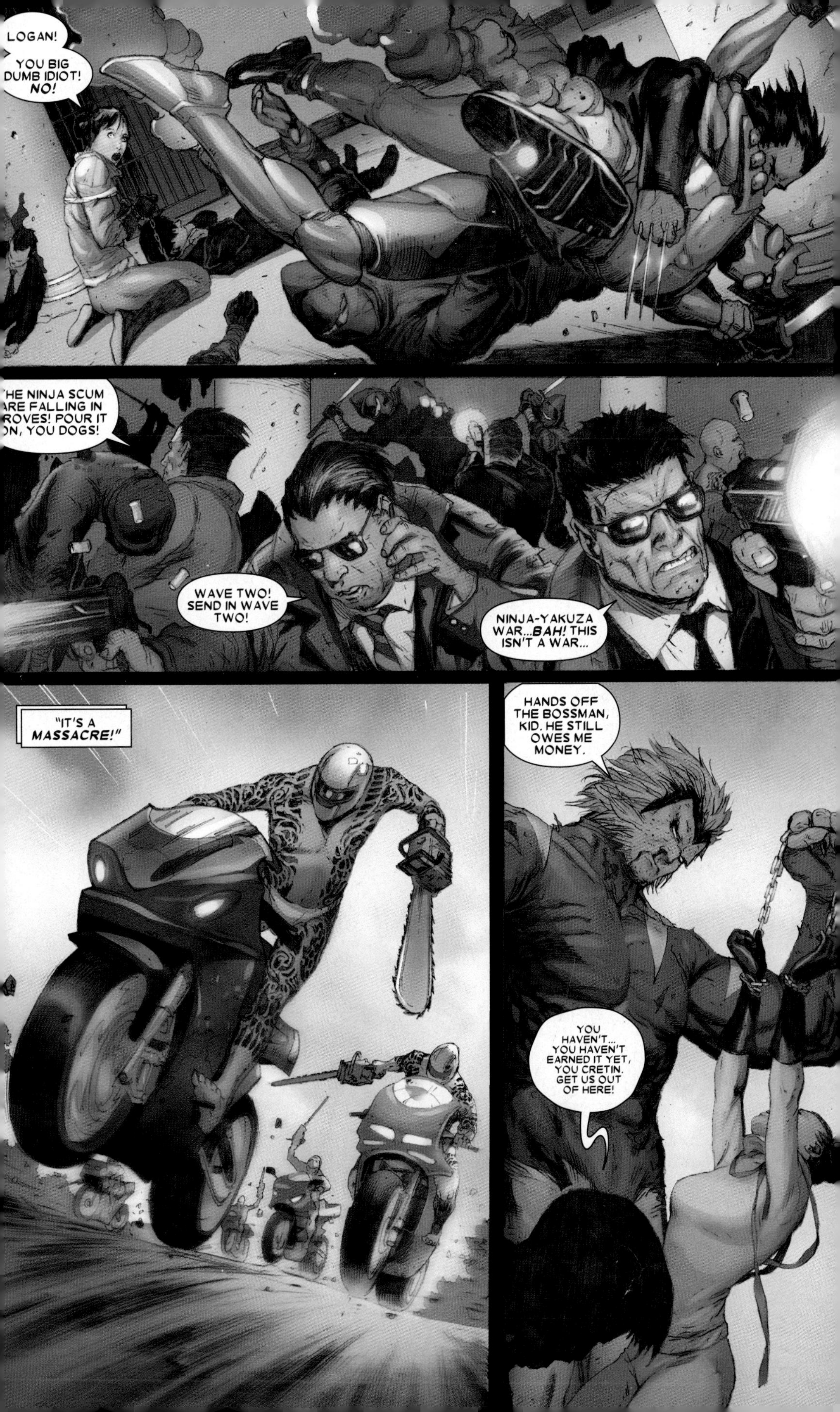
LOGAN!
YOU BIG DUMB IDIOT! NO!
THE NINJA SCUM ARE FALLING IN DROVES! POUR IT ON, YOU DOGS!
WAVE TWO! SEND IN WAVE TWO!
NINJA-YAKUZA WAR...BAH! THIS ISN'T A WAR...
"IT'S A MASSACRE!"
HANDS OFF THE BOSSMAN, KID. HE STILL OWES ME MONEY.
YOU HAVEN'T... YOU HAVEN'T EARNED IT YET, YOU CRETIN. GET US OUT OF HERE!

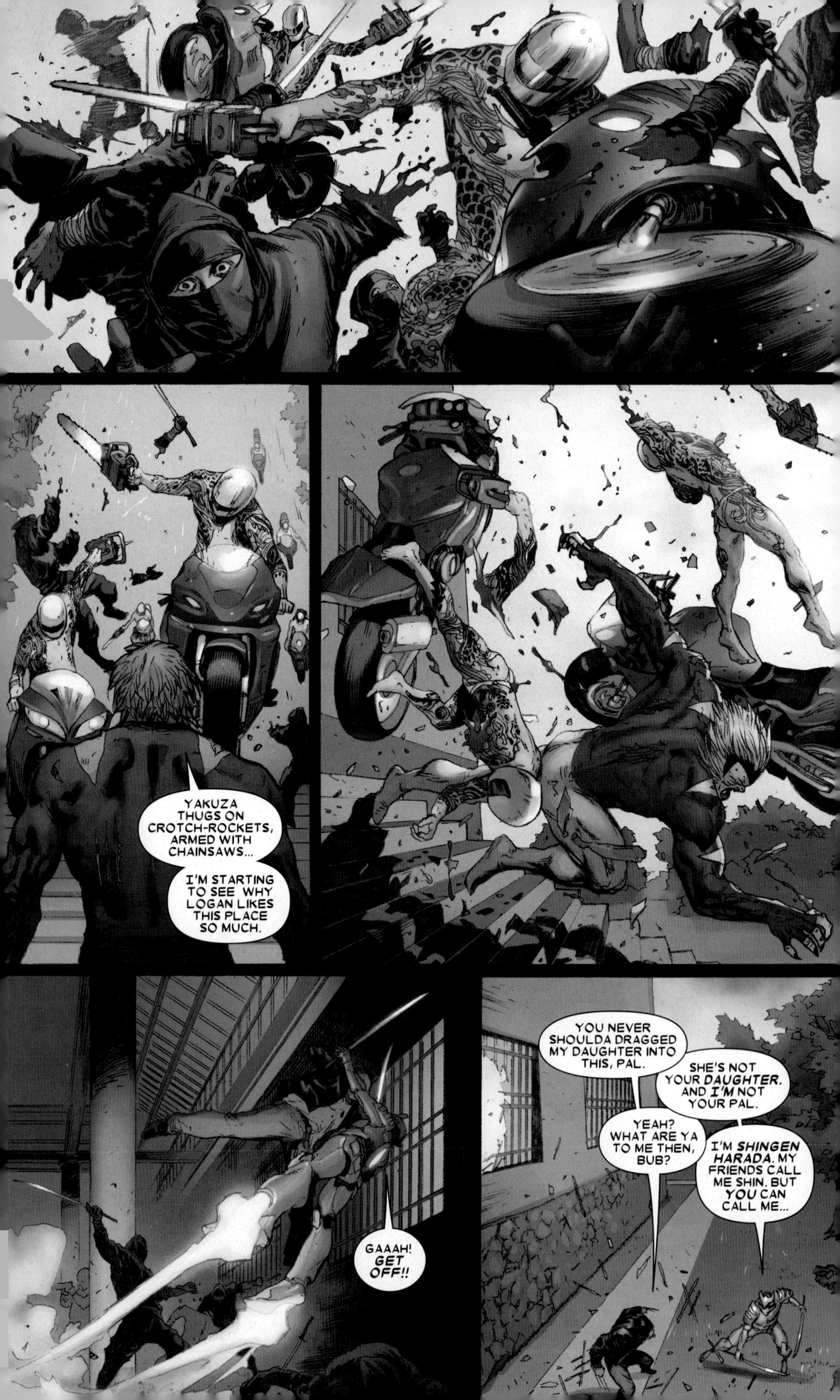
YAKUZA THUGS ON CROTCH-ROCKETS, ARMED WITH CHAINSAWS...
I'M STARTING TO SEE WHY LOGAN LIKES THIS PLACE SO MUCH.
GAAAH! GET OFF!!
YOU NEVER SHOULDA DRAGGED MY DAUGHTER INTO THIS, PAL.
SHE'S NOT YOUR DAUGHTER. AND I'M NOT YOUR PAL.
YEAH? WHAT ARE YA TO ME THEN, BUB?
I'M SHINGEN HARADA. MY FRIENDS CALL ME SHIN. BUT YOU CAN CALL ME...

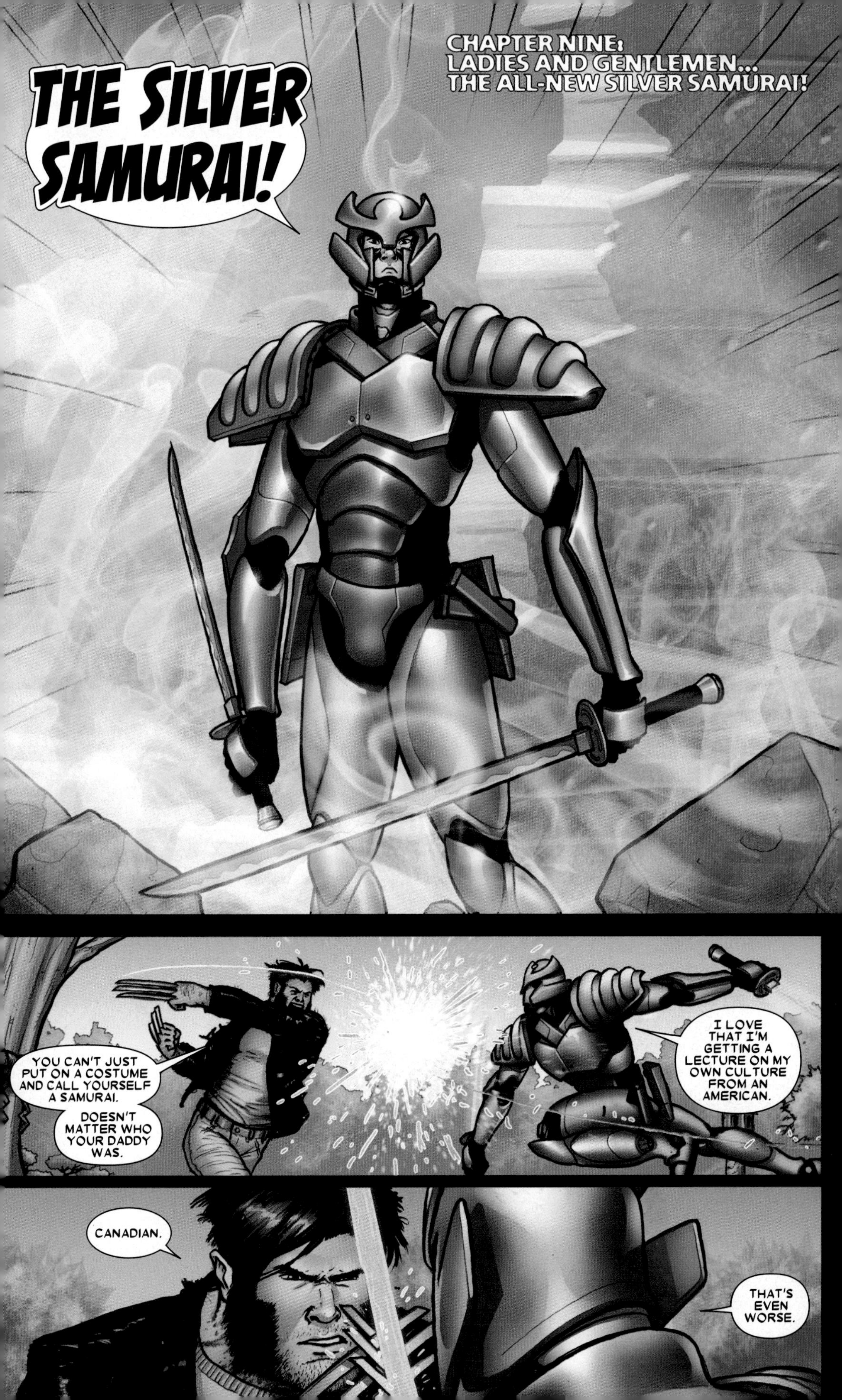
THE SILVER SAMURAI!
CHAPTER NINE: LADIES AND GENTLEMEN... THE ALL-NEW SILVER SAMURAI!
YOU CAN'T JUST PUT ON A COSTUME AND CALL YOURSELF A SAMURAI.
DOESN'T MATTER WHO YOUR DADDY WAS.
I LOVE THAT I'M GETTING A LECTURE ON MY OWN CULTURE FROM AN AMERICAN.
CANADIAN.
THAT'S EVEN WORSE.

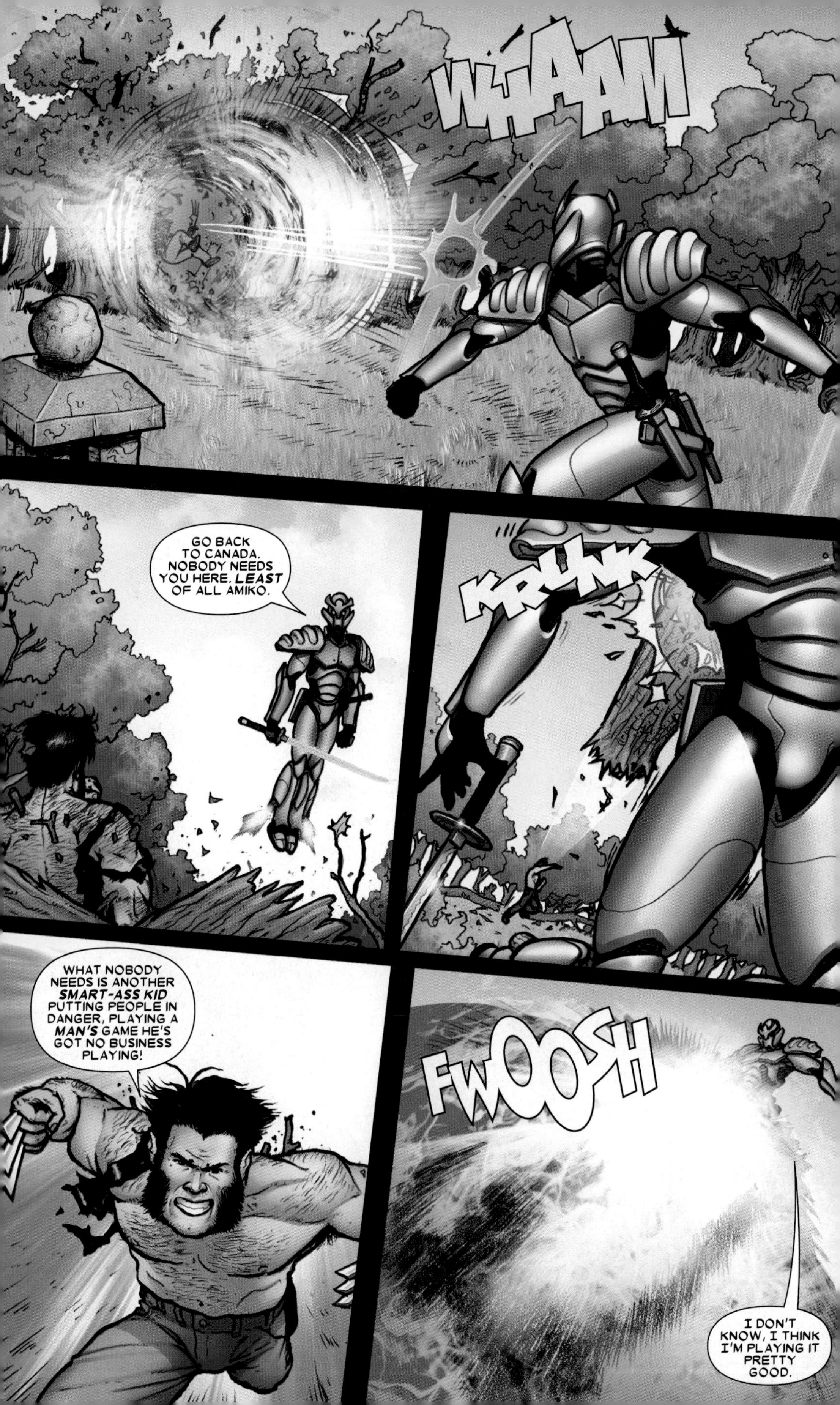
WHAAAM
GO BACK TO CANADA. NOBODY NEEDS YOU HERE. LEAST OF ALL AMIKO.
KRUNK
WHAT NOBODY NEEDS IS ANOTHER SMART-ASS KID PUTTING PEOPLE IN DANGER, PLAYING A MAN'S GAME HE'S GOT NO BUSINESS PLAYING!
FWOOSH
I DON'T KNOW, I THINK I'M PLAYING IT PRETTY GOOD.

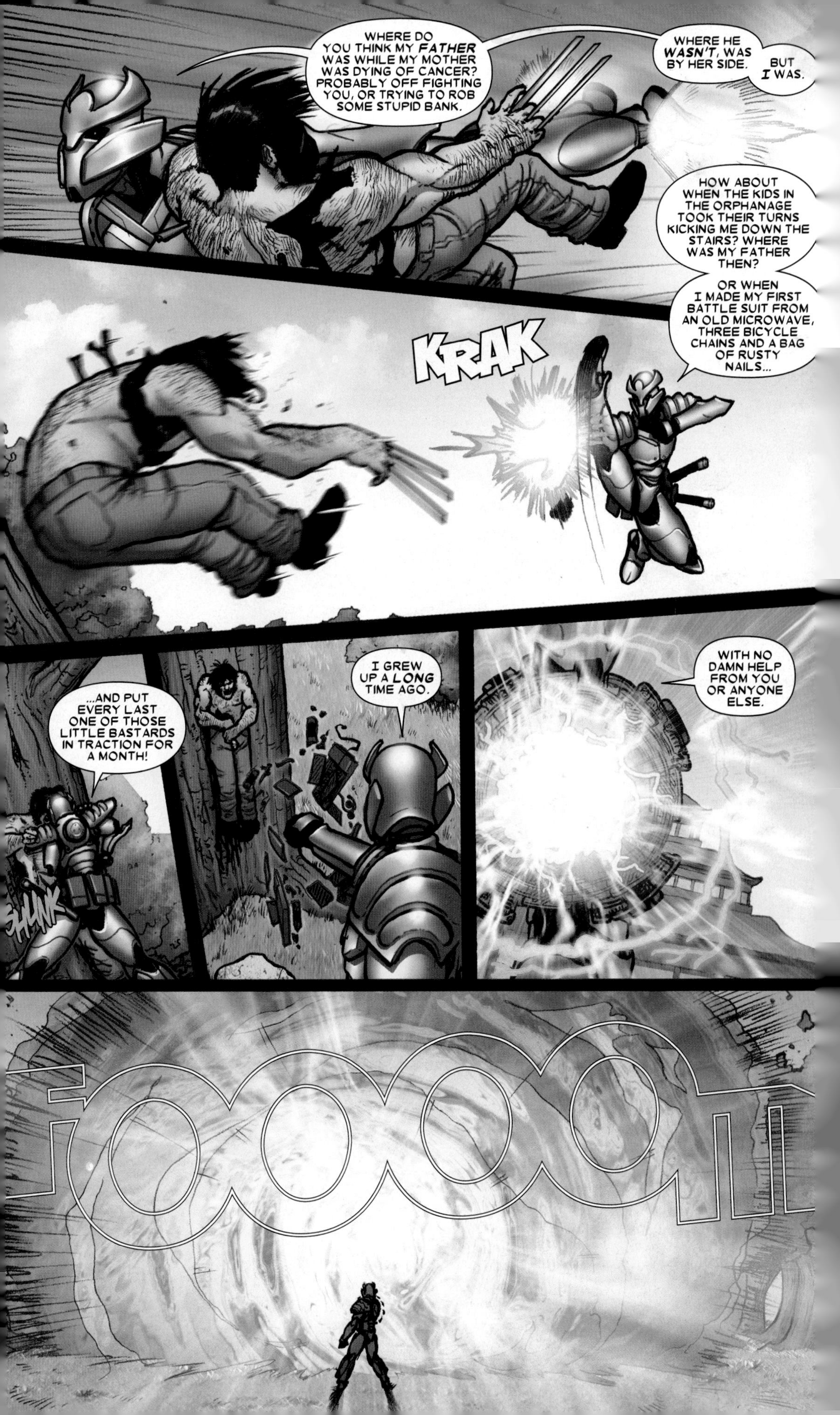
WHERE DO YOU THINK MY FATHER WAS WHILE MY MOTHER WAS DYING OF CANCER? PROBABLY OFF FIGHTING YOU, OR TRYING TO ROB SOME STUPID BANK.
WHERE HE WASN'T, WAS BY HER SIDE.
BUT I WAS.
HOW ABOUT WHEN THE KIDS IN THE ORPHANAGE TOOK THEIR TURNS KICKING ME DOWN THE STAIRS? WHERE WAS MY FATHER THEN?
OR WHEN I MADE MY FIRST BATTLE SUIT FROM AN OLD MICROWAVE, THREE BICYCLE CHAINS AND A BAG OF RUSTY NAILS...
KRAK
...AND PUT EVERY LAST ONE OF THOSE LITTLE BASTARDS IN TRACTION FOR A MONTH!
SHUNK
I GREW UP A LONG TIME AGO.
WITH NO DAMN HELP FROM YOU OR ANYONE ELSE.
FOOOOOM

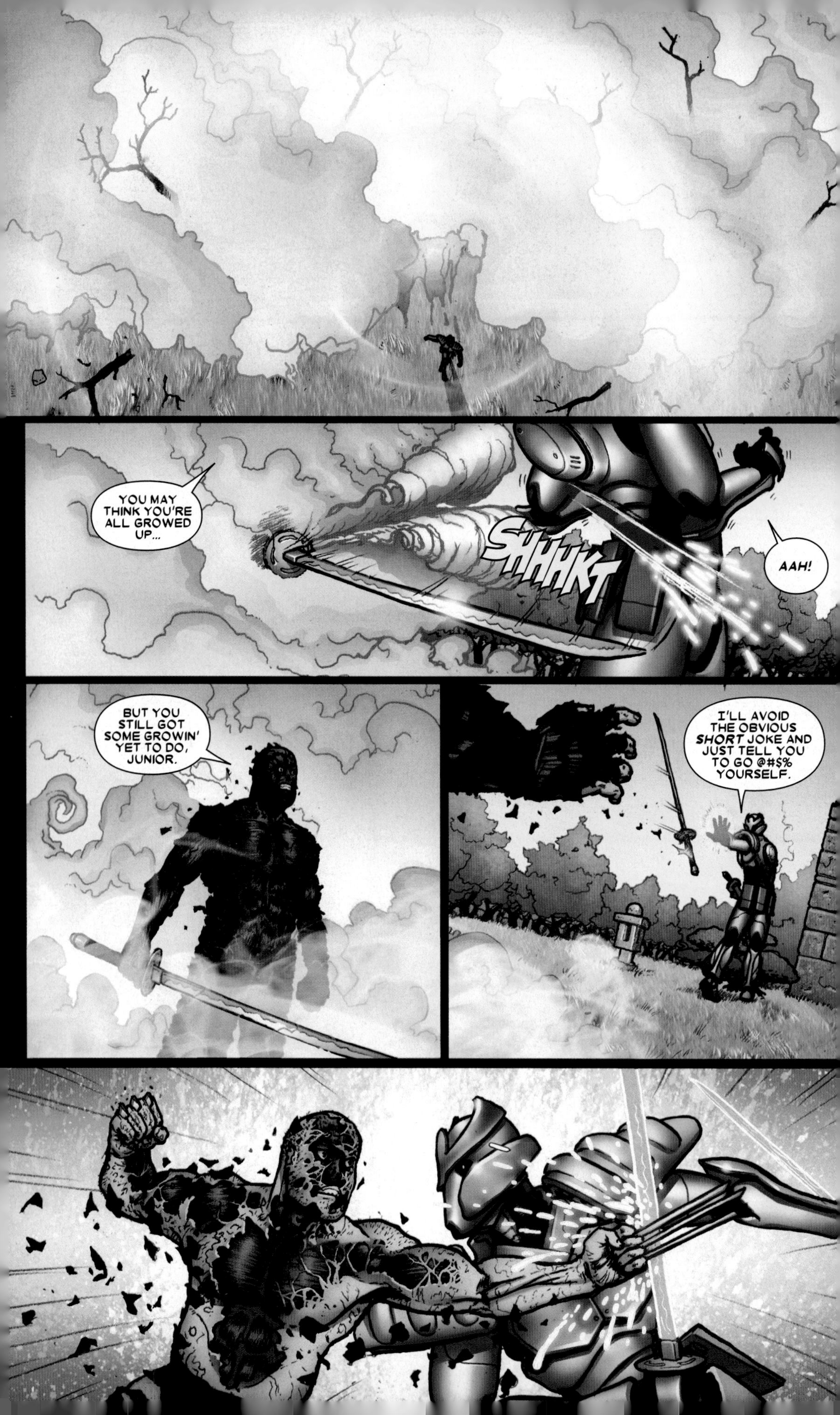
YOU MAY THINK YOU'RE ALL GROWED UP...
SHHHKT
AAH!
BUT YOU STILL GOT SOME GROWIN' YET TO DO, JUNIOR.
I'LL AVOID THE OBVIOUS SHORT JOKE AND JUST TELL YOU TO GO @#$% YOURSELF.

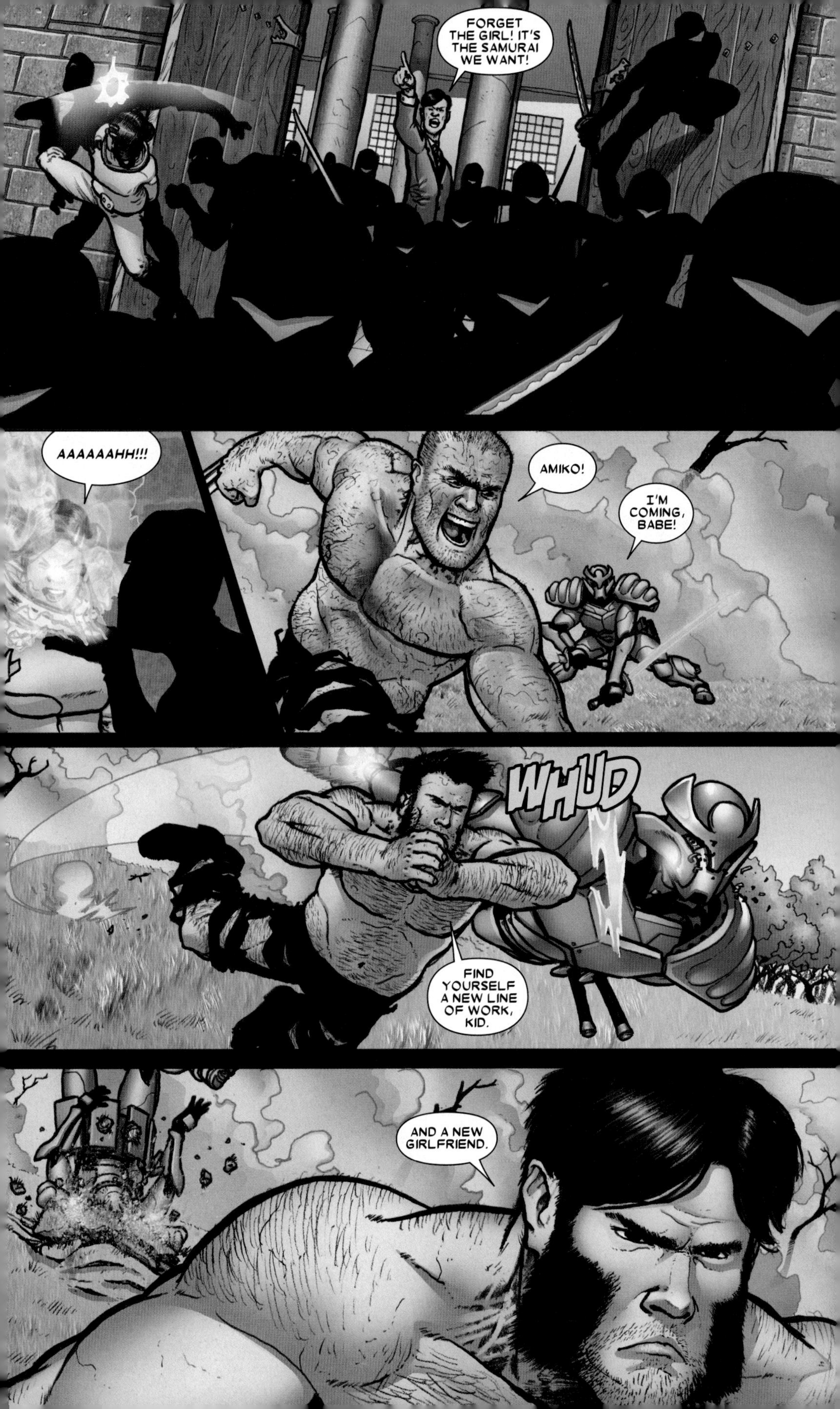
FORGET THE GIRL! IT'S THE SAMURAI WE WANT!
AAAAAAHH!!!
AMIKO!
I'M COMING, BABE!
WHUD
FIND YOURSELF A NEW LINE OF WORK, KID.
AND A NEW GIRLFRIEND.

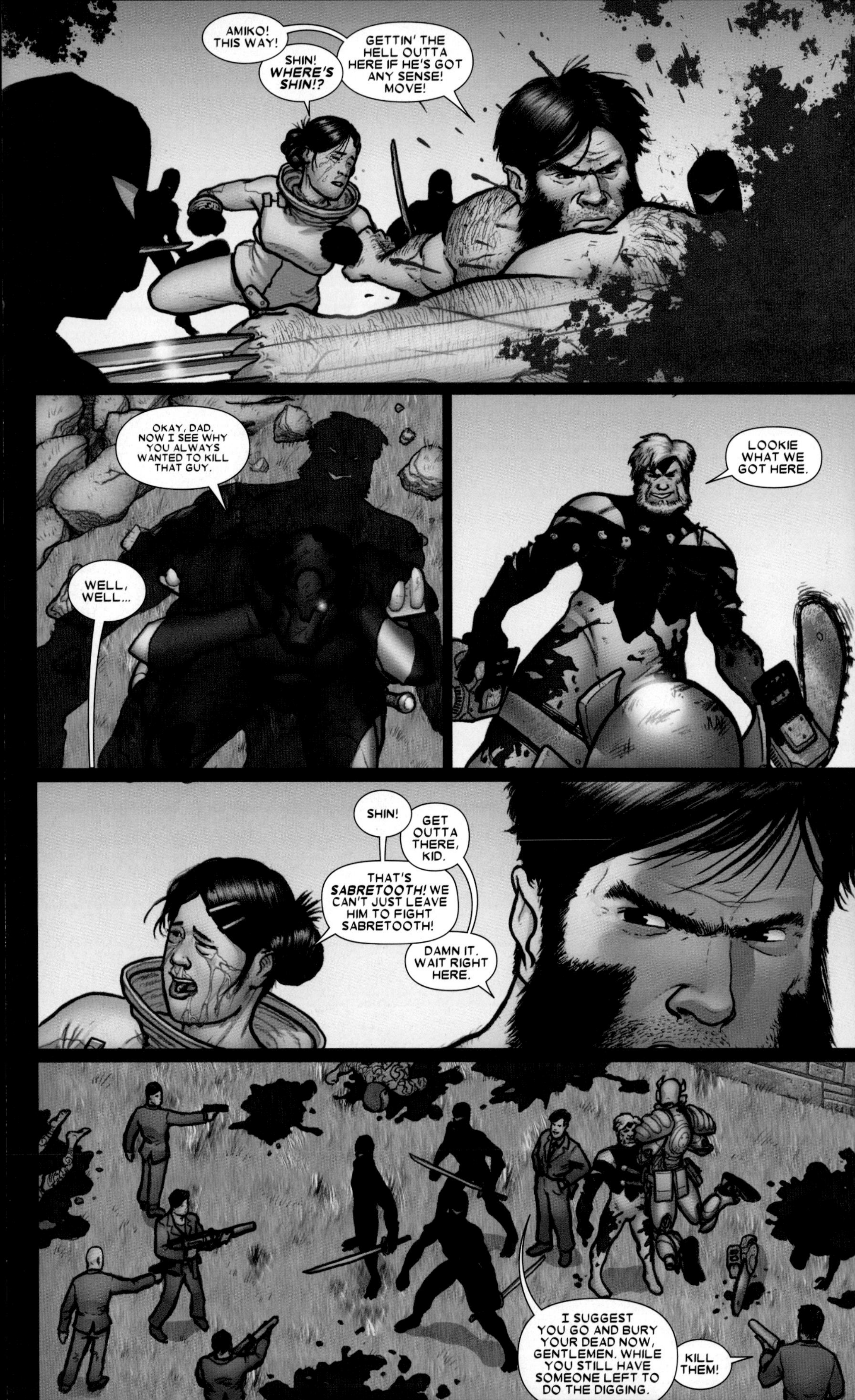
AMIKO! THIS WAY!
SHIN! WHERE'S SHIN!?
GETTIN' THE HELL OUTTA HERE IF HE'S GOT ANY SENSE! MOVE!
OKAY, DAD. NOW I SEE WHY YOU ALWAYS WANTED TO KILL THAT GUY.
WELL, WELL...
LOOKIE WHAT WE GOT HERE.
SHIN!
GET OUTTA THERE, KID.
THAT'S SABRETOOTH! WE CAN'T JUST LEAVE HIM TO FIGHT SABRETOOTH!
DAMN IT. WAIT RIGHT HERE.
I SUGGEST YOU GO AND BURY YOUR DEAD NOW, GENTLEMEN. WHILE YOU STILL HAVE SOMEONE LEFT TO DO THE DIGGING.
KILL THEM!

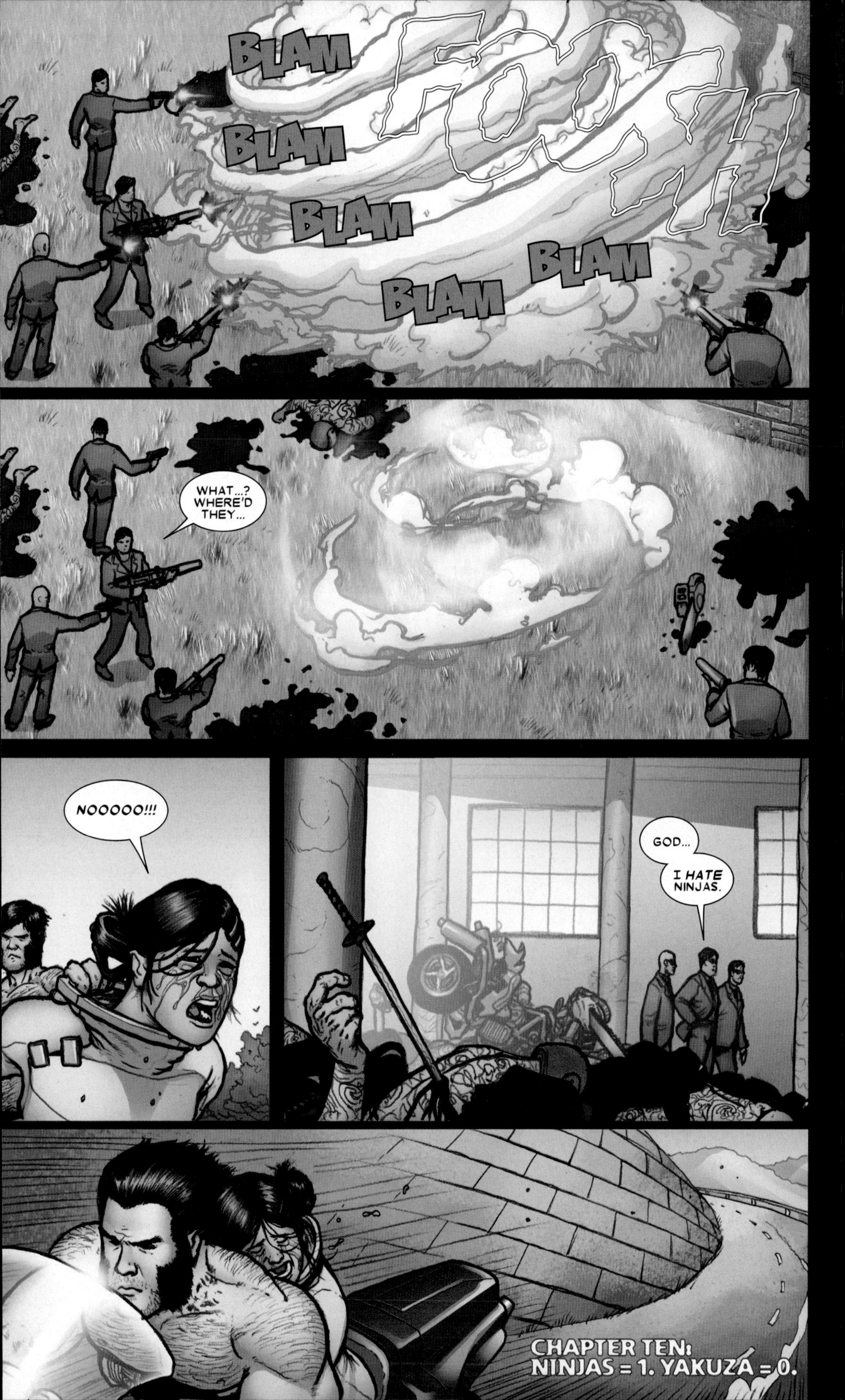
BLAM
BLAM
BLAM
BLAM
BLAM
FOOOM
WHAT...? WHERE'D THEY...
NOOOOO!!!
GOD...
I HATE NINJAS.
CHAPTER TEN:
NINJAS = 1. YAKUZA = 0.

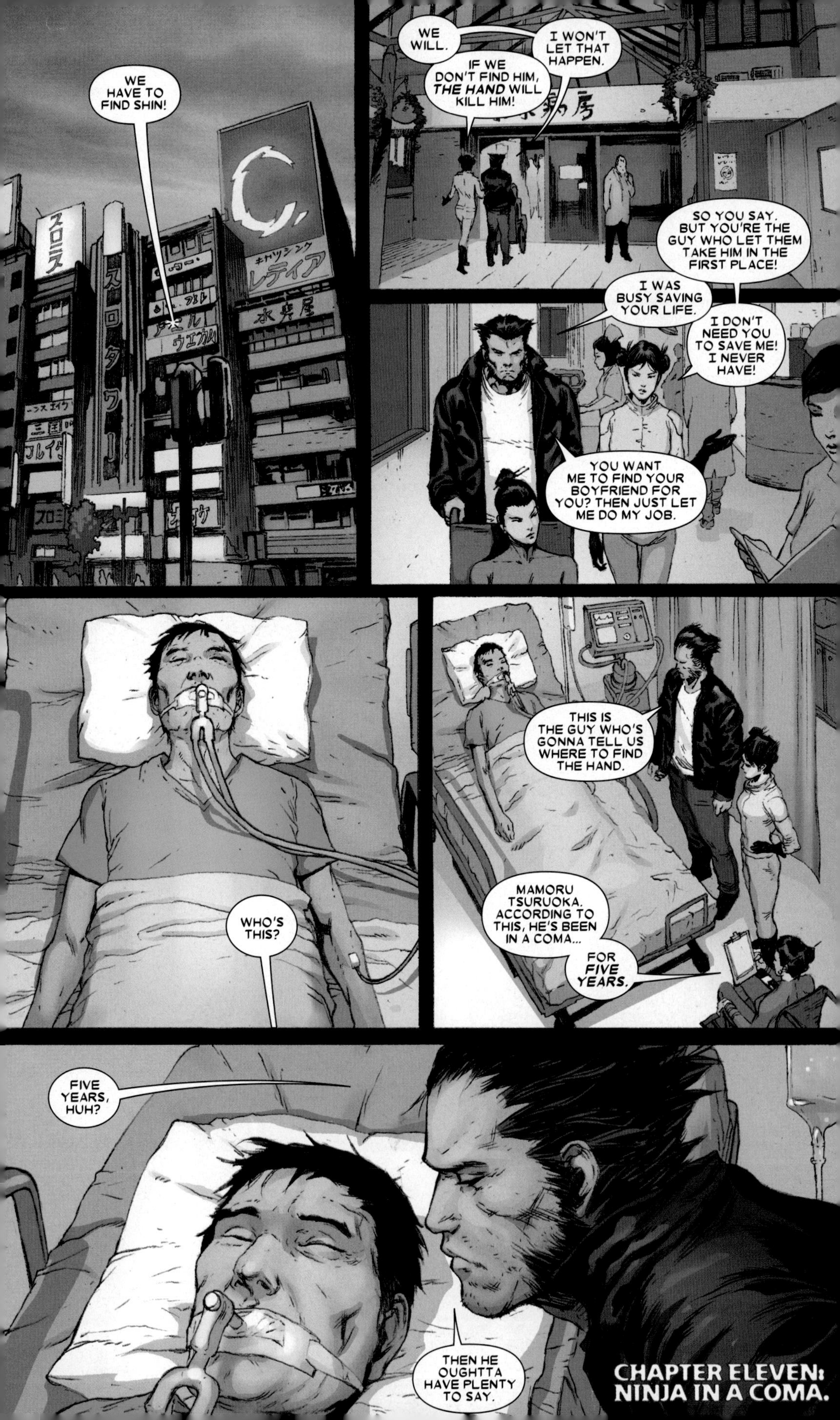
WE HAVE TO FIND SHIN!
WE WILL.
IF WE DON'T FIND HIM, *THE HAND* WILL KILL HIM!
I WON'T LET THAT HAPPEN.
SO YOU SAY. BUT YOU'RE THE GUY WHO LET THEM TAKE HIM IN THE FIRST PLACE!
I WAS BUSY SAVING YOUR LIFE.
I DON'T NEED YOU TO SAVE ME! I NEVER HAVE!
YOU WANT ME TO FIND YOUR BOYFRIEND FOR YOU? THEN JUST LET ME DO MY JOB.
WHO'S THIS?
THIS IS THE GUY WHO'S GONNA TELL US WHERE TO FIND THE HAND.
MAMORU TSURUOKA. ACCORDING TO THIS, HE'S BEEN IN A COMA...
FOR *FIVE YEARS.*
FIVE YEARS, HUH?
THEN HE OUGHTTA HAVE PLENTY TO SAY.
CHAPTER ELEVEN: NINJA IN A COMA.

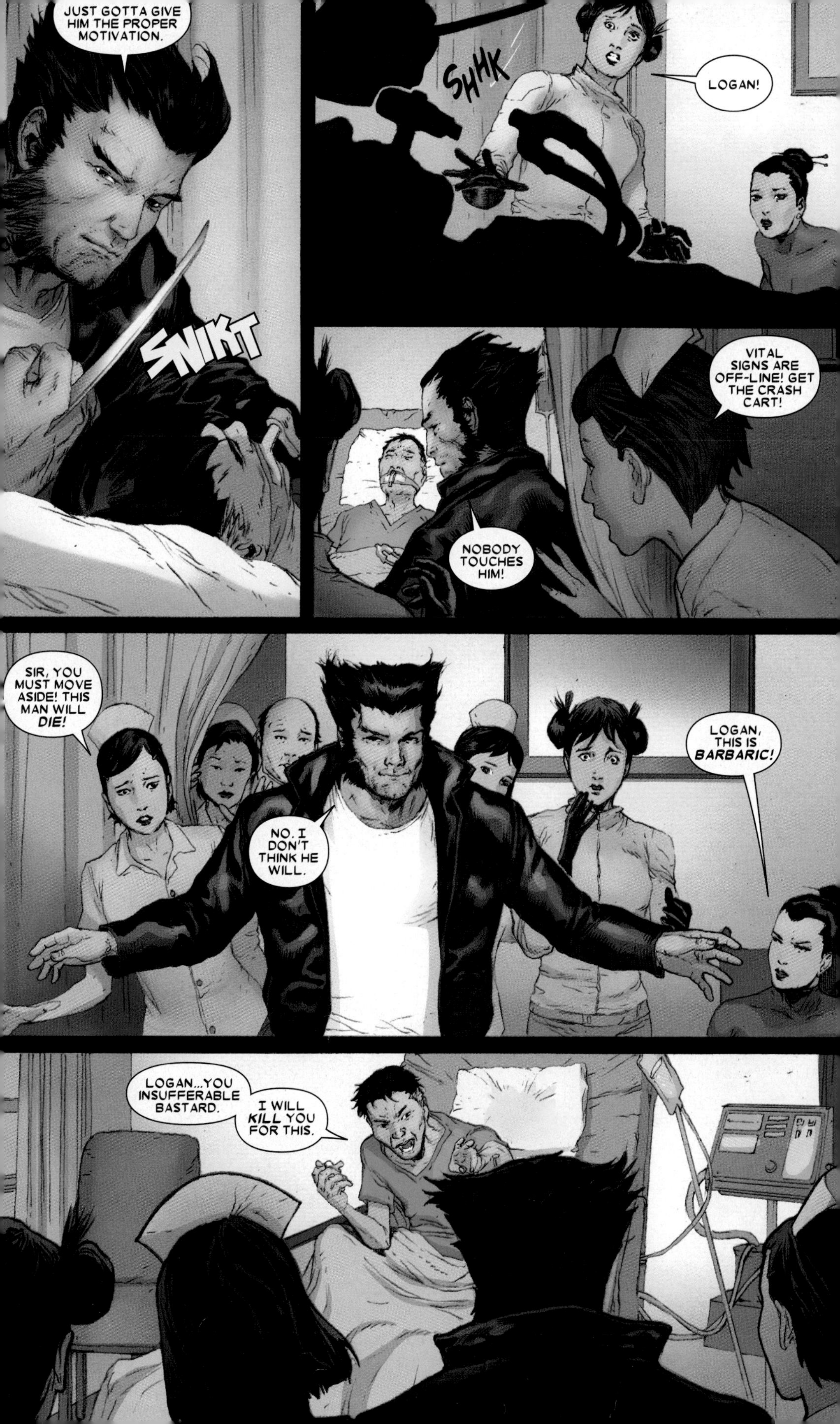
JUST GOTTA GIVE HIM THE PROPER MOTIVATION.
SNIKT
SHHK
LOGAN!
VITAL SIGNS ARE OFF-LINE! GET THE CRASH CART!
NOBODY TOUCHES HIM!
SIR, YOU MUST MOVE ASIDE! THIS MAN WILL *DIE!*
NO. I DON'T THINK HE WILL.
LOGAN, THIS IS *BARBARIC!*
LOGAN...YOU INSUFFERABLE BASTARD.
I WILL *KILL* YOU FOR THIS.

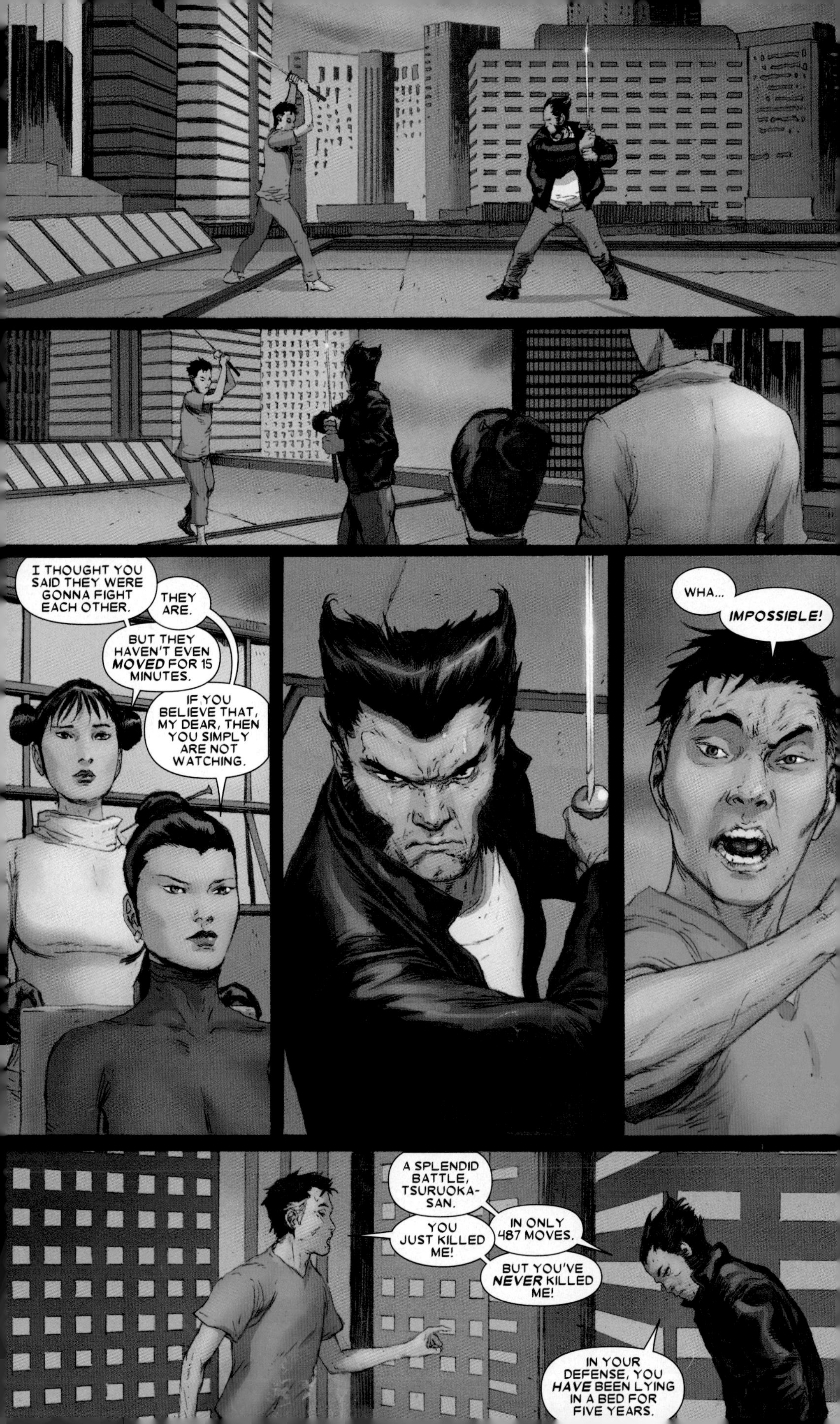

I THOUGHT YOU SAID THEY WERE GONNA FIGHT EACH OTHER.
THEY ARE.
BUT THEY HAVEN'T EVEN MOVED FOR 15 MINUTES.
IF YOU BELIEVE THAT, MY DEAR, THEN YOU SIMPLY ARE NOT WATCHING.
WHA...
IMPOSSIBLE!
A SPLENDID BATTLE, TSURUOKA-SAN.
YOU JUST KILLED ME!
IN ONLY 487 MOVES.
BUT YOU'VE NEVER KILLED ME!
IN YOUR DEFENSE, YOU HAVE BEEN LYING IN A BED FOR FIVE YEARS.

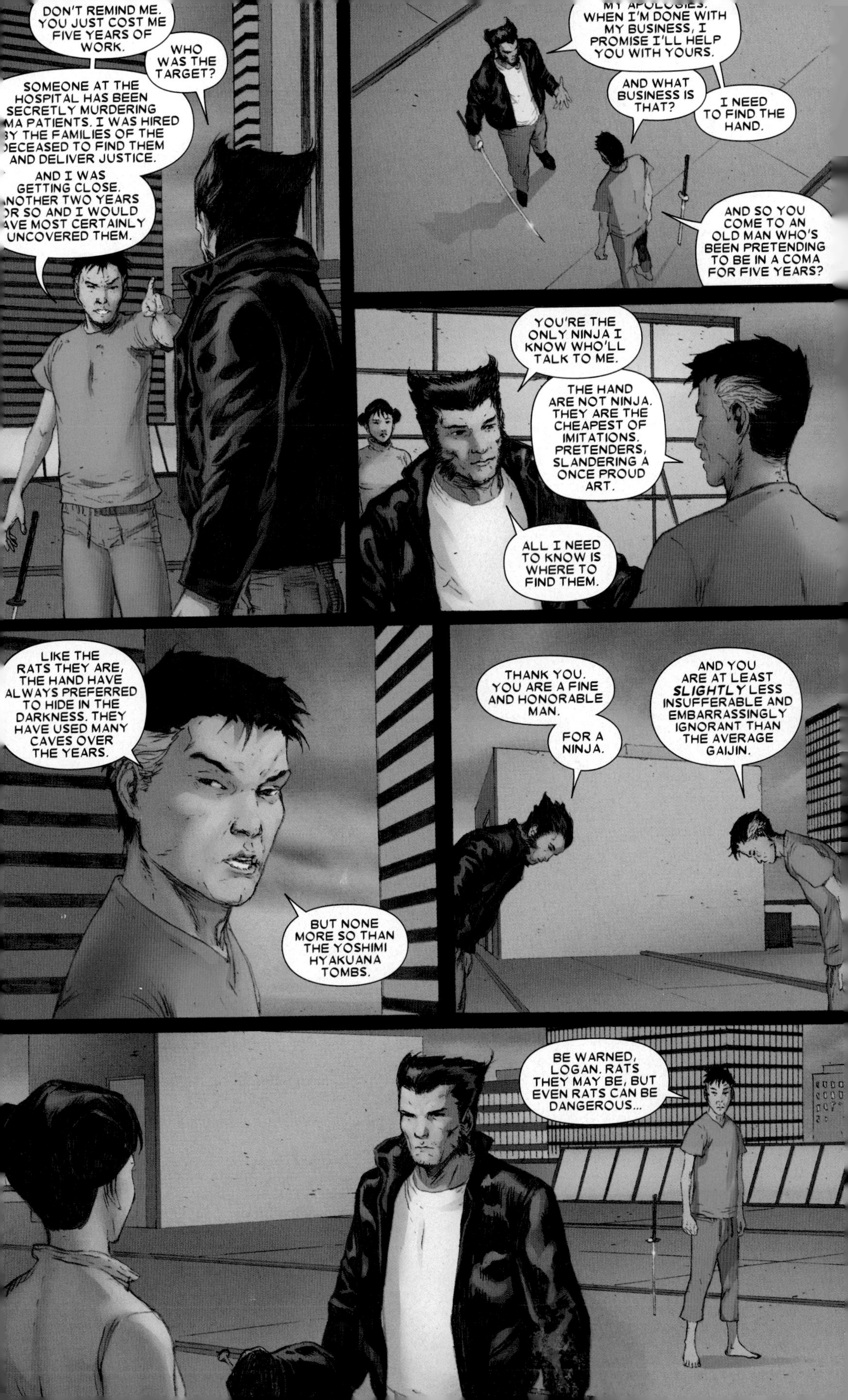
DON'T REMIND ME. YOU JUST COST ME FIVE YEARS OF WORK.
WHO WAS THE TARGET?
SOMEONE AT THE HOSPITAL HAS BEEN SECRETLY MURDERING MA PATIENTS. I WAS HIRED BY THE FAMILIES OF THE DECEASED TO FIND THEM AND DELIVER JUSTICE.
AND I WAS GETTING CLOSE. ANOTHER TWO YEARS OR SO AND I WOULD AVE MOST CERTAINLY UNCOVERED THEM.
WHEN I'M DONE WITH MY BUSINESS, I PROMISE I'LL HELP YOU WITH YOURS.
AND WHAT BUSINESS IS THAT?
I NEED TO FIND THE HAND.
AND SO YOU COME TO AN OLD MAN WHO'S BEEN PRETENDING TO BE IN A COMA FOR FIVE YEARS?
YOU'RE THE ONLY NINJA I KNOW WHO'LL TALK TO ME.
THE HAND ARE NOT NINJA. THEY ARE THE CHEAPEST OF IMITATIONS. PRETENDERS, SLANDERING A ONCE PROUD ART.
ALL I NEED TO KNOW IS WHERE TO FIND THEM.
LIKE THE RATS THEY ARE, THE HAND HAVE ALWAYS PREFERRED TO HIDE IN THE DARKNESS. THEY HAVE USED MANY CAVES OVER THE YEARS.
BUT NONE MORE SO THAN THE YOSHIMI HYAKUANA TOMBS.
THANK YOU. YOU ARE A FINE AND HONORABLE MAN.
FOR A NINJA.
AND YOU ARE AT LEAST *SLIGHTLY* LESS INSUFFERABLE AND EMBARRASSINGLY IGNORANT THAN THE AVERAGE GAIJIN.
BE WARNED, LOGAN. RATS THEY MAY BE, BUT EVEN RATS CAN BE DANGEROUS...

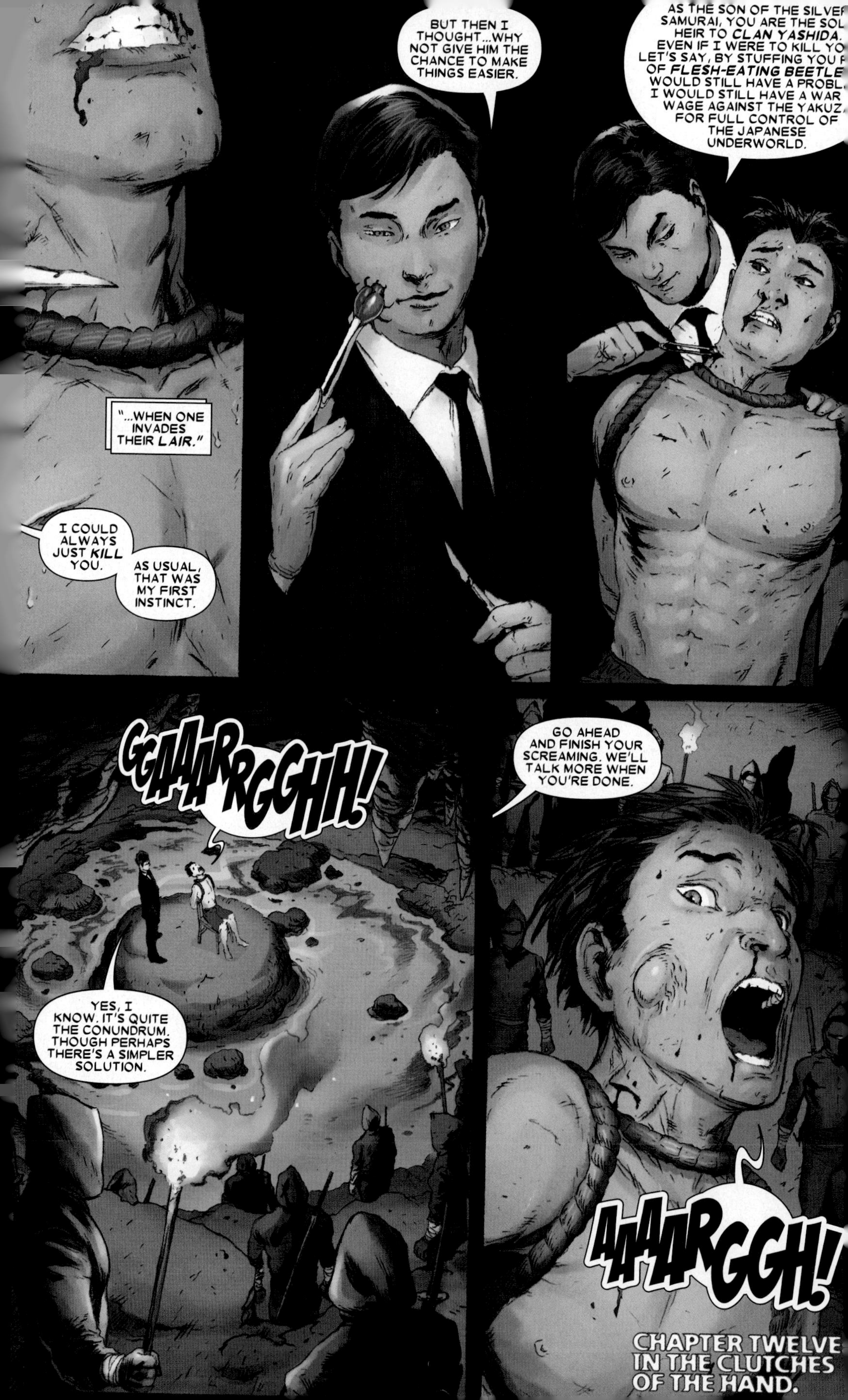
"...WHEN ONE INVADES THEIR LAIR."
I COULD ALWAYS JUST KILL YOU.
AS USUAL, THAT WAS MY FIRST INSTINCT.
BUT THEN I THOUGHT...WHY NOT GIVE HIM THE CHANCE TO MAKE THINGS EASIER.
AS THE SON OF THE SILVER SAMURAI, YOU ARE THE SOL HEIR TO CLAN YASHIDA. EVEN IF I WERE TO KILL YO LET'S SAY, BY STUFFING YOU F OF FLESH-EATING BEETLE WOULD STILL HAVE A PROBL. I WOULD STILL HAVE A WAR WAGE AGAINST THE YAKUZ FOR FULL CONTROL OF THE JAPANESE UNDERWORLD.
GGAAAARRGGHH!
YES, I KNOW. IT'S QUITE THE CONUNDRUM. THOUGH PERHAPS THERE'S A SIMPLER SOLUTION.
GO AHEAD AND FINISH YOUR SCREAMING. WE'LL TALK MORE WHEN YOU'RE DONE.
AAAARGGH!
CHAPTER TWELVE IN THE CLUTCHES OF THE HAND.

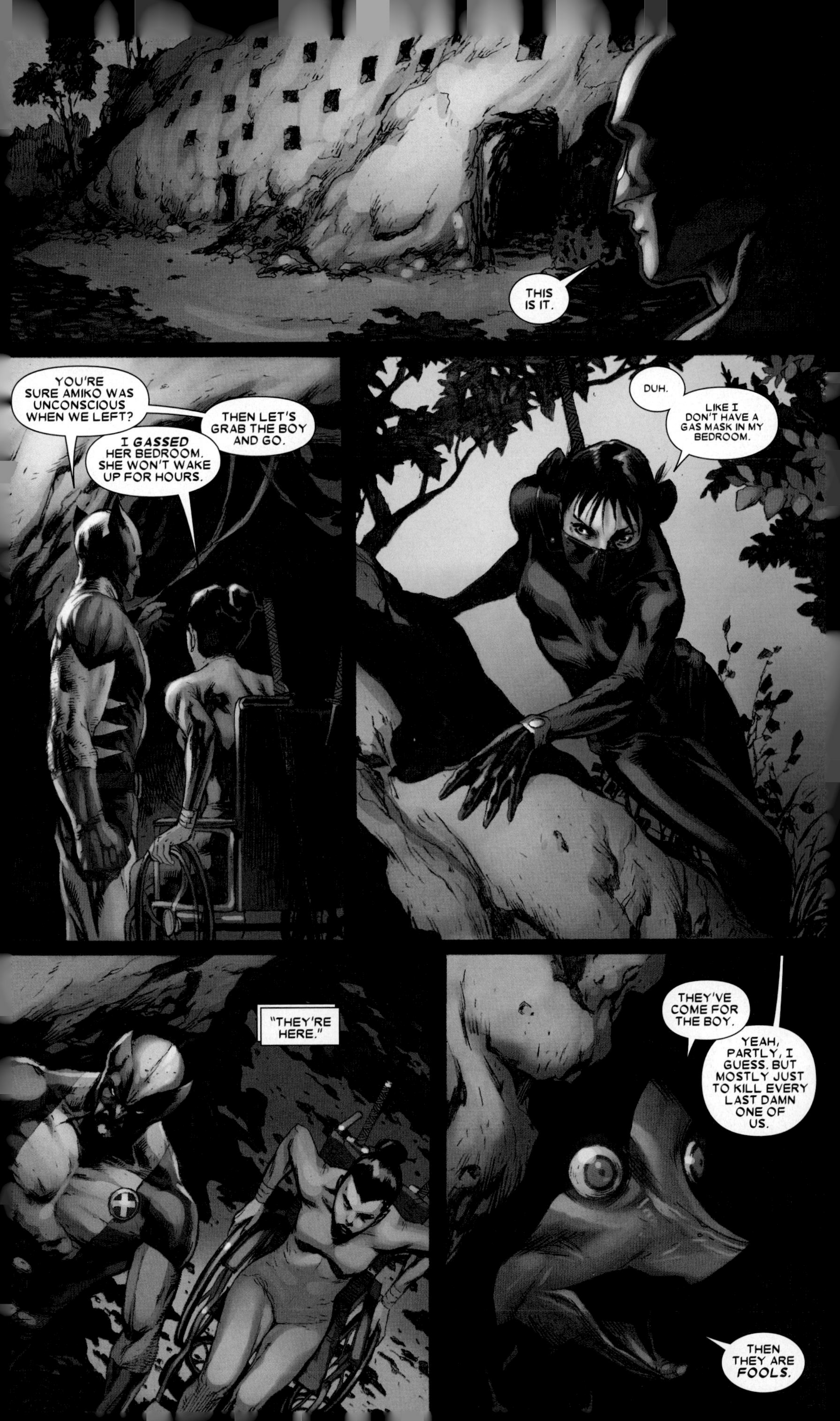
THIS IS IT.
YOU'RE SURE AMIKO WAS UNCONSCIOUS WHEN WE LEFT?
I *GASSED* HER BEDROOM. SHE WON'T WAKE UP FOR HOURS.
THEN LET'S GRAB THE BOY AND GO.
DUH.
LIKE I DON'T HAVE A GAS MASK IN MY BEDROOM.
"THEY'RE HERE."
THEY'VE COME FOR THE BOY.
YEAH, PARTLY, I GUESS. BUT MOSTLY JUST TO KILL EVERY LAST DAMN ONE OF US.
THEN THEY ARE *FOOLS*.

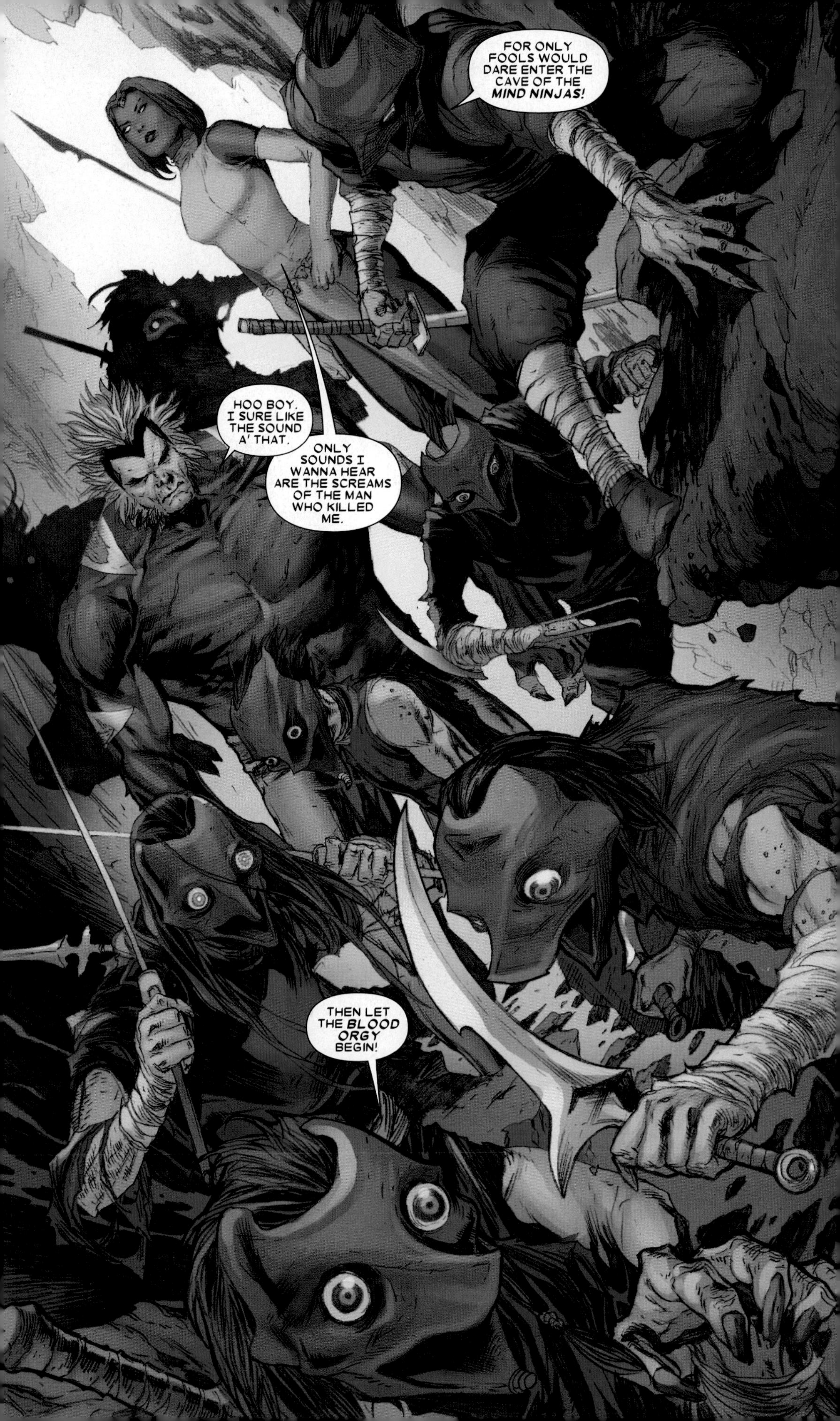
FOR ONLY FOOLS WOULD DARE ENTER THE CAVE OF THE *MIND NINJAS!*
HOO BOY. I SURE LIKE THE SOUND A' THAT.
ONLY SOUNDS I WANNA HEAR ARE THE SCREAMS OF THE MAN WHO KILLED ME.
THEN LET THE *BLOOD ORGY* BEGIN!

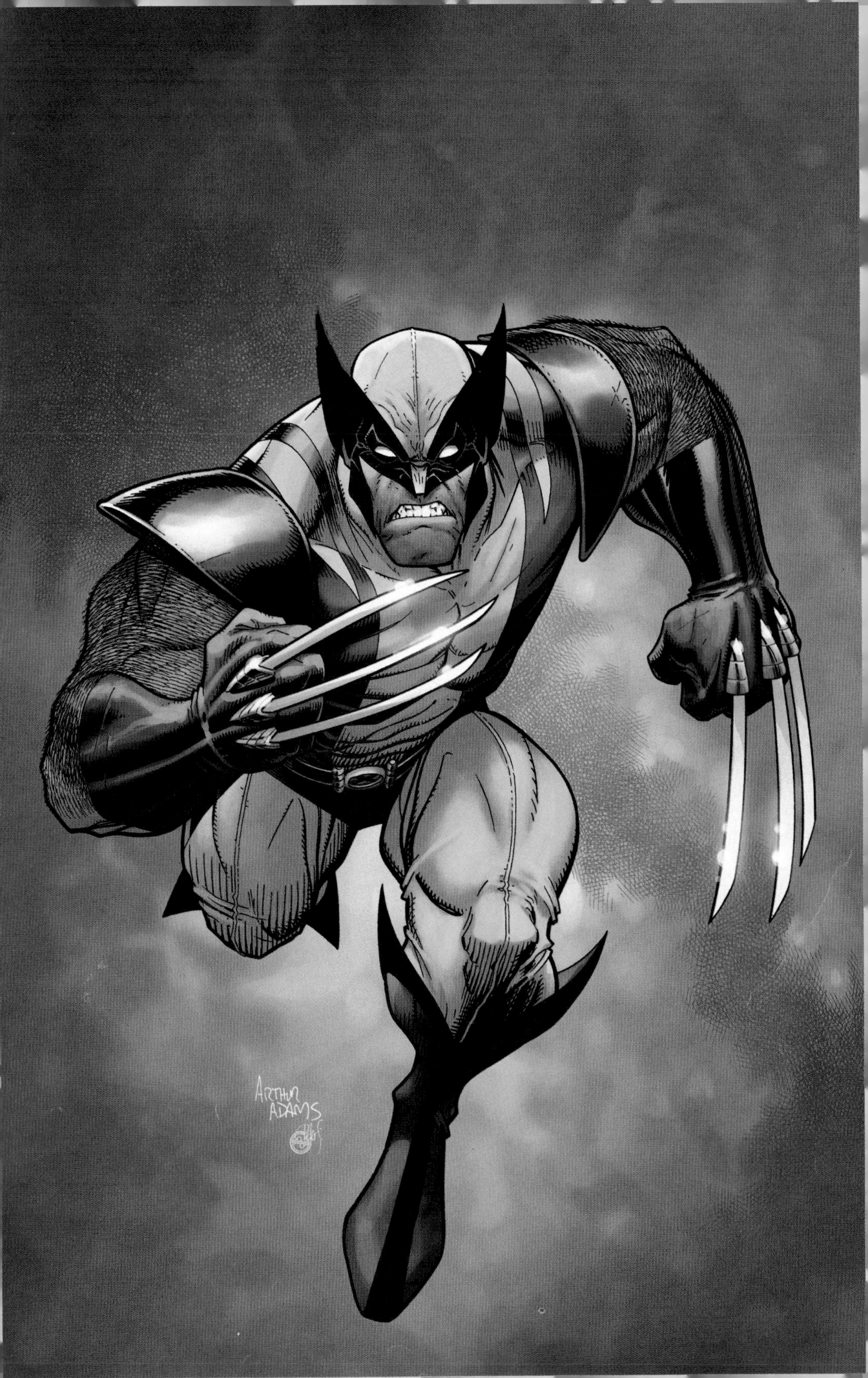
ARTHUR
ADAMS

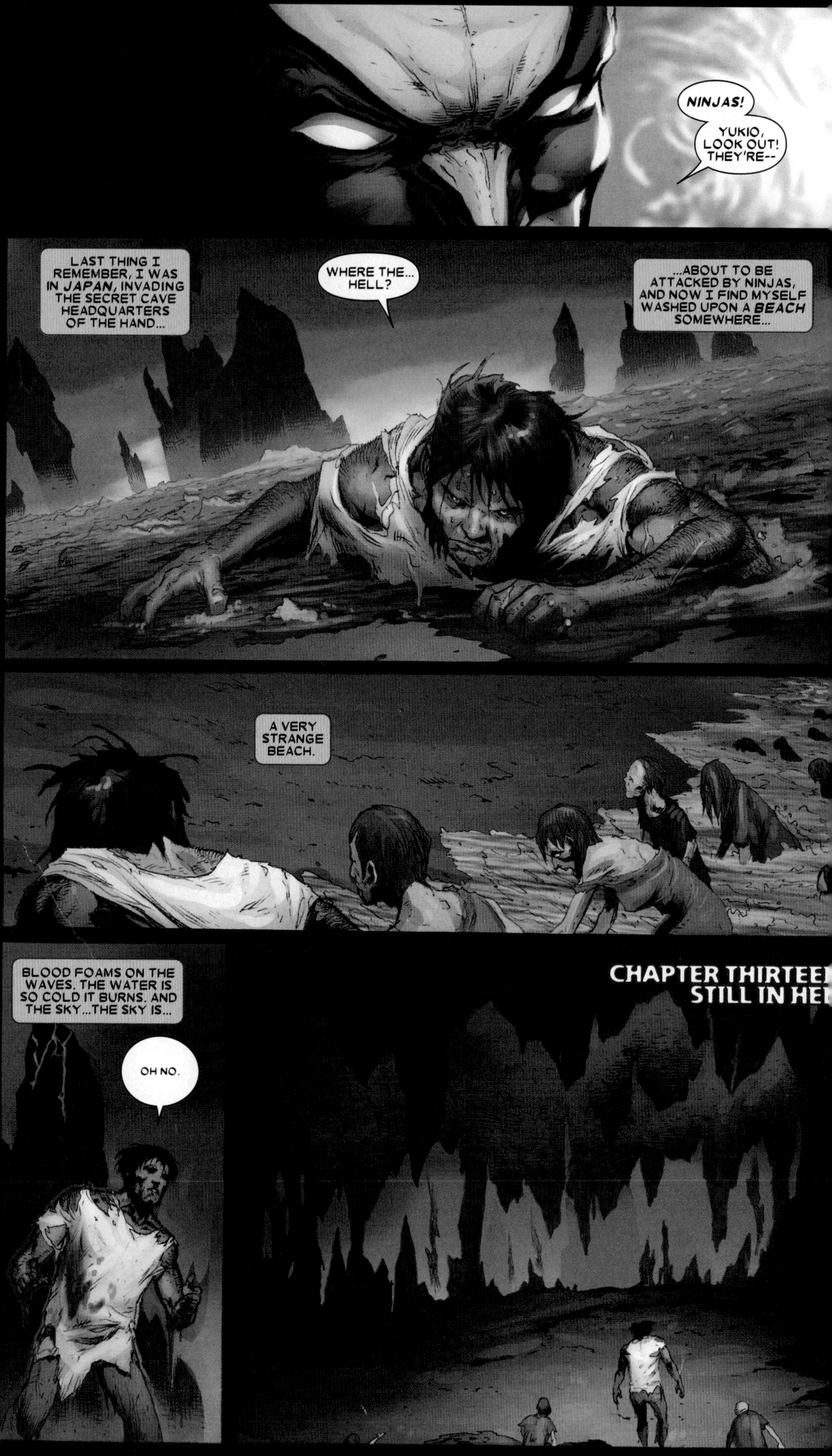
NINJAS!
YUKIO, LOOK OUT! THEY'RE--
LAST THING I REMEMBER, I WAS IN JAPAN, INVADING THE SECRET CAVE HEADQUARTERS OF THE HAND...
WHERE THE... HELL?
...ABOUT TO BE ATTACKED BY NINJAS, AND NOW I FIND MYSELF WASHED UPON A BEACH SOMEWHERE...
A VERY STRANGE BEACH.
BLOOD FOAMS ON THE WAVES. THE WATER IS SO COLD IT BURNS. AND THE SKY...THE SKY IS...
OH NO.

CHAPTER THIRTEE
STILL IN HE

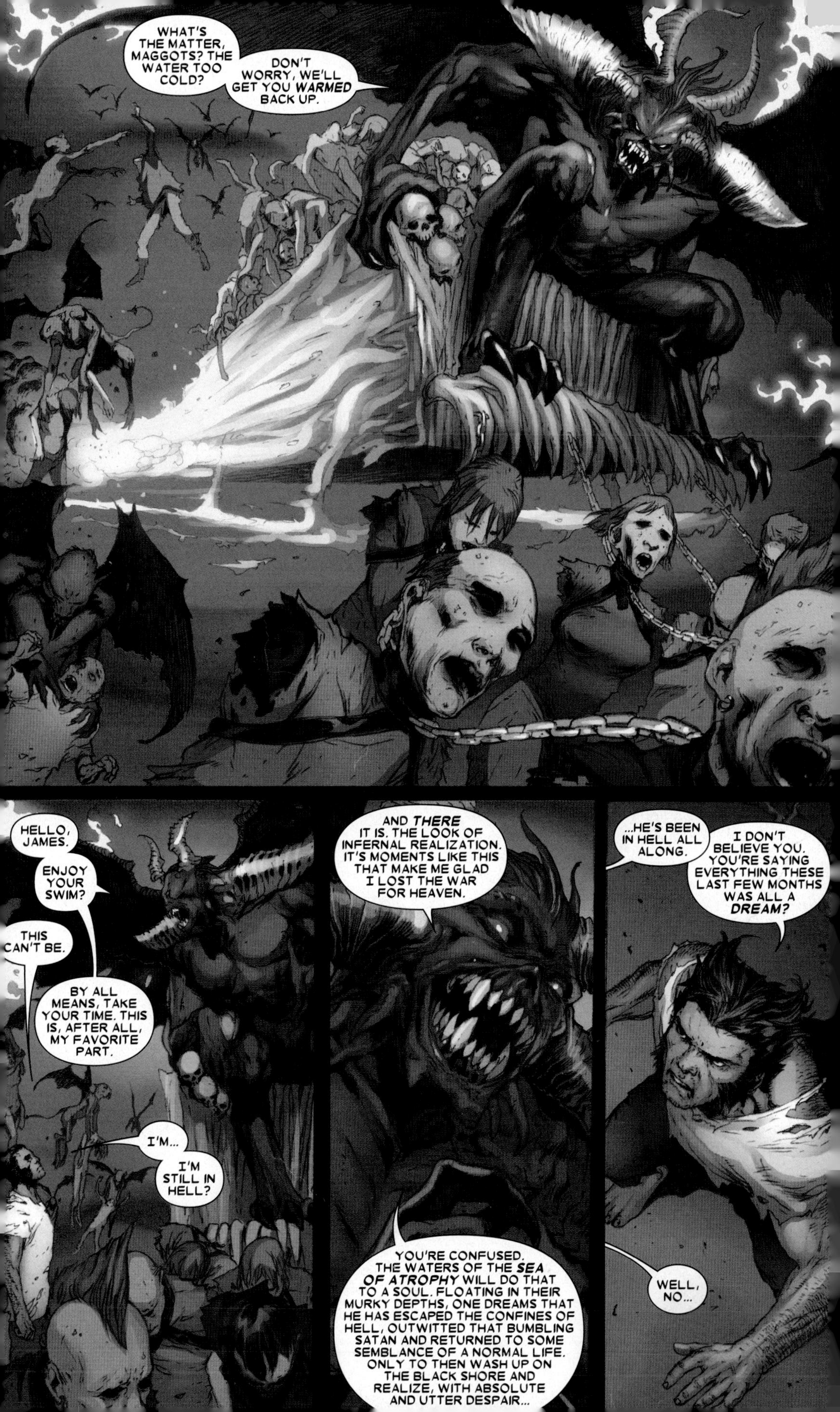
WHAT'S THE MATTER, MAGGOTS? THE WATER TOO COLD?
DON'T WORRY, WE'LL GET YOU WARMED BACK UP.
HELLO, JAMES.
ENJOY YOUR SWIM?
THIS CAN'T BE.
BY ALL MEANS, TAKE YOUR TIME. THIS IS, AFTER ALL, MY FAVORITE PART.
I'M...
I'M STILL IN HELL?
AND THERE IT IS. THE LOOK OF INFERNAL REALIZATION. IT'S MOMENTS LIKE THIS THAT MAKE ME GLAD I LOST THE WAR FOR HEAVEN.
YOU'RE CONFUSED. THE WATERS OF THE SEA OF ATROPHY WILL DO THAT TO A SOUL. FLOATING IN THEIR MURKY DEPTHS, ONE DREAMS THAT HE HAS ESCAPED THE CONFINES OF HELL, OUTWITTED THAT BUMBLING SATAN AND RETURNED TO SOME SEMBLANCE OF A NORMAL LIFE. ONLY TO THEN WASH UP ON THE BLACK SHORE AND REALIZE, WITH ABSOLUTE AND UTTER DESPAIR...
...HE'S BEEN IN HELL ALL ALONG.
I DON'T BELIEVE YOU. YOU'RE SAYING EVERYTHING THESE LAST FEW MONTHS WAS ALL A DREAM?
WELL, NO...

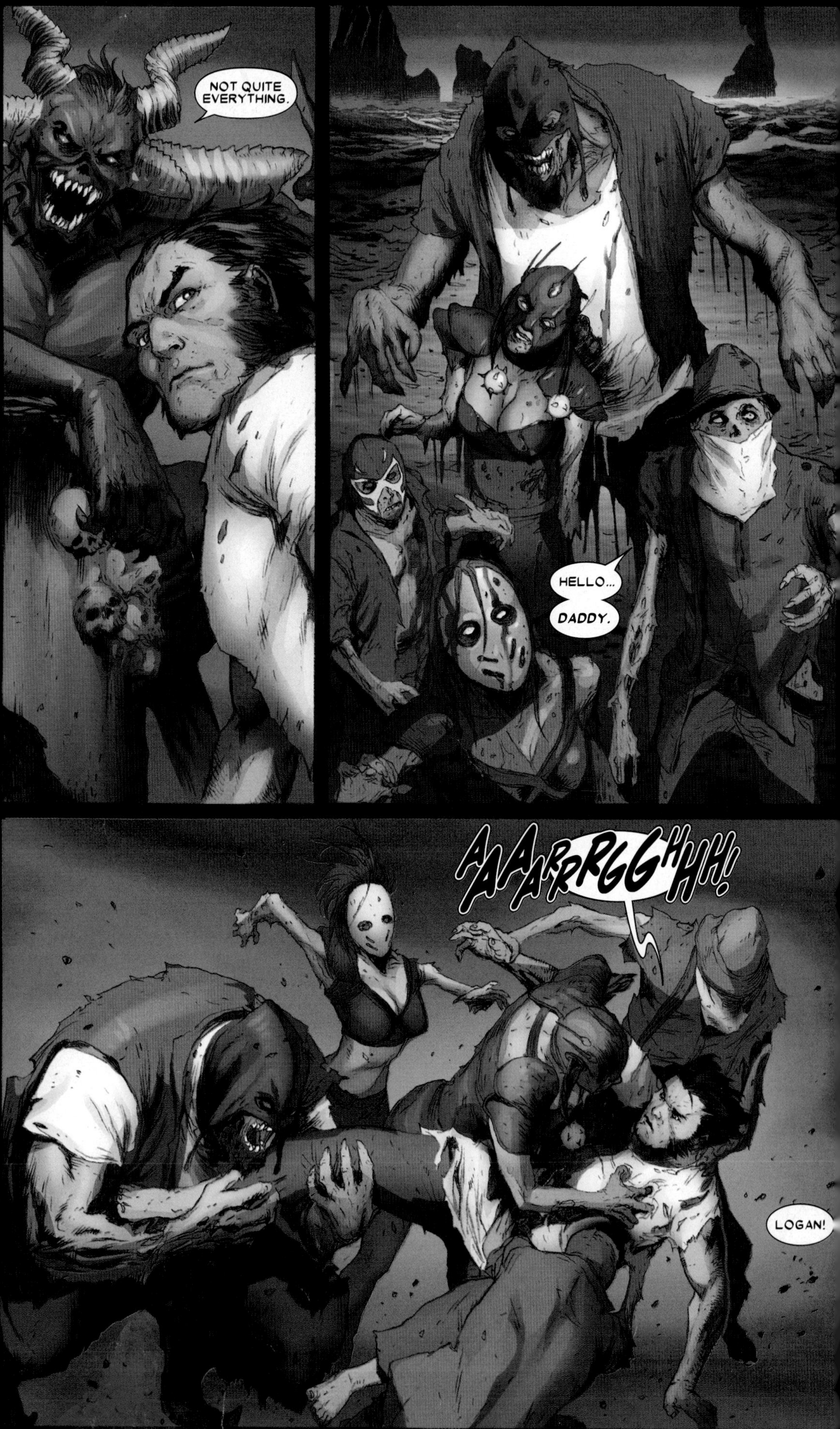
NOT QUITE EVERYTHING.
HELLO...
DADDY.
AAAARRRGGHHH!
LOGAN!

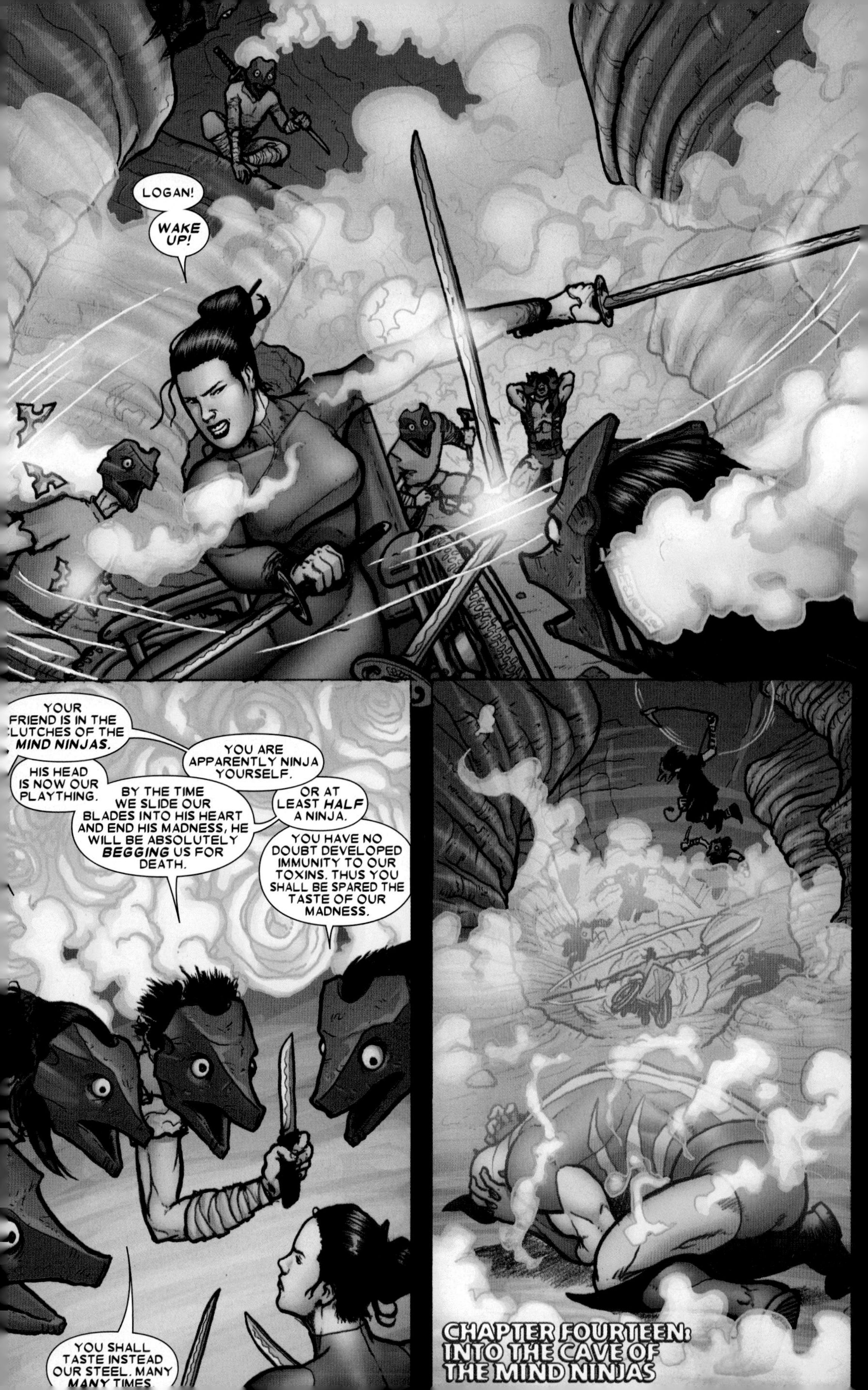
LOGAN!
WAKE UP!
YOUR FRIEND IS IN THE CLUTCHES OF THE MIND NINJAS.
HIS HEAD IS NOW OUR PLAYTHING.
BY THE TIME WE SLIDE OUR BLADES INTO HIS HEART AND END HIS MADNESS, HE WILL BE ABSOLUTELY BEGGING US FOR DEATH.
YOU ARE APPARENTLY NINJA YOURSELF.
OR AT LEAST HALF A NINJA.
YOU HAVE NO DOUBT DEVELOPED IMMUNITY TO OUR TOXINS. THUS YOU SHALL BE SPARED THE TASTE OF OUR MADNESS.
YOU SHALL TASTE INSTEAD OUR STEEL. MANY MANY TIMES.
CHAPTER FOURTEEN: INTO THE CAVE OF THE MIND NINJAS

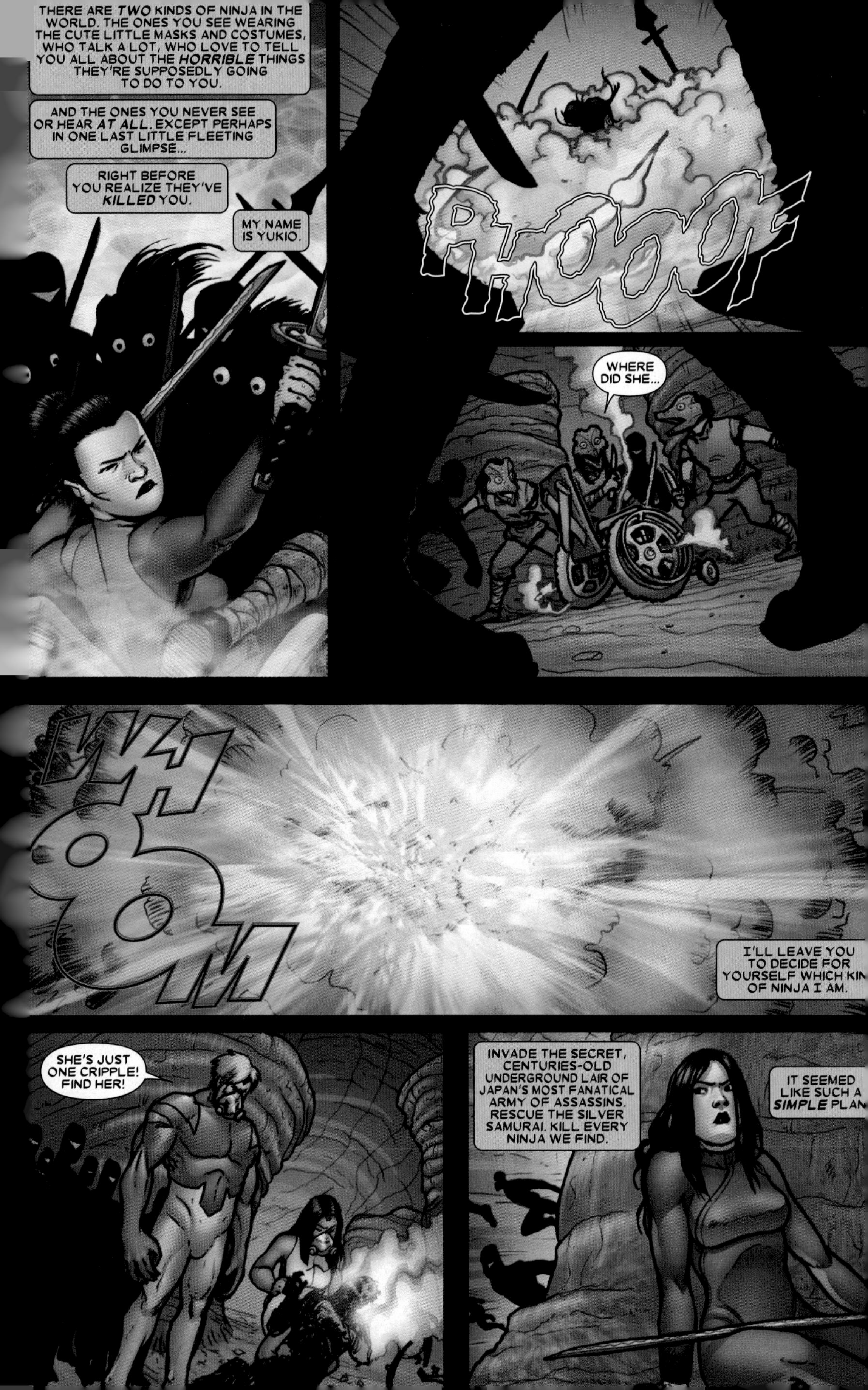
THERE ARE TWO KINDS OF NINJA IN THE WORLD. THE ONES YOU SEE WEARING THE CUTE LITTLE MASKS AND COSTUMES, WHO TALK A LOT, WHO LOVE TO TELL YOU ALL ABOUT THE HORRIBLE THINGS THEY'RE SUPPOSEDLY GOING TO DO TO YOU.
AND THE ONES YOU NEVER SEE OR HEAR AT ALL. EXCEPT PERHAPS IN ONE LAST LITTLE FLEETING GLIMPSE...
RIGHT BEFORE YOU REALIZE THEY'VE KILLED YOU.
MY NAME IS YUKIO.
PHOOOOF
WHERE DID SHE...
WHOOM
I'LL LEAVE YOU TO DECIDE FOR YOURSELF WHICH KIN OF NINJA I AM.
SHE'S JUST ONE CRIPPLE! FIND HER!
INVADE THE SECRET, CENTURIES-OLD UNDERGROUND LAIR OF JAPAN'S MOST FANATICAL ARMY OF ASSASSINS. RESCUE THE SILVER SAMURAI. KILL EVERY NINJA WE FIND.
IT SEEMED LIKE SUCH A SIMPLE PLAN

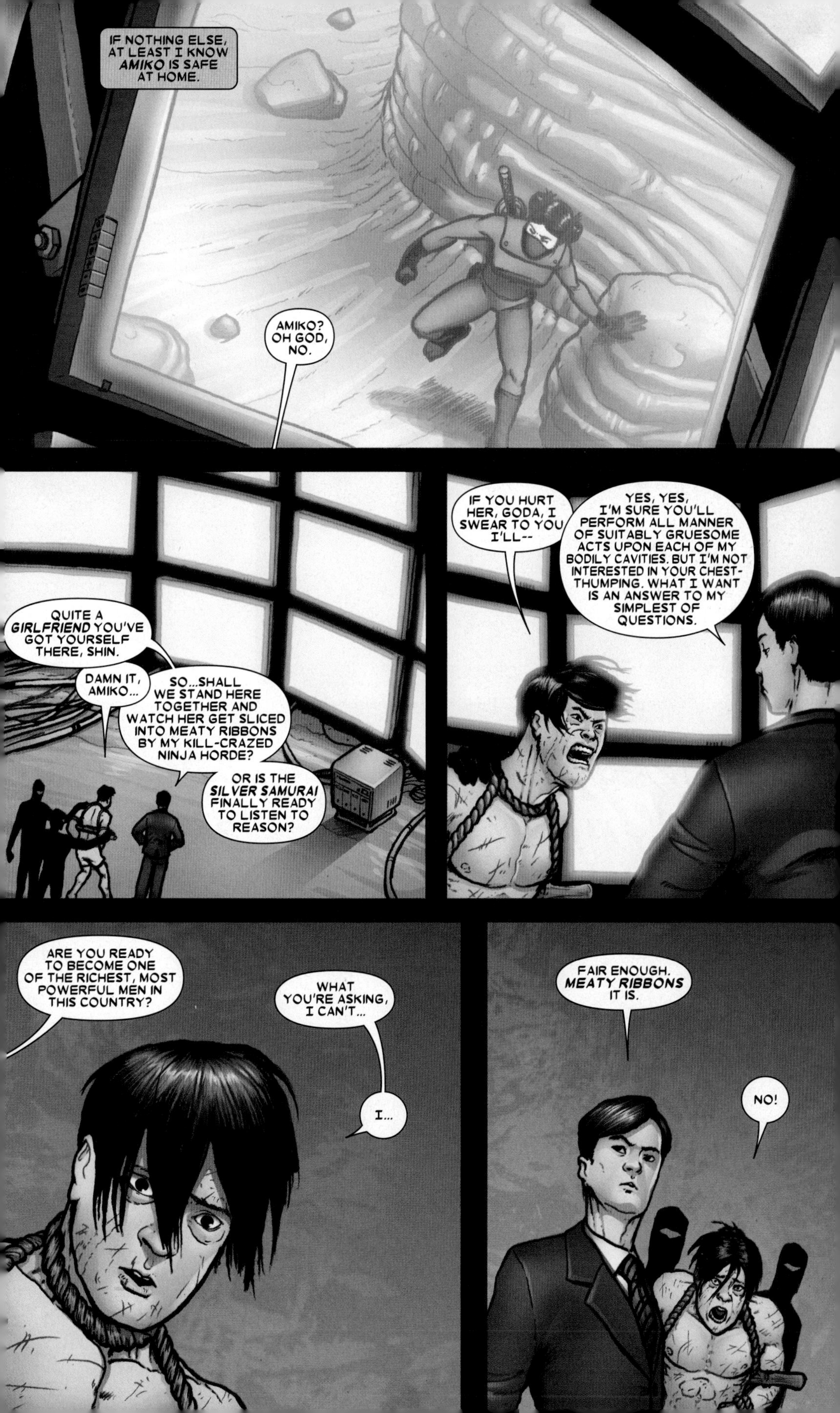

IF NOTHING ELSE, AT LEAST I KNOW AMIKO IS SAFE AT HOME.
AMIKO? OH GOD, NO.
QUITE A GIRLFRIEND YOU'VE GOT YOURSELF THERE, SHIN.
DAMN IT, AMIKO...
SO...SHALL WE STAND HERE TOGETHER AND WATCH HER GET SLICED INTO MEATY RIBBONS BY MY KILL-CRAZED NINJA HORDE?
OR IS THE SILVER SAMURAI FINALLY READY TO LISTEN TO REASON?
IF YOU HURT HER, GODA, I SWEAR TO YOU I'LL--
YES, YES, I'M SURE YOU'LL PERFORM ALL MANNER OF SUITABLY GRUESOME ACTS UPON EACH OF MY BODILY CAVITIES. BUT I'M NOT INTERESTED IN YOUR CHEST-THUMPING. WHAT I WANT IS AN ANSWER TO MY SIMPLEST OF QUESTIONS.
ARE YOU READY TO BECOME ONE OF THE RICHEST, MOST POWERFUL MEN IN THIS COUNTRY?
WHAT YOU'RE ASKING, I CAN'T...
I...
FAIR ENOUGH. MEATY RIBBONS IT IS.
NO!

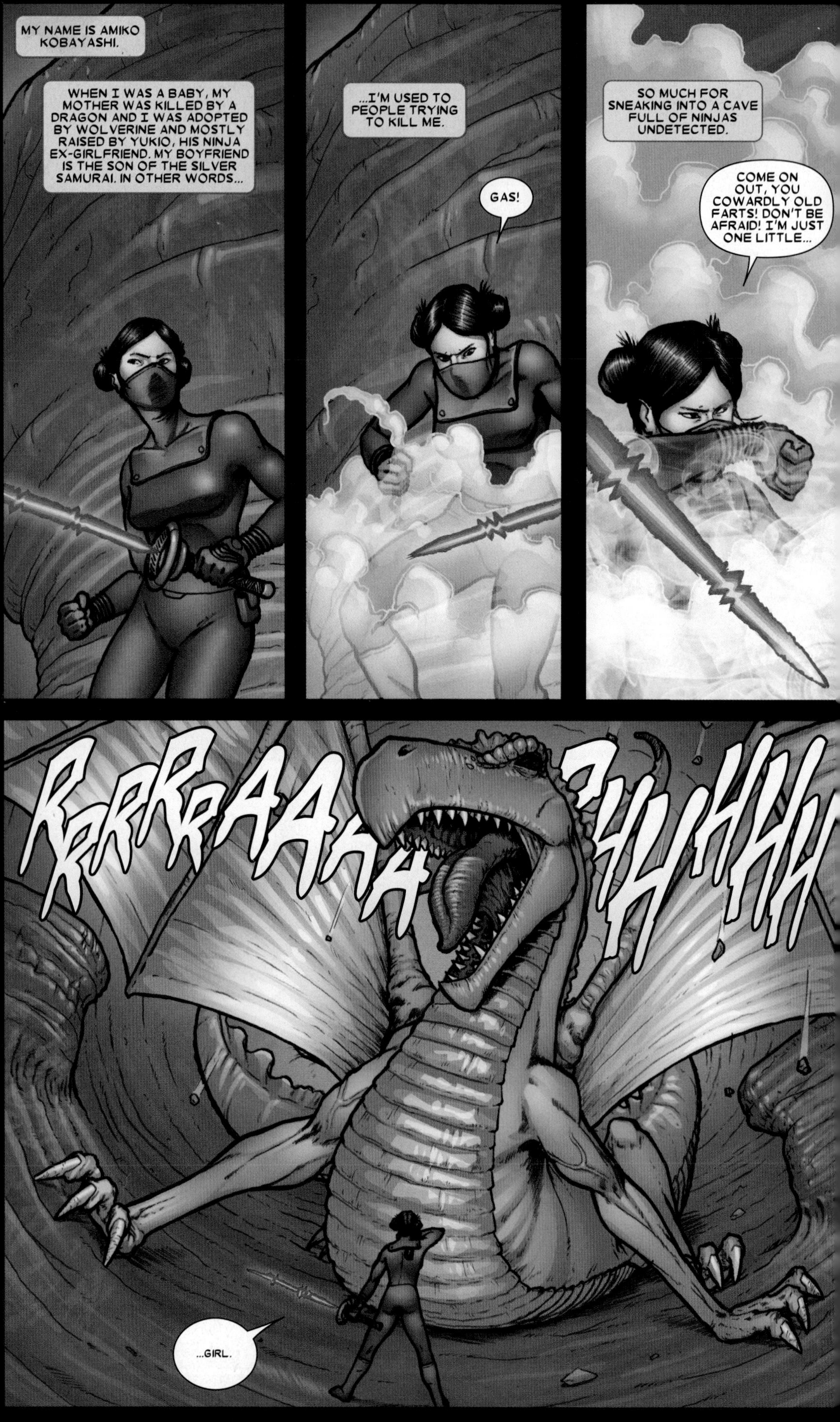
MY NAME IS AMIKO KOBAYASHI.
WHEN I WAS A BABY, MY MOTHER WAS KILLED BY A DRAGON AND I WAS ADOPTED BY WOLVERINE AND MOSTLY RAISED BY YUKIO, HIS NINJA EX-GIRLFRIEND. MY BOYFRIEND IS THE SON OF THE SILVER SAMURAI. IN OTHER WORDS...
...I'M USED TO PEOPLE TRYING TO KILL ME.
GAS!
SO MUCH FOR SNEAKING INTO A CAVE FULL OF NINJAS UNDETECTED.
COME ON OUT, YOU COWARDLY OLD FARTS! DON'T BE AFRAID! I'M JUST ONE LITTLE...
RRRRRRAAAAAHHHHHH
...GIRL.

IT'S THE DRAGON THAT KILLED MY MOTHER. THAT RUINED MY LIFE.

EVER SINCE I WAS A BABY, I'VE ALWAYS HOPED AND PRAYED...

...THAT SOMEDAY IT'D COME BACK.

DIE, YOU SONUVA BITCH!

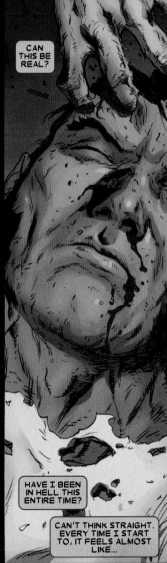

CAN THIS BE REAL?

HAVE I BEEN IN HELL THIS ENTIRE TIME?

CAN'T THINK STRAIGHT. EVERY TIME I START TO, IT FEELS ALMOST LIKE...

LIKE SOMEONE'S SHOOTING ME IN THE FACE.

BUDDA
BUDDA
BUDDA

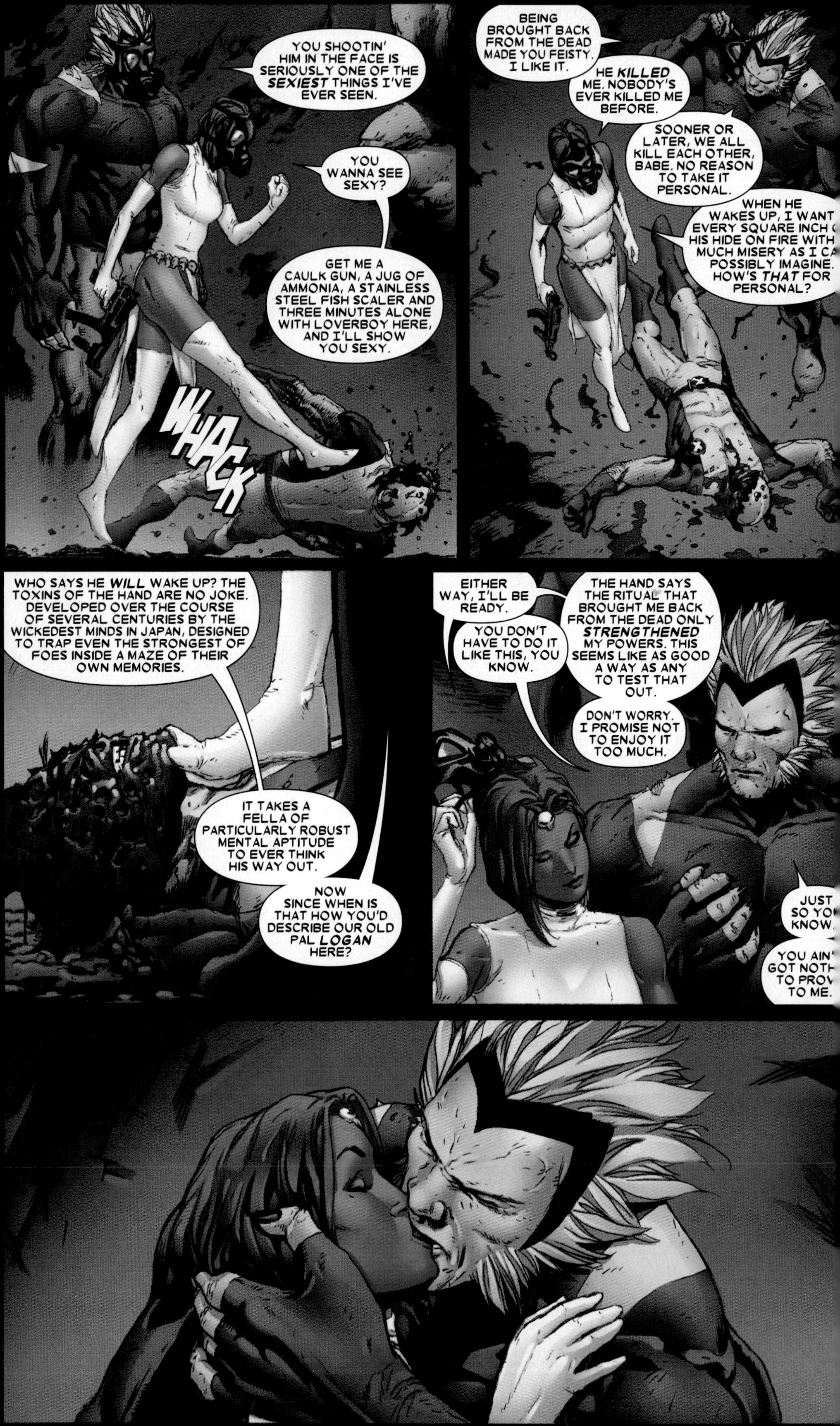
YOU SHOOTIN' HIM IN THE FACE IS SERIOUSLY ONE OF THE SEXIEST THINGS I'VE EVER SEEN.
YOU WANNA SEE SEXY?
GET ME A CAULK GUN, A JUG OF AMMONIA, A STAINLESS STEEL FISH SCALER AND THREE MINUTES ALONE WITH LOVERBOY HERE, AND I'LL SHOW YOU SEXY.
WHACK
BEING BROUGHT BACK FROM THE DEAD MADE YOU FEISTY. I LIKE IT.
HE KILLED ME. NOBODY'S EVER KILLED ME BEFORE.
SOONER OR LATER, WE ALL KILL EACH OTHER, BABE. NO REASON TO TAKE IT PERSONAL.
WHEN HE WAKES UP, I WANT EVERY SQUARE INCH HIS HIDE ON FIRE WITH MUCH MISERY AS I C POSSIBLY IMAGINE. HOW'S THAT FOR PERSONAL?
WHO SAYS HE WILL WAKE UP? THE TOXINS OF THE HAND ARE NO JOKE. DEVELOPED OVER THE COURSE OF SEVERAL CENTURIES BY THE WICKEDEST MINDS IN JAPAN, DESIGNED TO TRAP EVEN THE STRONGEST OF FOES INSIDE A MAZE OF THEIR OWN MEMORIES.
IT TAKES A FELLA OF PARTICULARLY ROBUST MENTAL APTITUDE TO EVER THINK HIS WAY OUT.
NOW SINCE WHEN IS THAT HOW YOU'D DESCRIBE OUR OLD PAL LOGAN HERE?
EITHER WAY, I'LL BE READY.
THE HAND SAYS THE RITUAL THAT BROUGHT ME BACK FROM THE DEAD ONLY STRENGTHENED MY POWERS. THIS SEEMS LIKE AS GOOD A WAY AS ANY TO TEST THAT OUT.
YOU DON'T HAVE TO DO IT LIKE THIS, YOU KNOW.
DON'T WORRY. I PROMISE NOT TO ENJOY IT TOO MUCH.
JUST SO YO KNOW.
YOU AIN' GOT NOTH TO PROV TO ME.

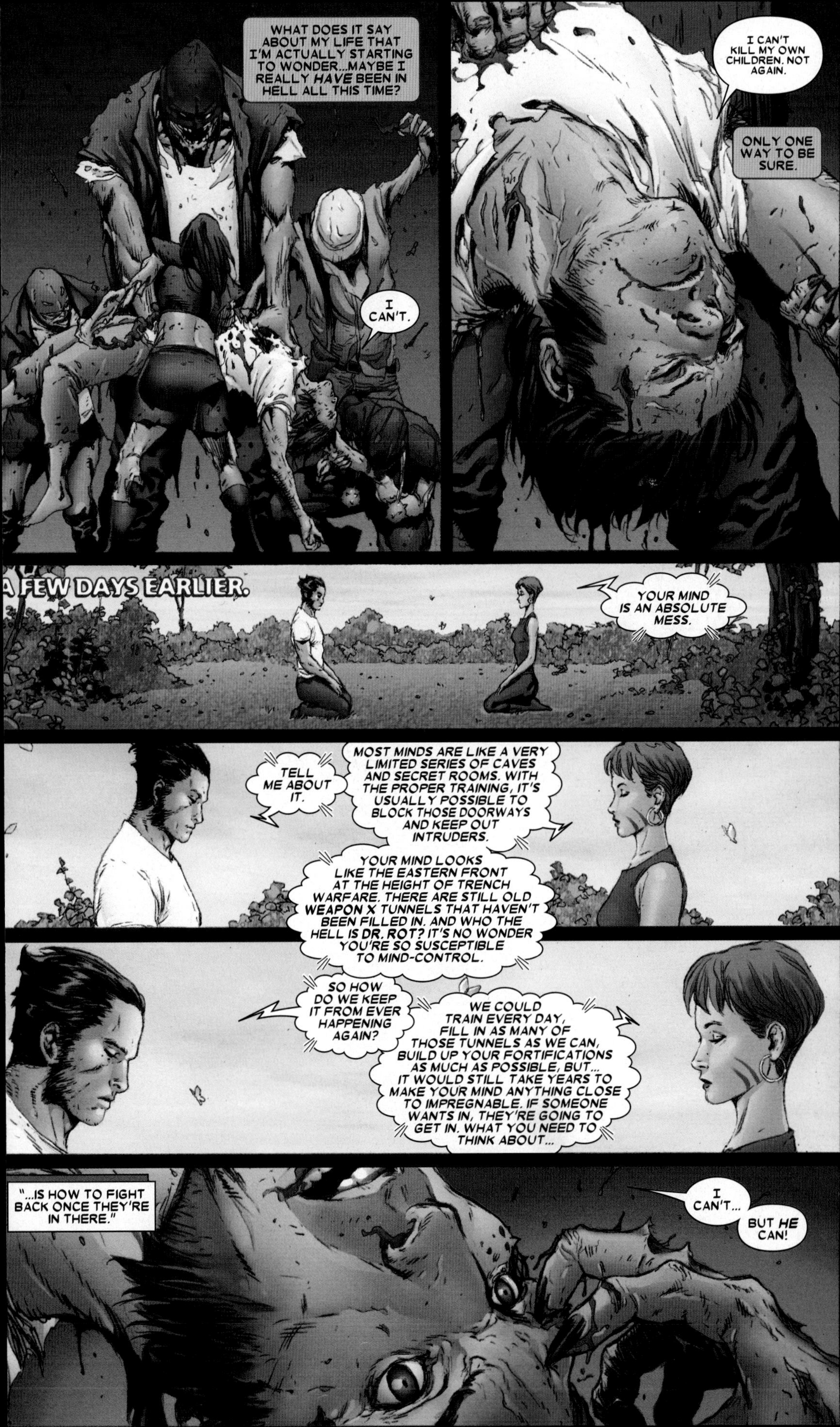
WHAT DOES IT SAY ABOUT MY LIFE THAT I'M ACTUALLY STARTING TO WONDER...MAYBE I REALLY *HAVE* BEEN IN HELL ALL THIS TIME?
I CAN'T.
I CAN'T KILL MY OWN CHILDREN. NOT AGAIN.
ONLY ONE WAY TO BE SURE.
A FEW DAYS EARLIER.
YOUR MIND IS AN ABSOLUTE MESS.
TELL ME ABOUT IT.
MOST MINDS ARE LIKE A VERY LIMITED SERIES OF CAVES AND SECRET ROOMS. WITH THE PROPER TRAINING, IT'S USUALLY POSSIBLE TO BLOCK THOSE DOORWAYS AND KEEP OUT INTRUDERS.
YOUR MIND LOOKS LIKE THE EASTERN FRONT AT THE HEIGHT OF TRENCH WARFARE. THERE ARE STILL OLD **WEAPON X** TUNNELS THAT HAVEN'T BEEN FILLED IN. AND WHO THE HELL IS **DR. ROT**? IT'S NO WONDER YOU'RE SO SUSCEPTIBLE TO MIND-CONTROL.
SO HOW DO WE KEEP IT FROM EVER HAPPENING AGAIN?
WE COULD TRAIN EVERY DAY, FILL IN AS MANY OF THOSE TUNNELS AS WE CAN, BUILD UP YOUR FORTIFICATIONS AS MUCH AS POSSIBLE, BUT... IT WOULD STILL TAKE YEARS TO MAKE YOUR MIND ANYTHING CLOSE TO IMPREGNABLE. IF SOMEONE WANTS IN, THEY'RE GOING TO GET IN. WHAT YOU NEED TO THINK ABOUT...
"...IS HOW TO FIGHT BACK ONCE THEY'RE IN THERE."
I CAN'T...
BUT *HE* CAN!

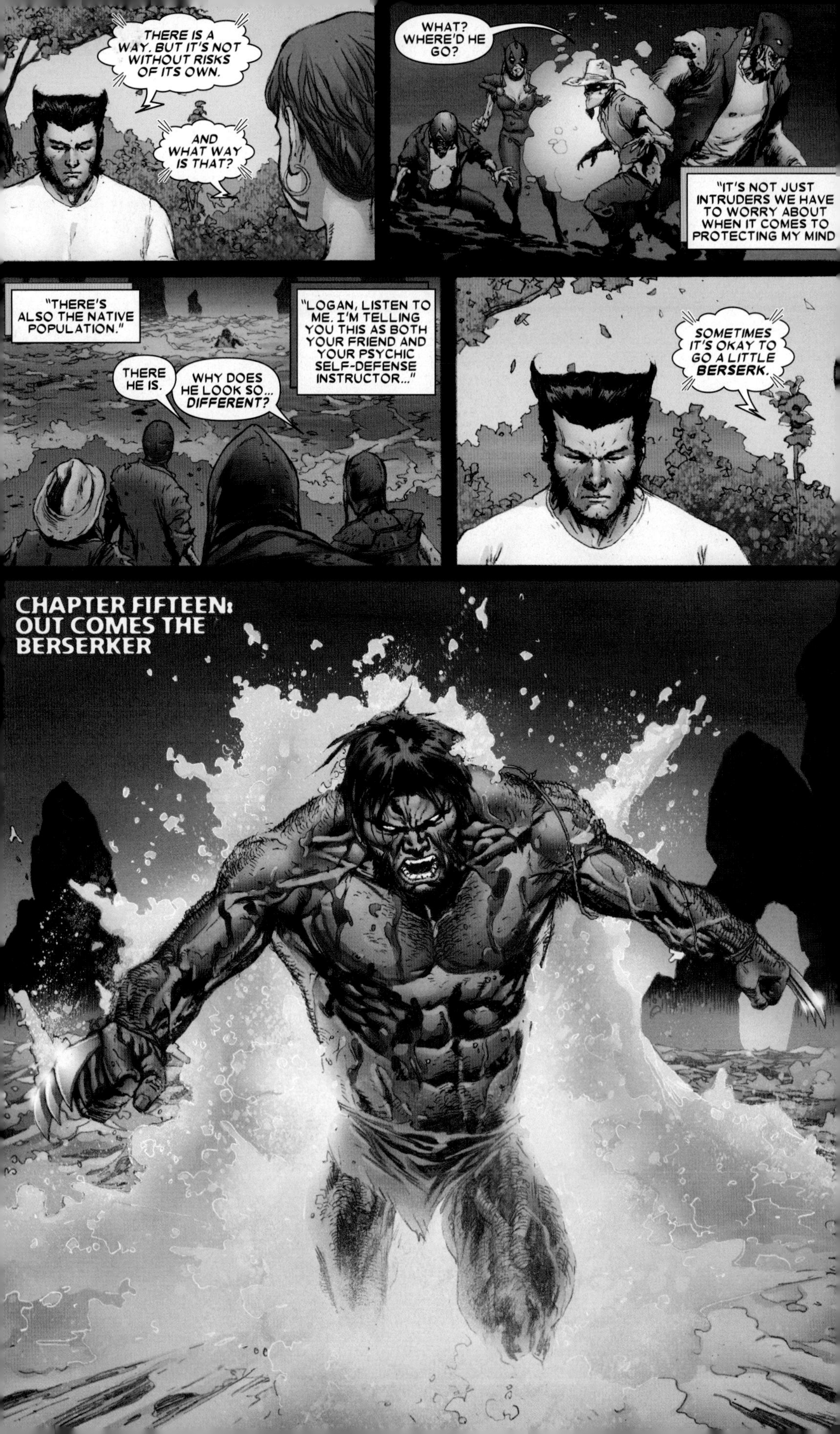
THERE IS A WAY. BUT IT'S NOT WITHOUT RISKS OF ITS OWN.
AND WHAT WAY IS THAT?
WHAT? WHERE'D HE GO?
"IT'S NOT JUST INTRUDERS WE HAVE TO WORRY ABOUT WHEN IT COMES TO PROTECTING MY MIND
"THERE'S ALSO THE NATIVE POPULATION."
THERE HE IS.
WHY DOES HE LOOK SO... DIFFERENT?
"LOGAN, LISTEN TO ME. I'M TELLING YOU THIS AS BOTH YOUR FRIEND AND YOUR PSYCHIC SELF-DEFENSE INSTRUCTOR..."
SOMETIMES IT'S OKAY TO GO A LITTLE BERSERK.
CHAPTER FIFTEEN: OUT COMES THE BERSERKER

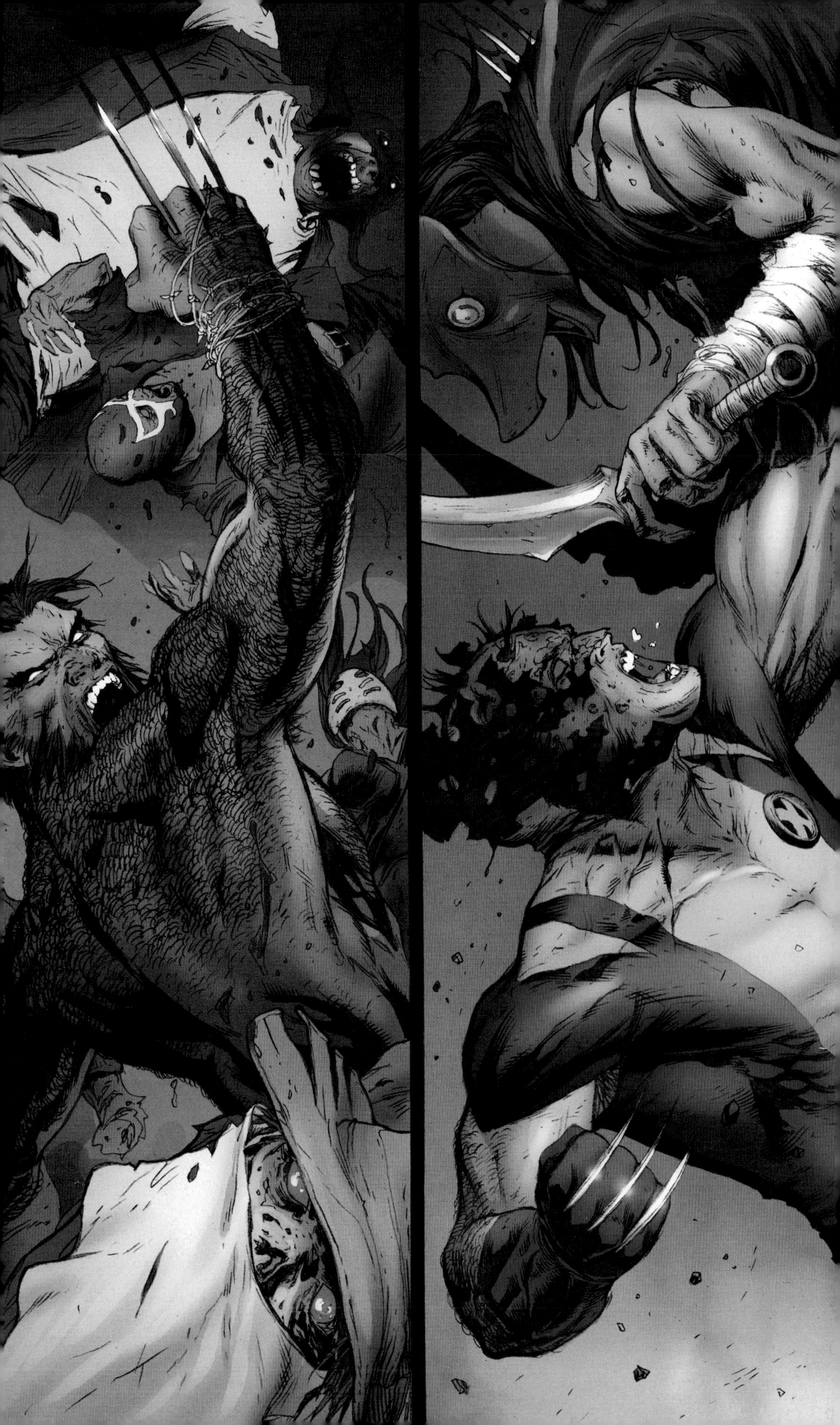

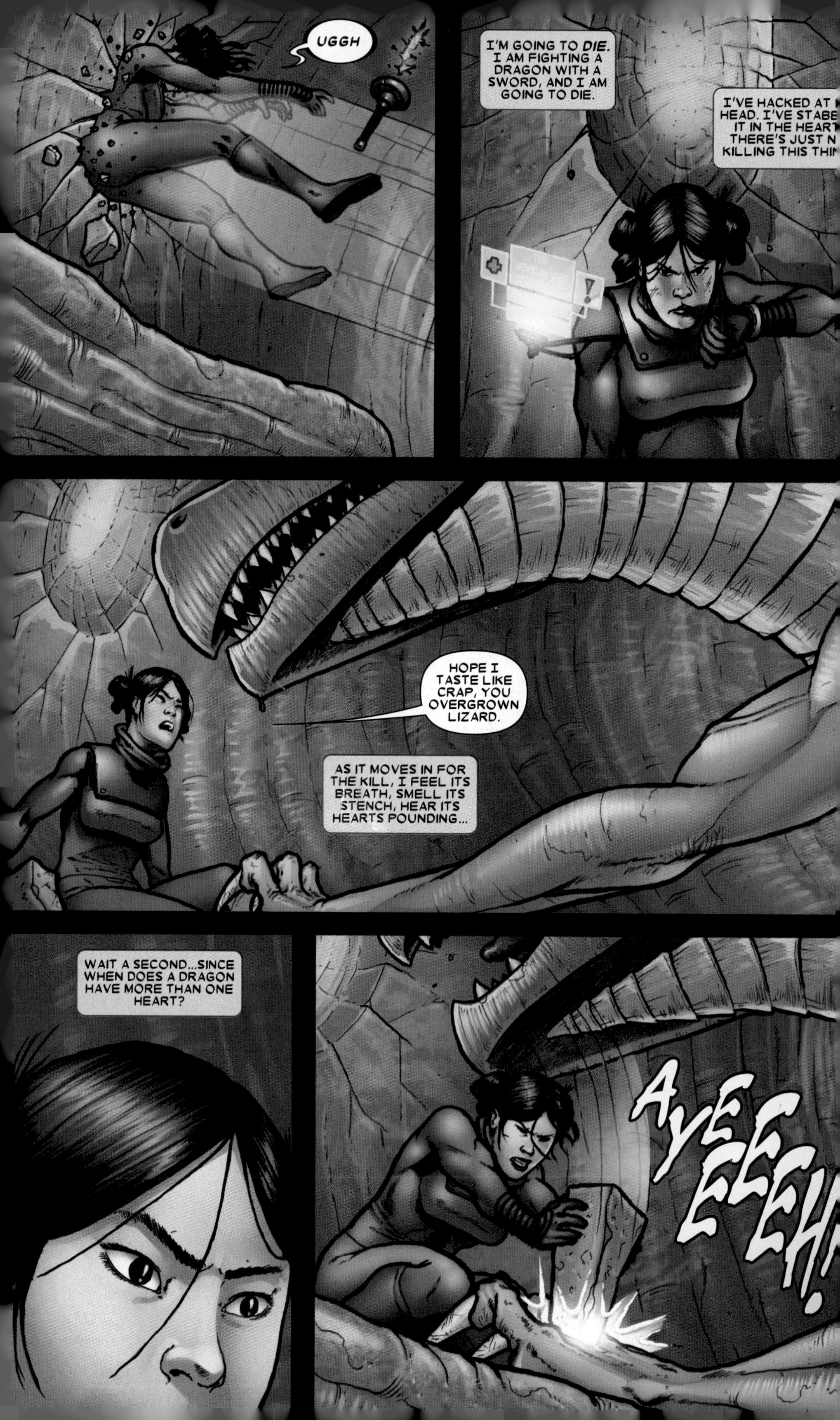
UGGH
I'M GOING TO *DIE.* I AM FIGHTING A DRAGON WITH A SWORD, AND I AM GOING TO DIE.
I'VE HACKED AT HEAD. I'VE IT IN THE HEART THERE'S JUST KILLING THIS
HOPE I TASTE LIKE CRAP, YOU OVERGROWN LIZARD.
AS IT MOVES IN FOR THE KILL, I FEEL ITS BREATH, SMELL ITS STENCH, HEAR ITS HEARTS POUNDING...
WAIT A SECOND...SINCE WHEN DOES A DRAGON HAVE MORE THAN ONE HEART?
AYEEEEEH!

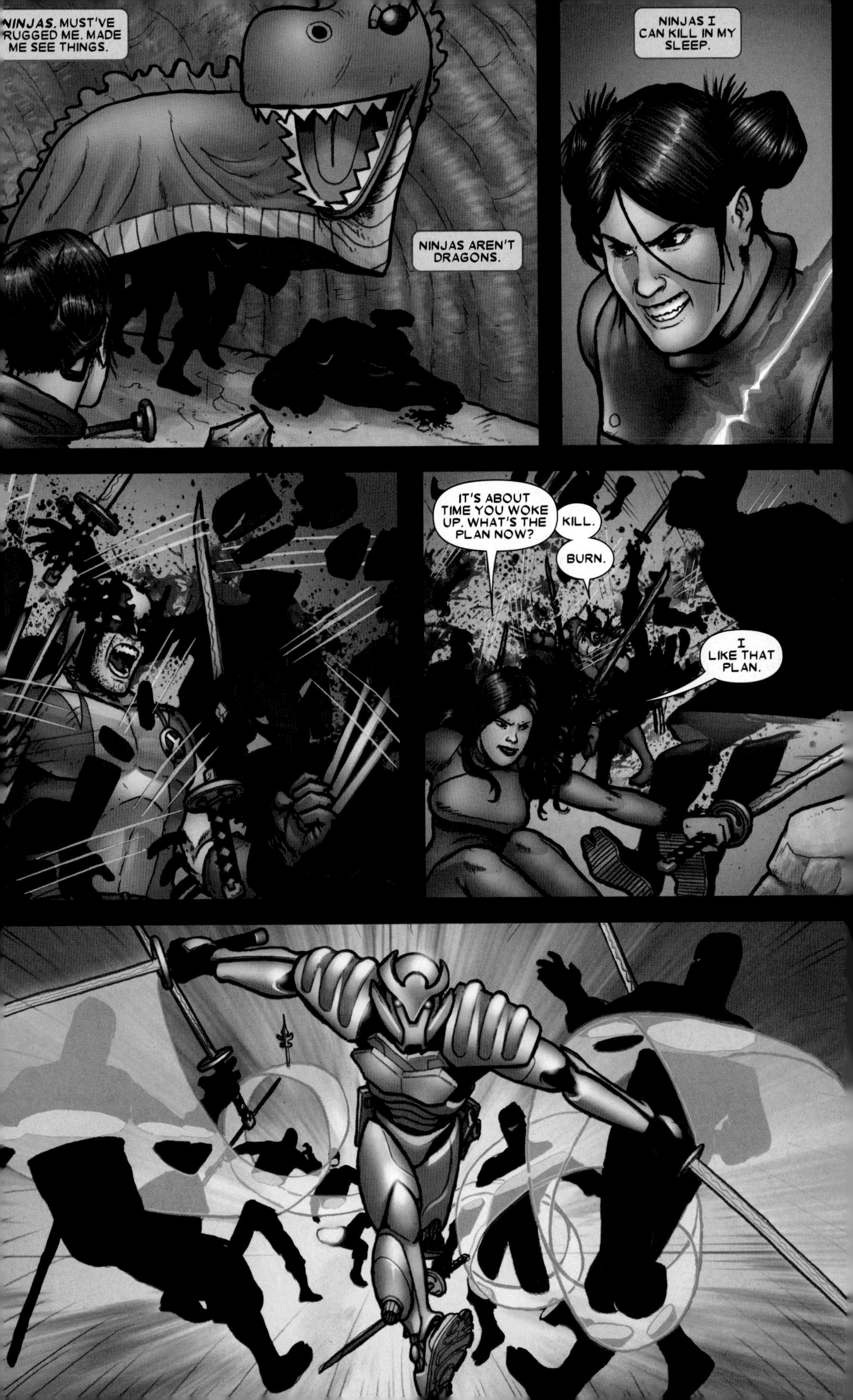

NINJAS. MUST'VE RUGGED ME. MADE ME SEE THINGS.
NINJAS AREN'T DRAGONS.
NINJAS I CAN KILL IN MY SLEEP.
IT'S ABOUT TIME YOU WOKE UP. WHAT'S THE PLAN NOW?
KILL.
BURN.
I LIKE THAT PLAN.

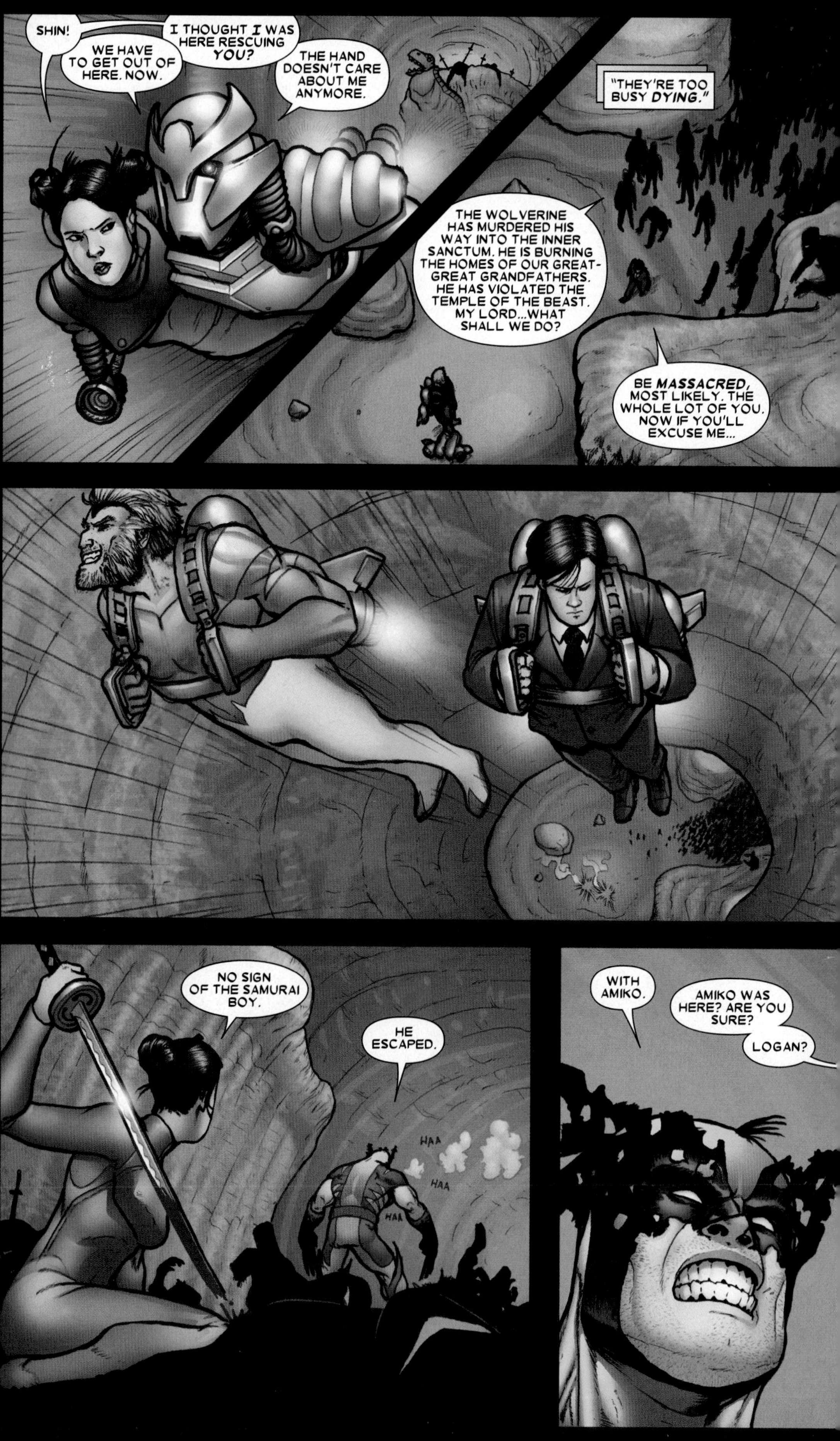
SHIN!
WE HAVE TO GET OUT OF HERE. NOW.
I THOUGHT I WAS HERE RESCUING YOU?
THE HAND DOESN'T CARE ABOUT ME ANYMORE.
"THEY'RE TOO BUSY DYING."
THE WOLVERINE HAS MURDERED HIS WAY INTO THE INNER SANCTUM. HE IS BURNING THE HOMES OF OUR GREAT-GREAT GRANDFATHERS. HE HAS VIOLATED THE TEMPLE OF THE BEAST. MY LORD...WHAT SHALL WE DO?
BE MASSACRED, MOST LIKELY. THE WHOLE LOT OF YOU. NOW IF YOU'LL EXCUSE ME...
NO SIGN OF THE SAMURAI BOY.
HE ESCAPED.
HAA
HAA
HAA
WITH AMIKO.
AMIKO WAS HERE? ARE YOU SURE?
LOGAN?

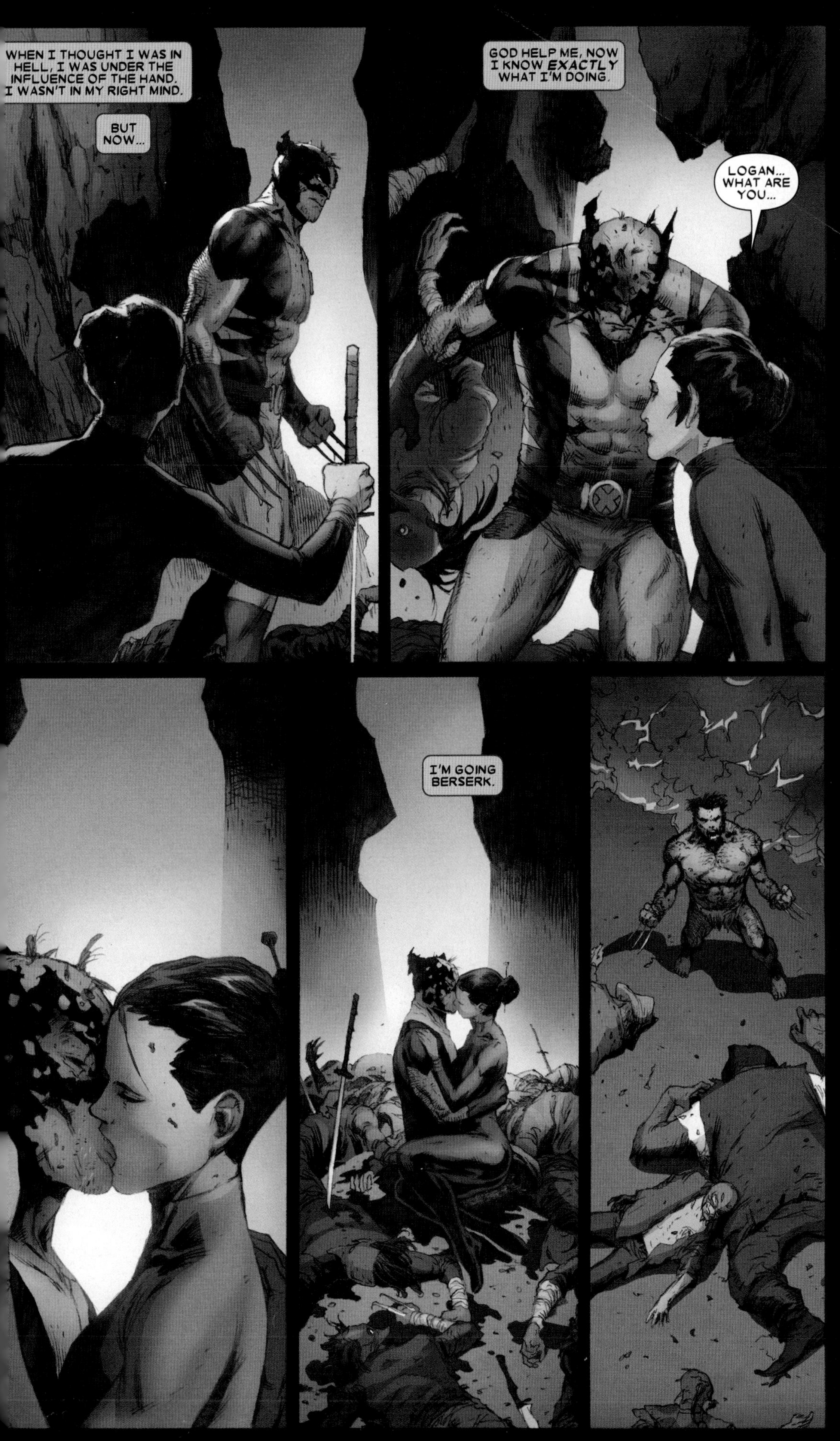
WHEN I THOUGHT I WAS IN HELL, I WAS UNDER THE INFLUENCE OF THE HAND. I WASN'T IN MY RIGHT MIND.
BUT NOW...
GOD HELP ME, NOW I KNOW EXACTLY WHAT I'M DOING.
LOGAN... WHAT ARE YOU...
I'M GOING BERSERK.

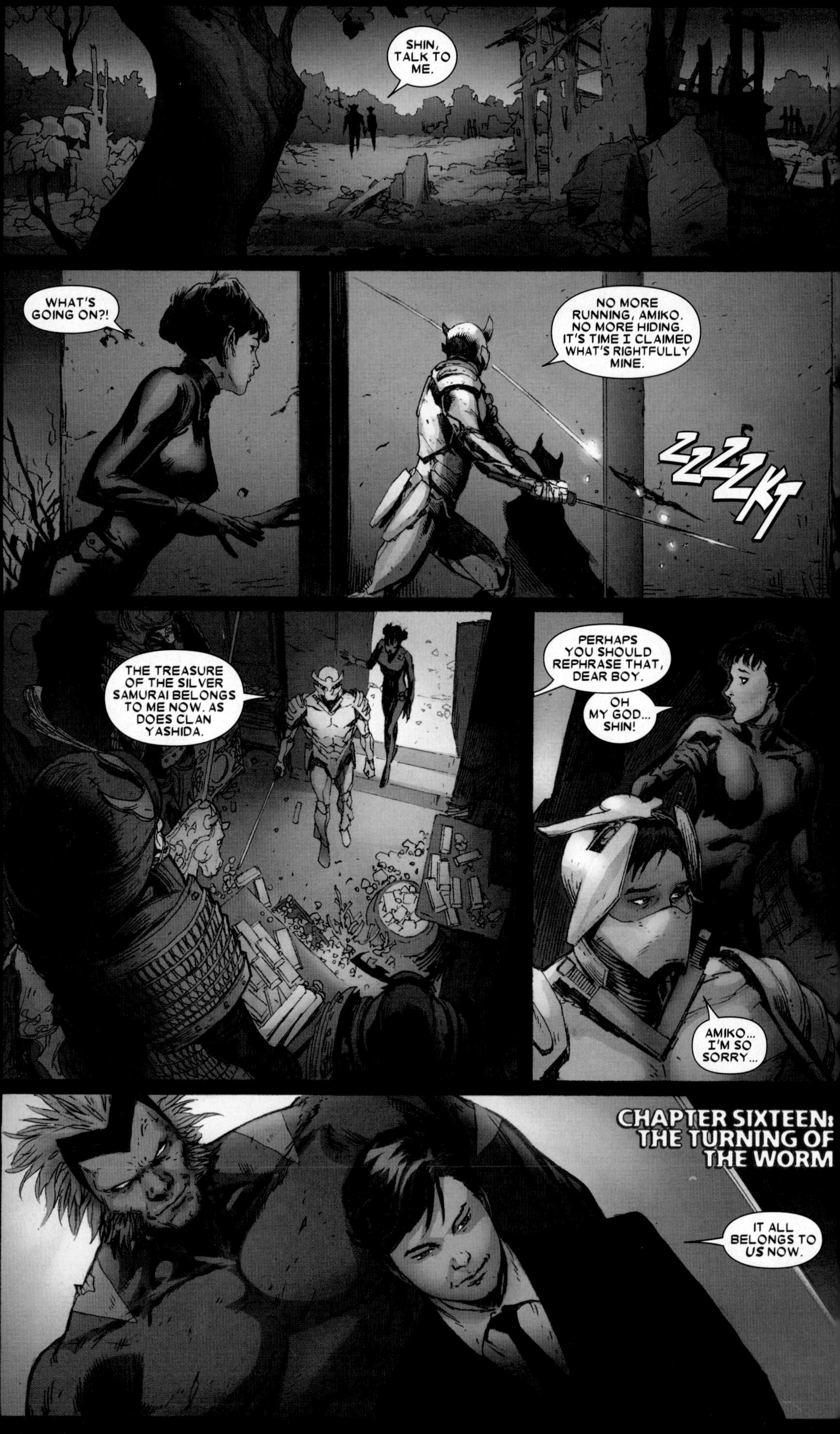

SHIN, TALK TO ME.
WHAT'S GOING ON?!
NO MORE RUNNING, AMIKO. NO MORE HIDING. IT'S TIME I CLAIMED WHAT'S RIGHTFULLY MINE.
ZZZZKT
THE TREASURE OF THE SILVER SAMURAI BELONGS TO ME NOW. AS DOES CLAN YASHIDA.
PERHAPS YOU SHOULD REPHRASE THAT, DEAR BOY.
OH MY GOD... SHIN!
AMIKO... I'M SO SORRY...
CHAPTER SIXTEEN: THE TURNING OF THE WORM
IT ALL BELONGS TO US NOW.

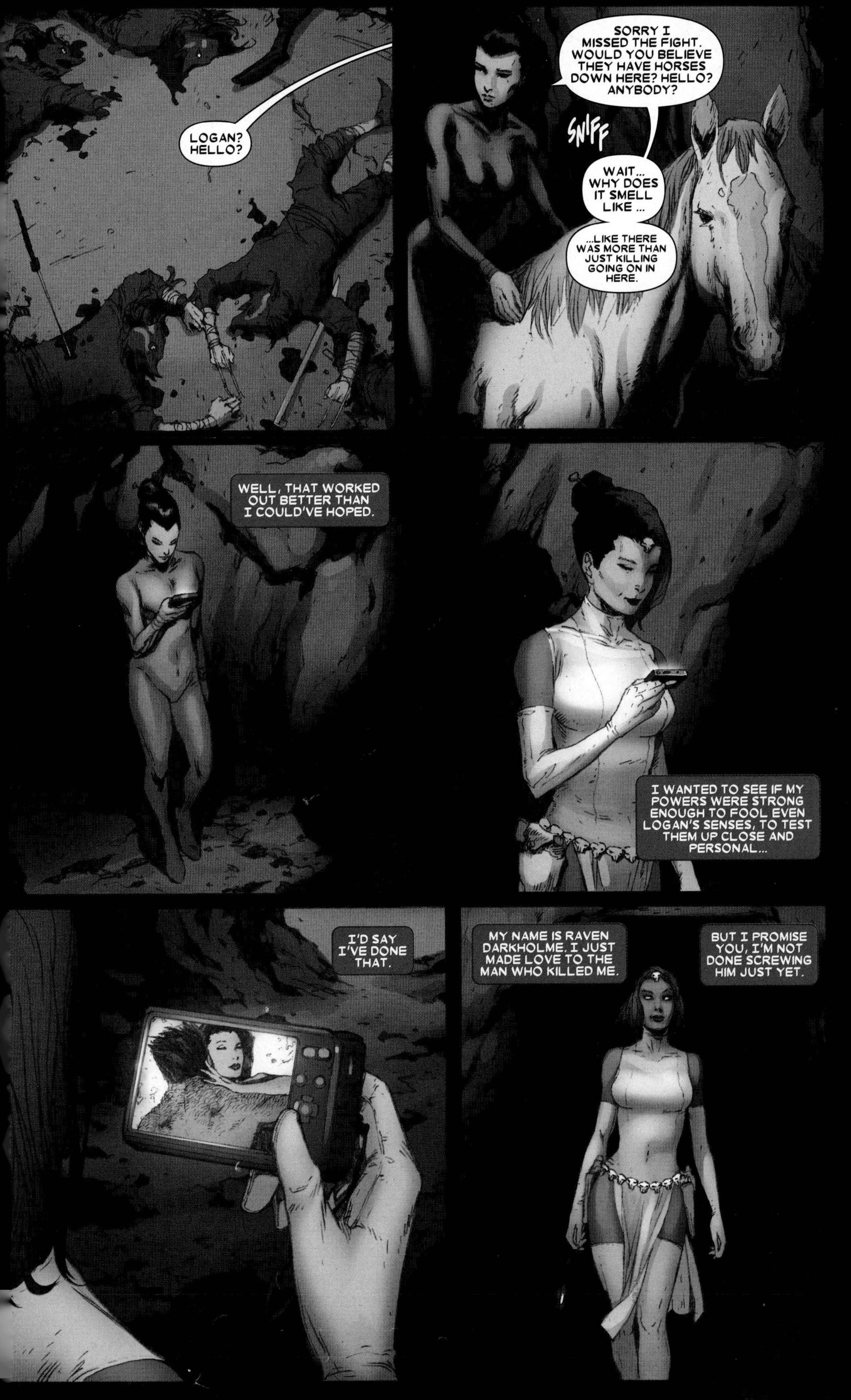
LOGAN? HELLO?
SORRY I MISSED THE FIGHT. WOULD YOU BELIEVE THEY HAVE HORSES DOWN HERE? HELLO? ANYBODY?
SNIFF
WAIT... WHY DOES IT SMELL LIKE ...
...LIKE THERE WAS MORE THAN JUST KILLING GOING ON IN HERE.
WELL, THAT WORKED OUT BETTER THAN I COULD'VE HOPED.
I WANTED TO SEE IF MY POWERS WERE STRONG ENOUGH TO FOOL EVEN LOGAN'S SENSES, TO TEST THEM UP CLOSE AND PERSONAL...
I'D SAY I'VE DONE THAT.
MY NAME IS RAVEN DARKHOLME. I JUST MADE LOVE TO THE MAN WHO KILLED ME.
BUT I PROMISE YOU, I'M NOT DONE SCREWING HIM JUST YET.

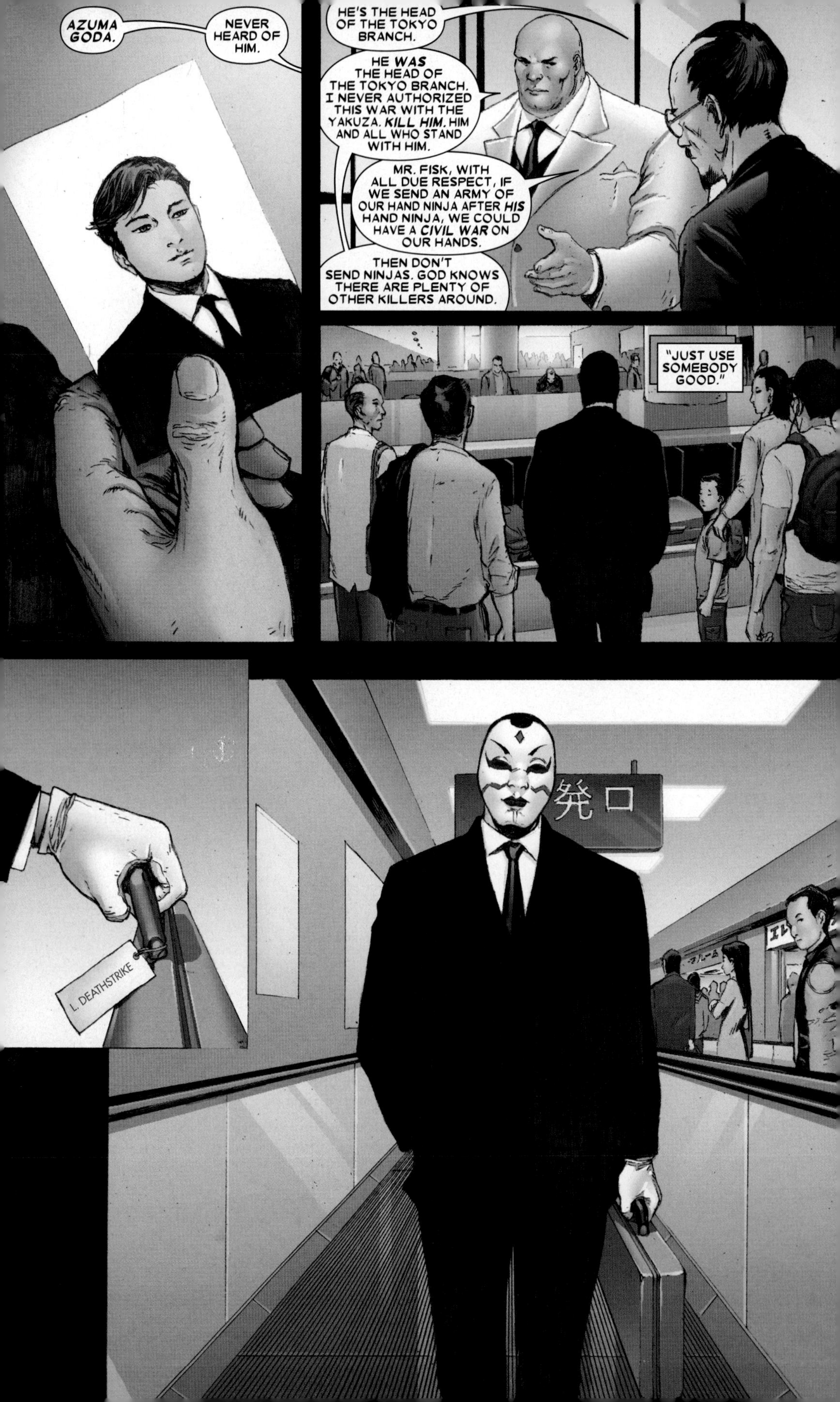

AZUMA GODA.
NEVER HEARD OF HIM.
HE'S THE HEAD OF THE TOKYO BRANCH.
HE *WAS* THE HEAD OF THE TOKYO BRANCH. I NEVER AUTHORIZED THIS WAR WITH THE YAKUZA. ***KILL HIM.*** HIM AND ALL WHO STAND WITH HIM.
MR. FISK, WITH ALL DUE RESPECT, IF WE SEND AN ARMY OF OUR HAND NINJA AFTER *HIS* HAND NINJA, WE COULD HAVE A *CIVIL WAR* ON OUR HANDS.
THEN DON'T SEND NINJAS. GOD KNOWS THERE ARE PLENTY OF OTHER KILLERS AROUND.
"JUST USE SOMEBODY GOOD."
L. DEATHSTRIKE
発口

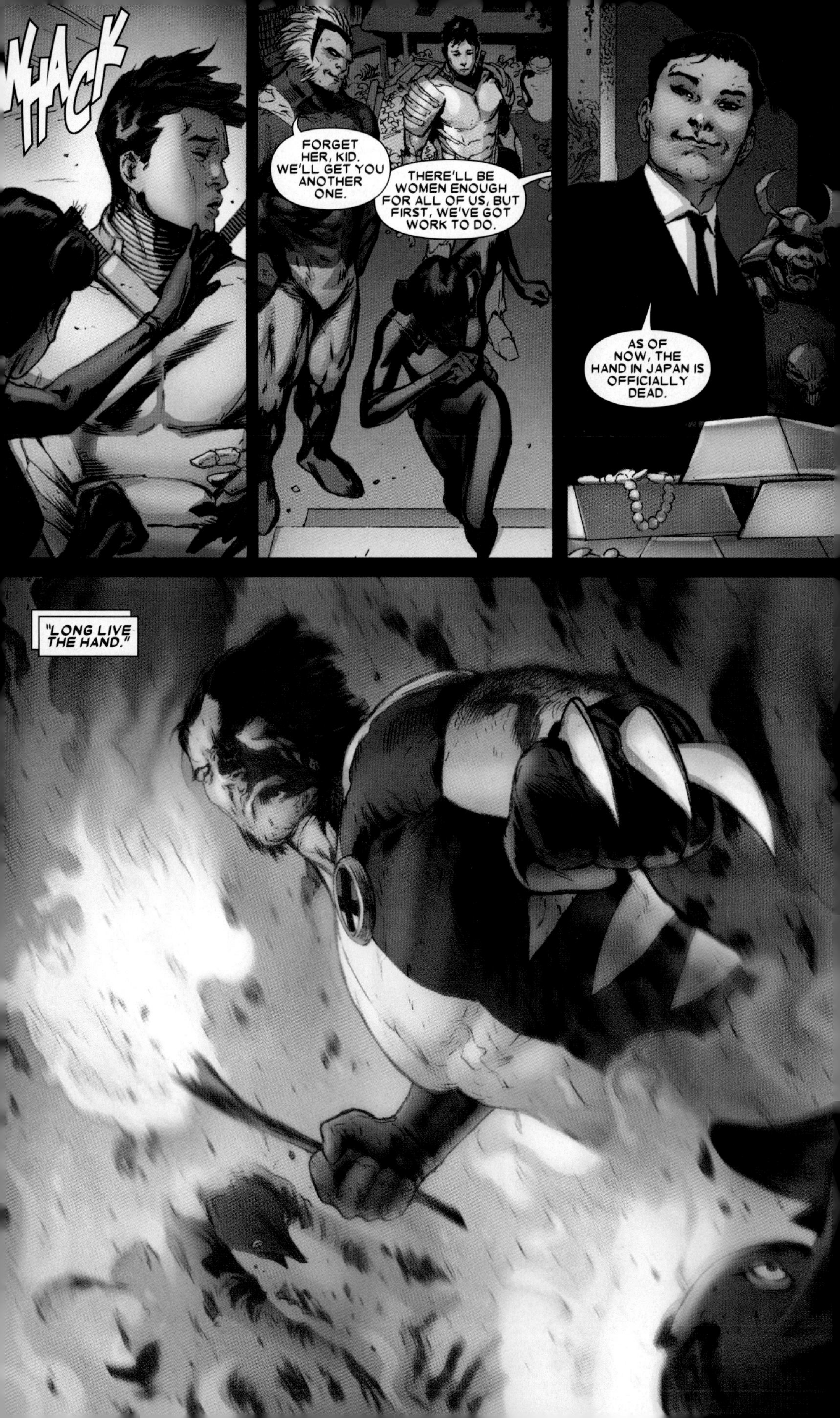
WHACK
FORGET HER, KID. WE'LL GET YOU ANOTHER ONE.
THERE'LL BE WOMEN ENOUGH FOR ALL OF US, BUT FIRST, WE'VE GOT WORK TO DO.
AS OF NOW, THE HAND IN JAPAN IS OFFICIALLY DEAD.
"LONG LIVE THE HAND."

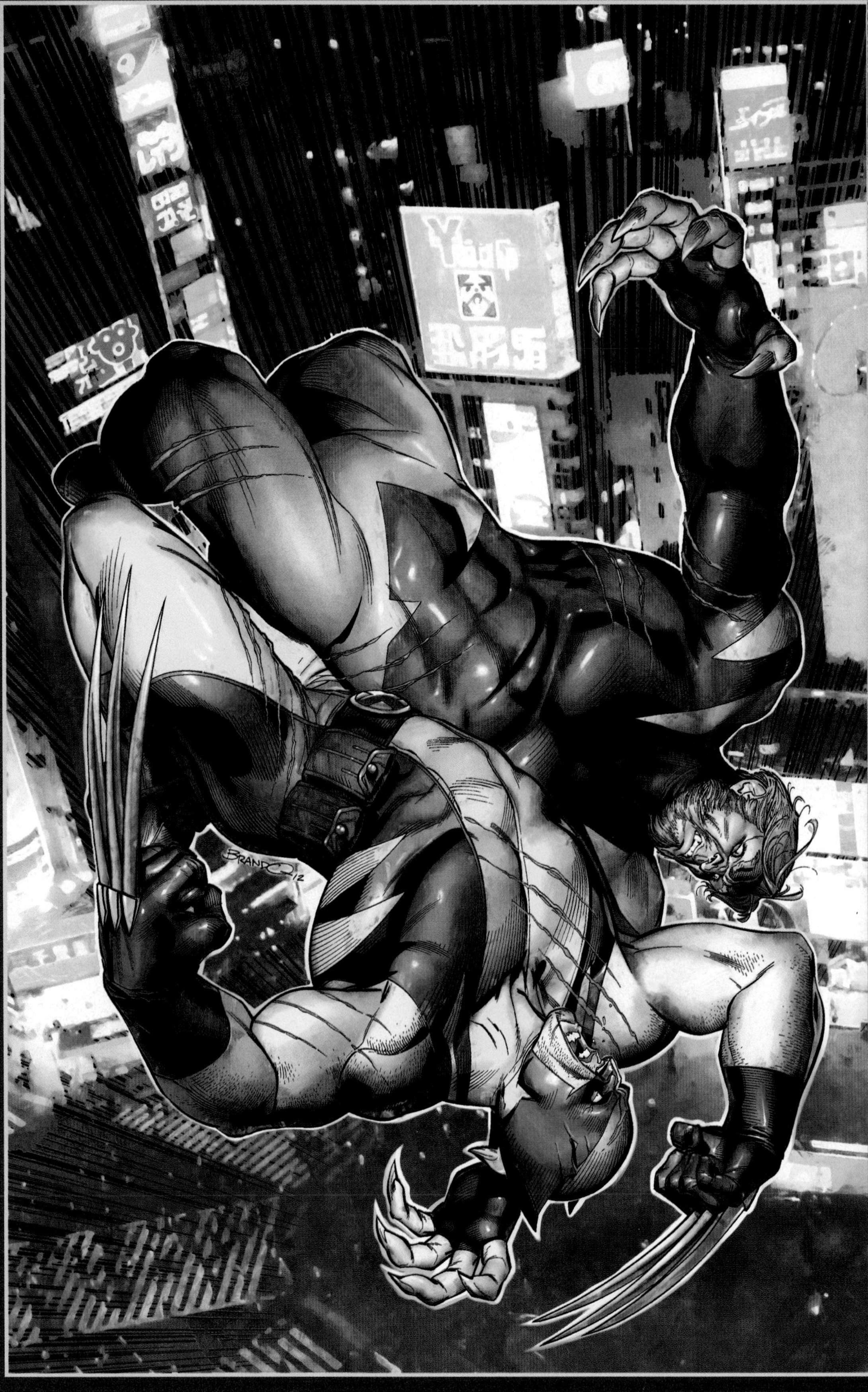

303

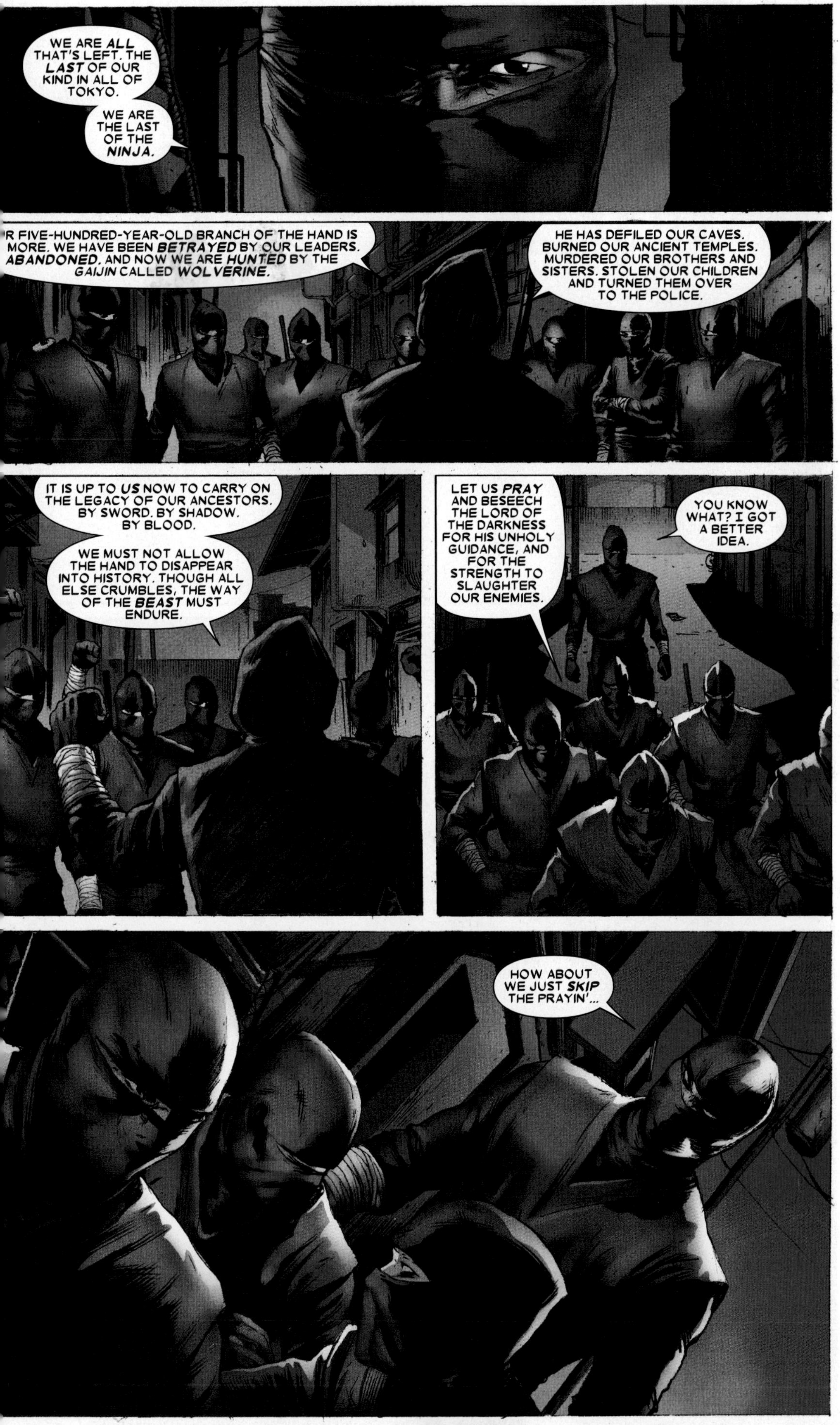
WE ARE ALL THAT'S LEFT. THE LAST OF OUR KIND IN ALL OF TOKYO.
WE ARE THE LAST OF THE NINJA.
R FIVE-HUNDRED-YEAR-OLD BRANCH OF THE HAND IS MORE. WE HAVE BEEN BETRAYED BY OUR LEADERS. ABANDONED. AND NOW WE ARE HUNTED BY THE GAIJIN CALLED WOLVERINE.
HE HAS DEFILED OUR CAVES. BURNED OUR ANCIENT TEMPLES. MURDERED OUR BROTHERS AND SISTERS. STOLEN OUR CHILDREN AND TURNED THEM OVER TO THE POLICE.
IT IS UP TO US NOW TO CARRY ON THE LEGACY OF OUR ANCESTORS. BY SWORD. BY SHADOW. BY BLOOD.
WE MUST NOT ALLOW THE HAND TO DISAPPEAR INTO HISTORY. THOUGH ALL ELSE CRUMBLES, THE WAY OF THE BEAST MUST ENDURE.
LET US PRAY AND BESEECH THE LORD OF THE DARKNESS FOR HIS UNHOLY GUIDANCE, AND FOR THE STRENGTH TO SLAUGHTER OUR ENEMIES.
YOU KNOW WHAT? I GOT A BETTER IDEA.
HOW ABOUT WE JUST SKIP THE PRAYIN'...

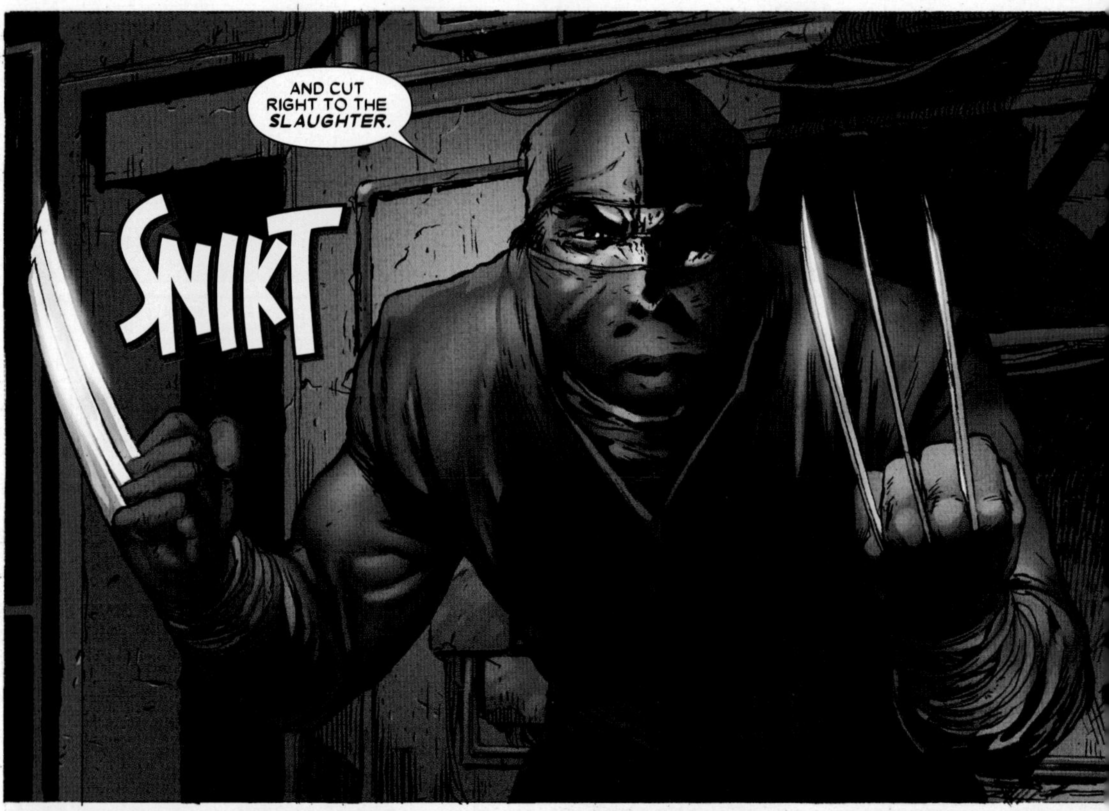
AND CUT RIGHT TO THE SLAUGHTER.
SNIKT

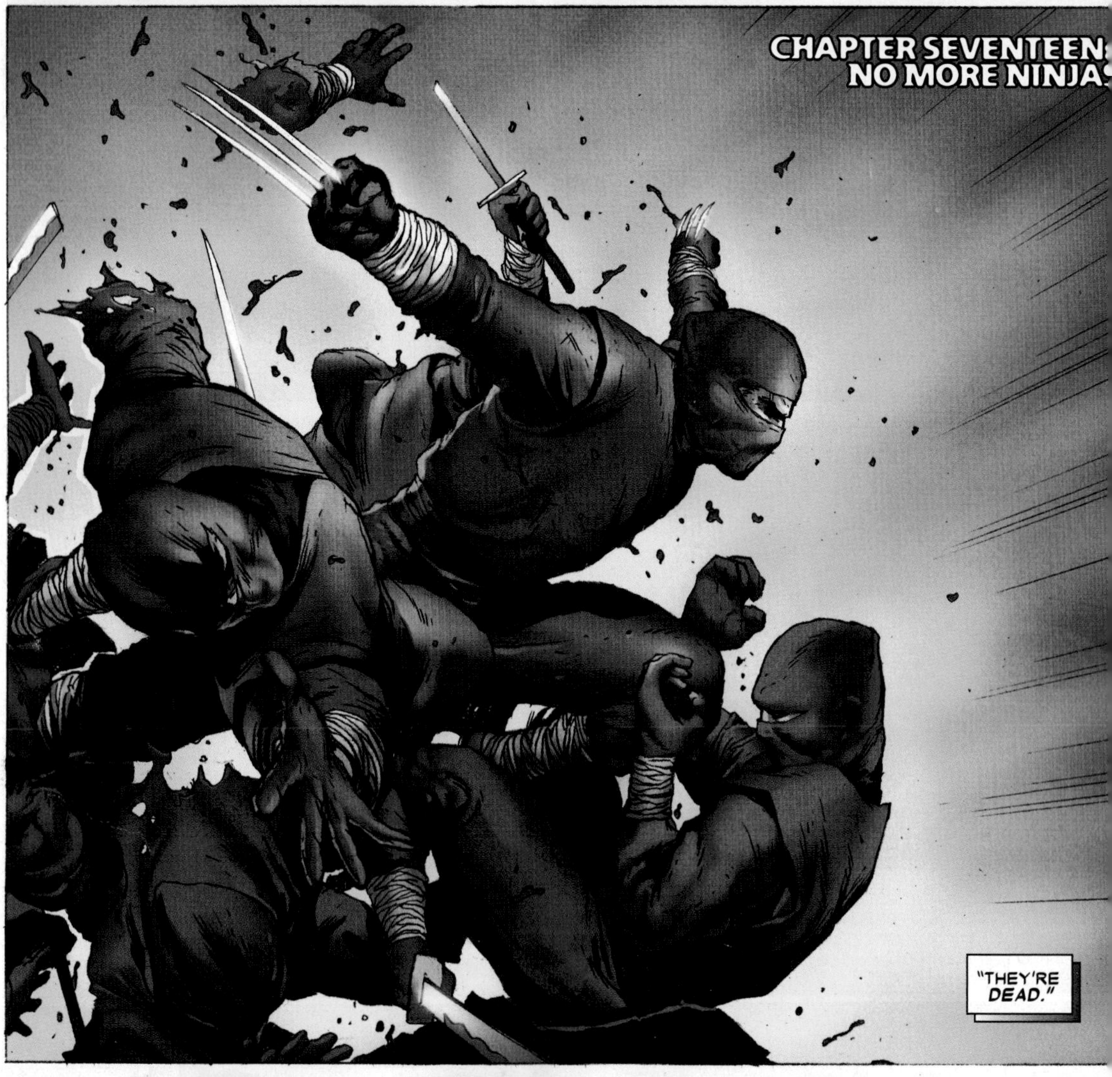
CHAPTER SEVENTEEN: NO MORE NINJA:
"THEY'RE DEAD."

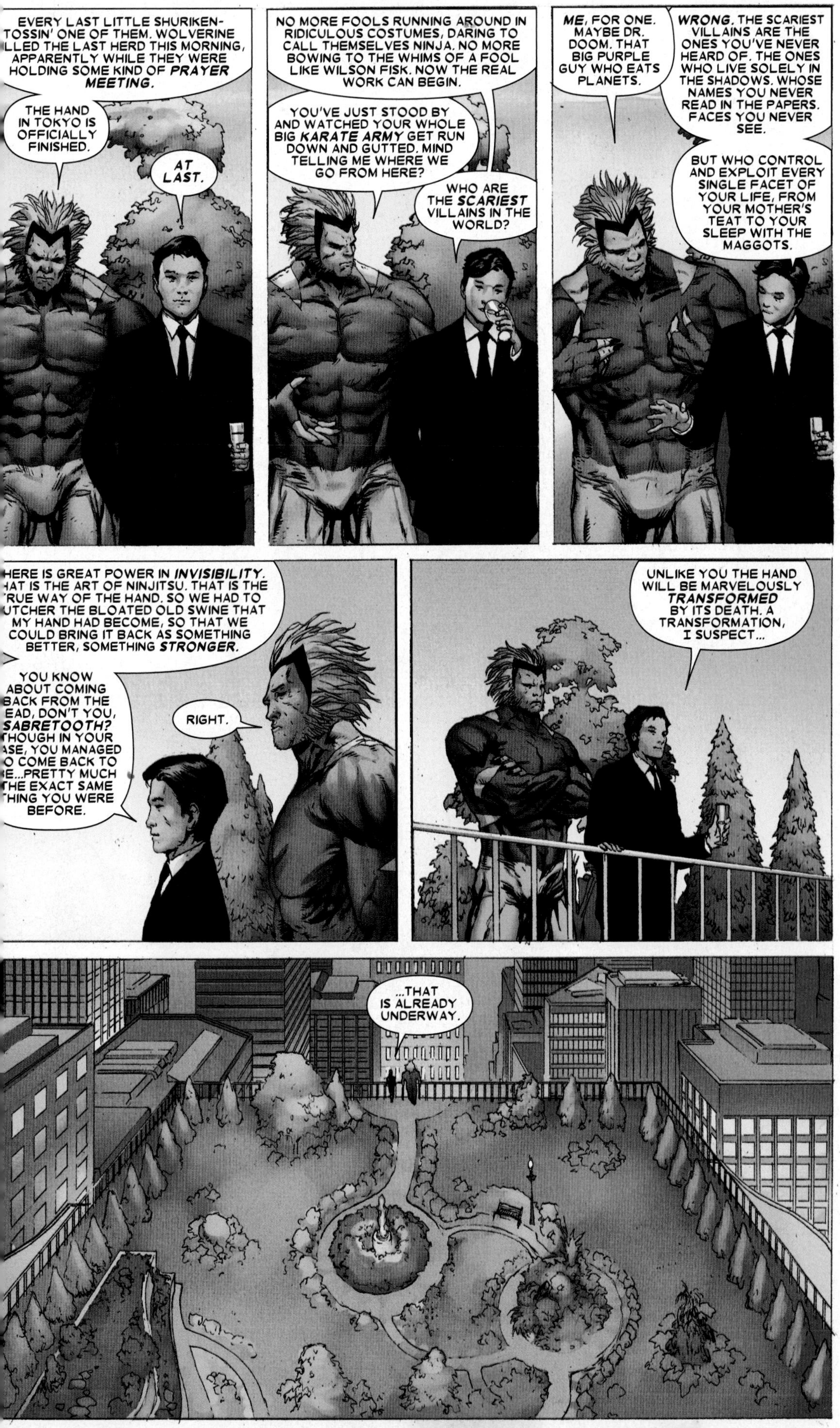

EVERY LAST LITTLE SHURIKEN-TOSSIN' ONE OF THEM. WOLVERINE LLED THE LAST HERD THIS MORNING, APPARENTLY WHILE THEY WERE HOLDING SOME KIND OF PRAYER MEETING.
THE HAND IN TOKYO IS OFFICIALLY FINISHED.
AT LAST.
NO MORE FOOLS RUNNING AROUND IN RIDICULOUS COSTUMES, DARING TO CALL THEMSELVES NINJA. NO MORE BOWING TO THE WHIMS OF A FOOL LIKE WILSON FISK. NOW THE REAL WORK CAN BEGIN.
YOU'VE JUST STOOD BY AND WATCHED YOUR WHOLE BIG KARATE ARMY GET RUN DOWN AND GUTTED. MIND TELLING ME WHERE WE GO FROM HERE?
WHO ARE THE SCARIEST VILLAINS IN THE WORLD?
ME, FOR ONE. MAYBE DR. DOOM. THAT BIG PURPLE GUY WHO EATS PLANETS.
WRONG. THE SCARIEST VILLAINS ARE THE ONES YOU'VE NEVER HEARD OF. THE ONES WHO LIVE SOLELY IN THE SHADOWS. WHOSE NAMES YOU NEVER READ IN THE PAPERS. FACES YOU NEVER SEE.
BUT WHO CONTROL AND EXPLOIT EVERY SINGLE FACET OF YOUR LIFE, FROM YOUR MOTHER'S TEAT TO YOUR SLEEP WITH THE MAGGOTS.
HERE IS GREAT POWER IN INVISIBILITY. HAT IS THE ART OF NINJITSU. THAT IS THE TRUE WAY OF THE HAND. SO WE HAD TO UTCHER THE BLOATED OLD SWINE THAT MY HAND HAD BECOME, SO THAT WE COULD BRING IT BACK AS SOMETHING BETTER, SOMETHING STRONGER.
YOU KNOW ABOUT COMING BACK FROM THE EAD, DON'T YOU, SABRETOOTH? THOUGH IN YOUR ASE, YOU MANAGED O COME BACK TO E...PRETTY MUCH THE EXACT SAME THING YOU WERE BEFORE.
RIGHT.
UNLIKE YOU THE HAND WILL BE MARVELOUSLY TRANSFORMED BY ITS DEATH. A TRANSFORMATION, I SUSPECT...
...THAT IS ALREADY UNDERWAY.

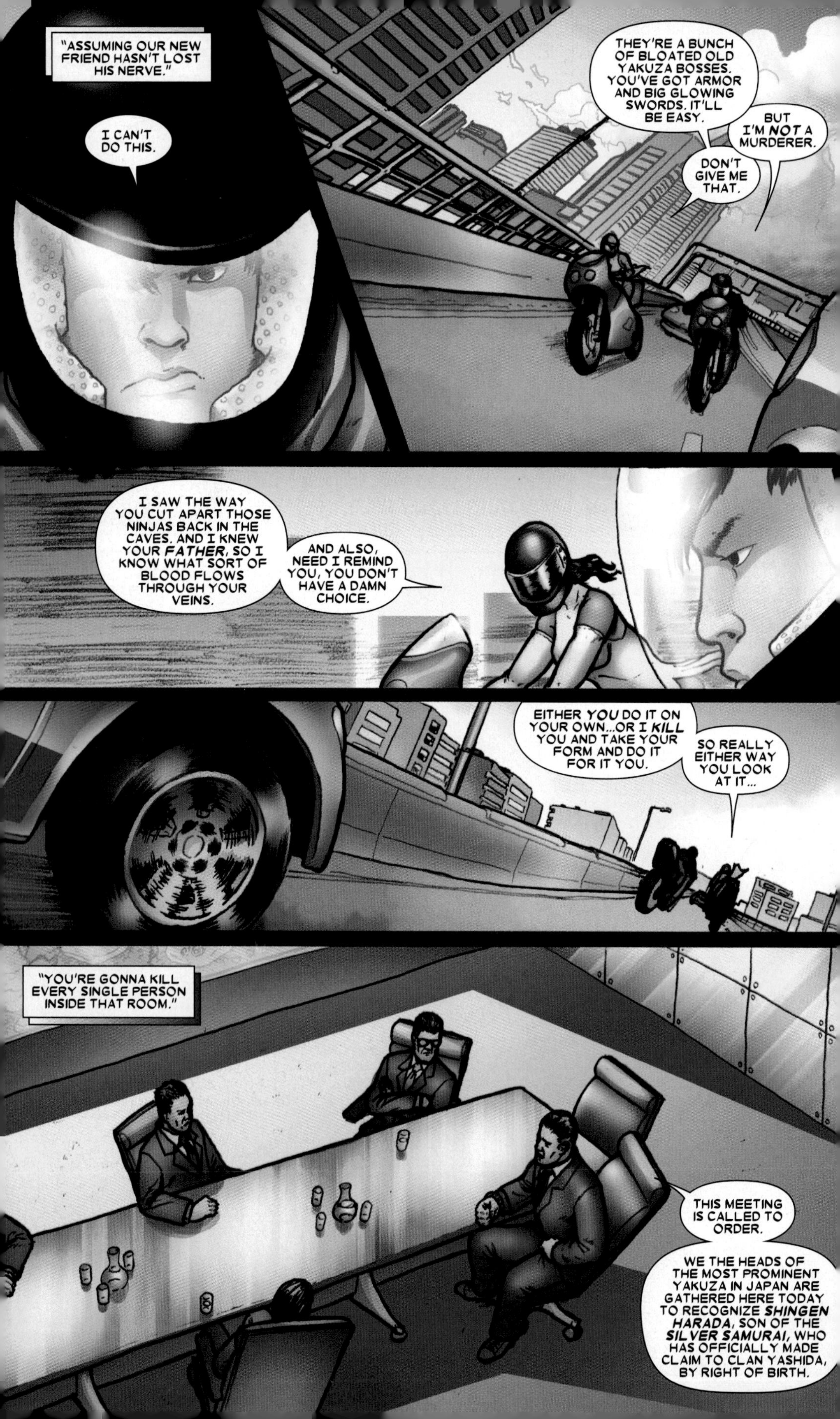

"ASSUMING OUR NEW FRIEND HASN'T LOST HIS NERVE."
I CAN'T DO THIS.
THEY'RE A BUNCH OF BLOATED OLD YAKUZA BOSSES. YOU'VE GOT ARMOR AND BIG GLOWING SWORDS. IT'LL BE EASY.
BUT I'M NOT A MURDERER.
DON'T GIVE ME THAT.
I SAW THE WAY YOU CUT APART THOSE NINJAS BACK IN THE CAVES. AND I KNEW YOUR FATHER, SO I KNOW WHAT SORT OF BLOOD FLOWS THROUGH YOUR VEINS.
AND ALSO, NEED I REMIND YOU, YOU DON'T HAVE A DAMN CHOICE.
EITHER YOU DO IT ON YOUR OWN...OR I KILL YOU AND TAKE YOUR FORM AND DO IT FOR IT YOU.
SO REALLY EITHER WAY YOU LOOK AT IT...
"YOU'RE GONNA KILL EVERY SINGLE PERSON INSIDE THAT ROOM."
THIS MEETING IS CALLED TO ORDER.
WE THE HEADS OF THE MOST PROMINENT YAKUZA IN JAPAN ARE GATHERED HERE TODAY TO RECOGNIZE SHINGEN HARADA, SON OF THE SILVER SAMURAI, WHO HAS OFFICIALLY MADE CLAIM TO CLAN YASHIDA, BY RIGHT OF BIRTH.

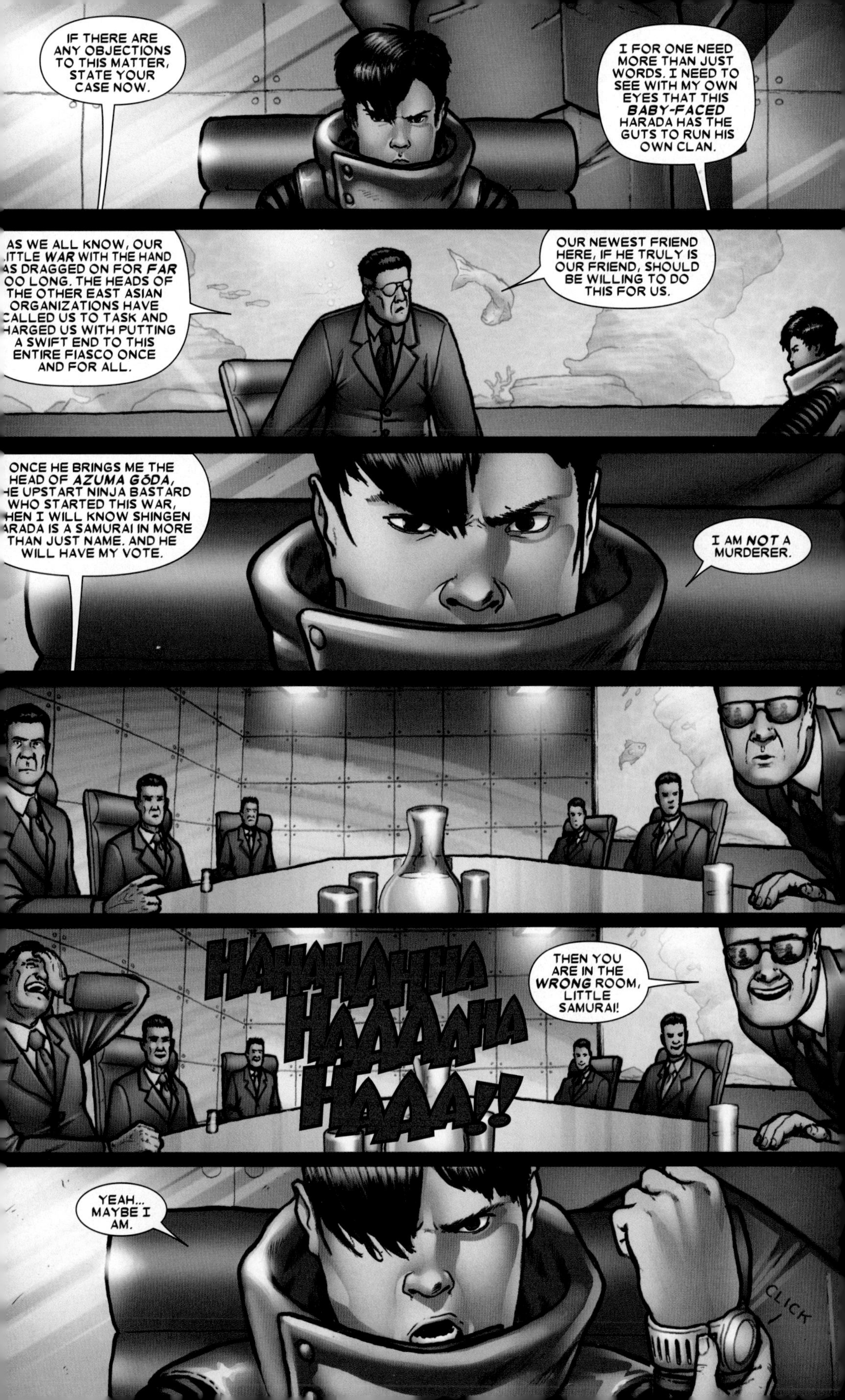
IF THERE ARE ANY OBJECTIONS TO THIS MATTER, STATE YOUR CASE NOW.
I FOR ONE NEED MORE THAN JUST WORDS. I NEED TO SEE WITH MY OWN EYES THAT THIS BABY-FACED HARADA HAS THE GUTS TO RUN HIS OWN CLAN.
AS WE ALL KNOW, OUR ITTLE WAR WITH THE HAND AS DRAGGED ON FOR FAR OO LONG. THE HEADS OF THE OTHER EAST ASIAN ORGANIZATIONS HAVE CALLED US TO TASK AND HARGED US WITH PUTTING A SWIFT END TO THIS ENTIRE FIASCO ONCE AND FOR ALL.
OUR NEWEST FRIEND HERE, IF HE TRULY IS OUR FRIEND, SHOULD BE WILLING TO DO THIS FOR US.
ONCE HE BRINGS ME THE HEAD OF AZUMA GŌDA, HE UPSTART NINJA BASTARD WHO STARTED THIS WAR, HEN I WILL KNOW SHINGEN ARADA IS A SAMURAI IN MORE THAN JUST NAME. AND HE WILL HAVE MY VOTE.
I AM NOT A MURDERER.
HAHAHAHHA HAAAAHA HAAA!!
THEN YOU ARE IN THE WRONG ROOM, LITTLE SAMURAI!
YEAH... MAYBE I AM.
CLICK

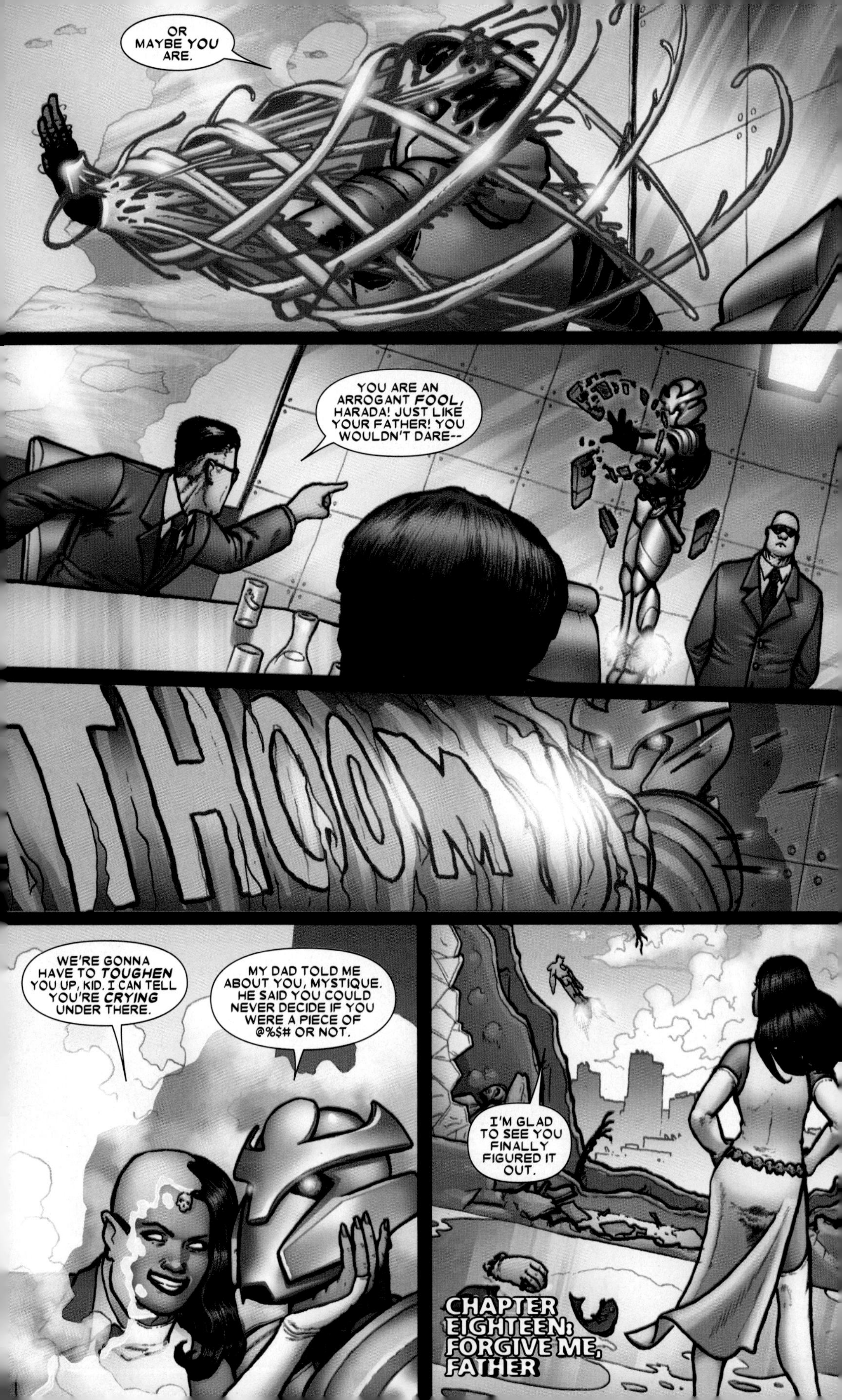

OR MAYBE YOU ARE.
YOU ARE AN ARROGANT FOOL, HARADA! JUST LIKE YOUR FATHER! YOU WOULDN'T DARE--
WHOOOM
WE'RE GONNA HAVE TO TOUGHEN YOU UP, KID. I CAN TELL YOU'RE CRYING UNDER THERE.
MY DAD TOLD ME ABOUT YOU, MYSTIQUE. HE SAID YOU COULD NEVER DECIDE IF YOU WERE A PIECE OF @%$# OR NOT.
I'M GLAD TO SEE YOU FINALLY FIGURED IT OUT.
CHAPTER EIGHTEEN: FORGIVE ME, FATHER

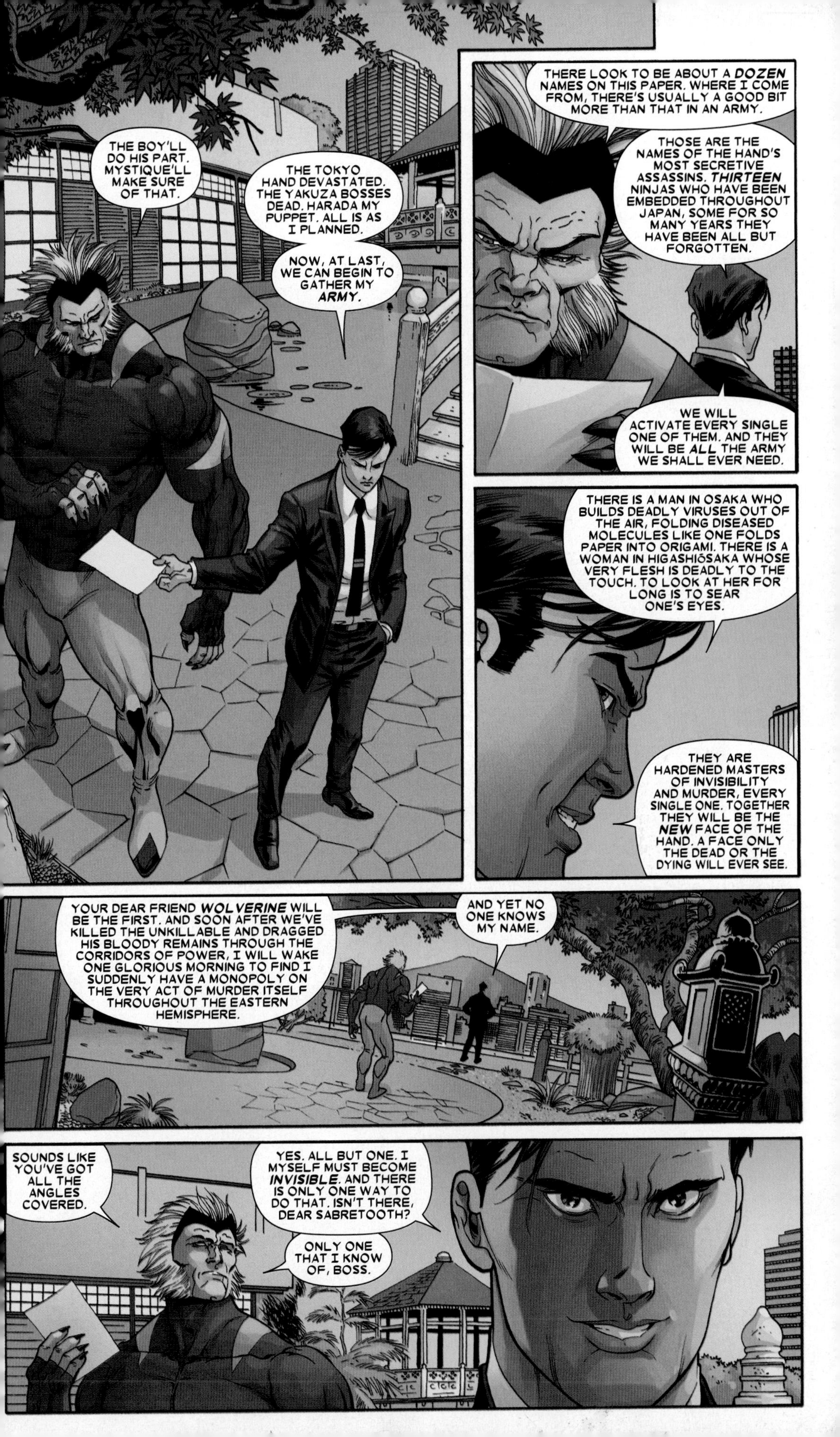
THE BOY'LL DO HIS PART. MYSTIQUE'LL MAKE SURE OF THAT.
THE TOKYO HAND DEVASTATED. THE YAKUZA BOSSES DEAD. HARADA MY PUPPET. ALL IS AS I PLANNED.
NOW, AT LAST, WE CAN BEGIN TO GATHER MY *ARMY.*
THERE LOOK TO BE ABOUT A *DOZEN* NAMES ON THIS PAPER. WHERE I COME FROM, THERE'S USUALLY A GOOD BIT MORE THAN THAT IN AN ARMY.
THOSE ARE THE NAMES OF THE HAND'S MOST SECRETIVE ASSASSINS. *THIRTEEN* NINJAS WHO HAVE BEEN EMBEDDED THROUGHOUT JAPAN, SOME FOR SO MANY YEARS THEY HAVE BEEN ALL BUT FORGOTTEN.
WE WILL ACTIVATE EVERY SINGLE ONE OF THEM. AND THEY WILL BE *ALL* THE ARMY WE SHALL EVER NEED.
THERE IS A MAN IN OSAKA WHO BUILDS DEADLY VIRUSES OUT OF THE AIR, FOLDING DISEASED MOLECULES LIKE ONE FOLDS PAPER INTO ORIGAMI. THERE IS A WOMAN IN HIGASHIŌSAKA WHOSE VERY FLESH IS DEADLY TO THE TOUCH. TO LOOK AT HER FOR LONG IS TO SEAR ONE'S EYES.
THEY ARE HARDENED MASTERS OF INVISIBILITY AND MURDER, EVERY SINGLE ONE. TOGETHER THEY WILL BE THE *NEW* FACE OF THE HAND. A FACE ONLY THE DEAD OR THE DYING WILL EVER SEE.
YOUR DEAR FRIEND *WOLVERINE* WILL BE THE FIRST. AND SOON AFTER WE'VE KILLED THE UNKILLABLE AND DRAGGED HIS BLOODY REMAINS THROUGH THE CORRIDORS OF POWER, I WILL WAKE ONE GLORIOUS MORNING TO FIND I SUDDENLY HAVE A MONOPOLY ON THE VERY ACT OF MURDER ITSELF THROUGHOUT THE EASTERN HEMISPHERE.
AND YET NO ONE KNOWS MY NAME.
SOUNDS LIKE YOU'VE GOT ALL THE ANGLES COVERED.
YES. ALL BUT ONE. I MYSELF MUST BECOME *INVISIBLE*. AND THERE IS ONLY ONE WAY TO DO THAT. ISN'T THERE, DEAR SABRETOOTH?
ONLY ONE THAT I KNOW OF, BOSS.

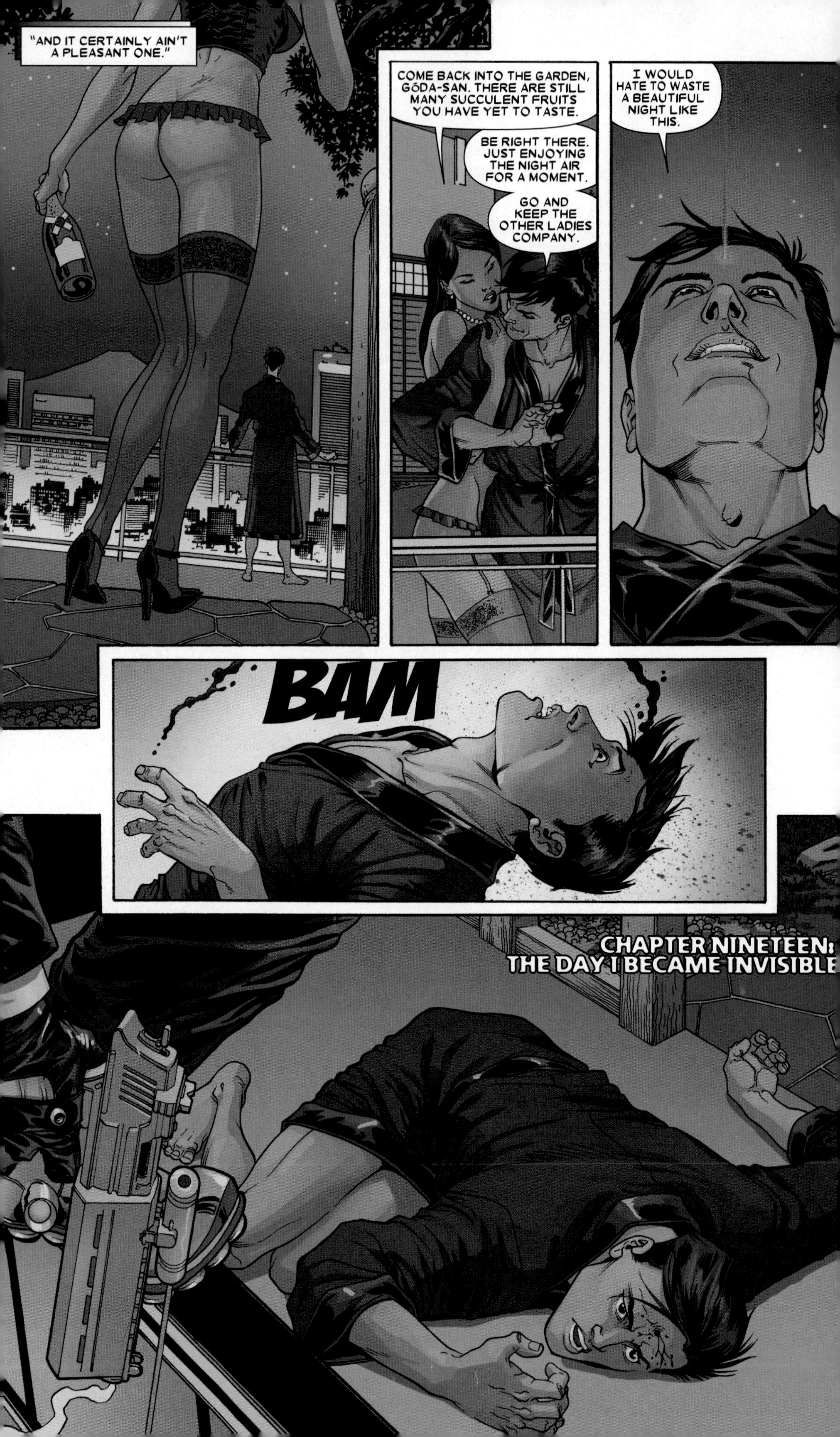
"AND IT CERTAINLY AIN'T A PLEASANT ONE."
COME BACK INTO THE GARDEN, GŌDA-SAN. THERE ARE STILL MANY SUCCULENT FRUITS YOU HAVE YET TO TASTE.
BE RIGHT THERE. JUST ENJOYING THE NIGHT AIR FOR A MOMENT.
GO AND KEEP THE OTHER LADIES COMPANY.
I WOULD HATE TO WASTE A BEAUTIFUL NIGHT LIKE THIS.
BAM
CHAPTER NINETEEN: THE DAY I BECAME INVISIBLE

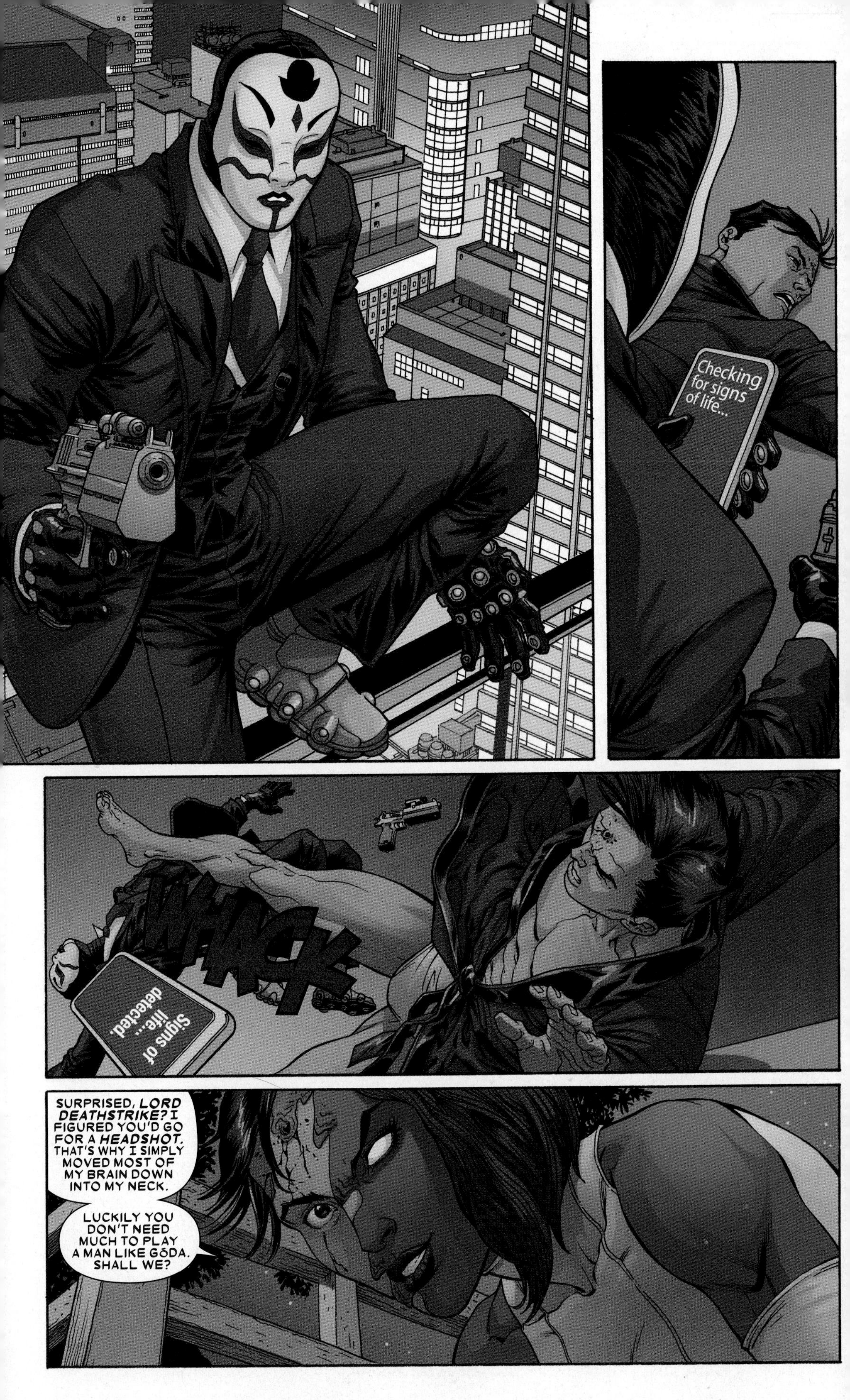
Checking for signs of life...
WHACK
Signs of life... detected.
SURPRISED, *LORD DEATHSTRIKE?* I FIGURED YOU'D GO FOR A *HEADSHOT*. THAT'S WHY I SIMPLY MOVED MOST OF MY BRAIN DOWN INTO MY NECK.
LUCKILY YOU DON'T NEED MUCH TO PLAY A MAN LIKE GŌDA. SHALL WE?

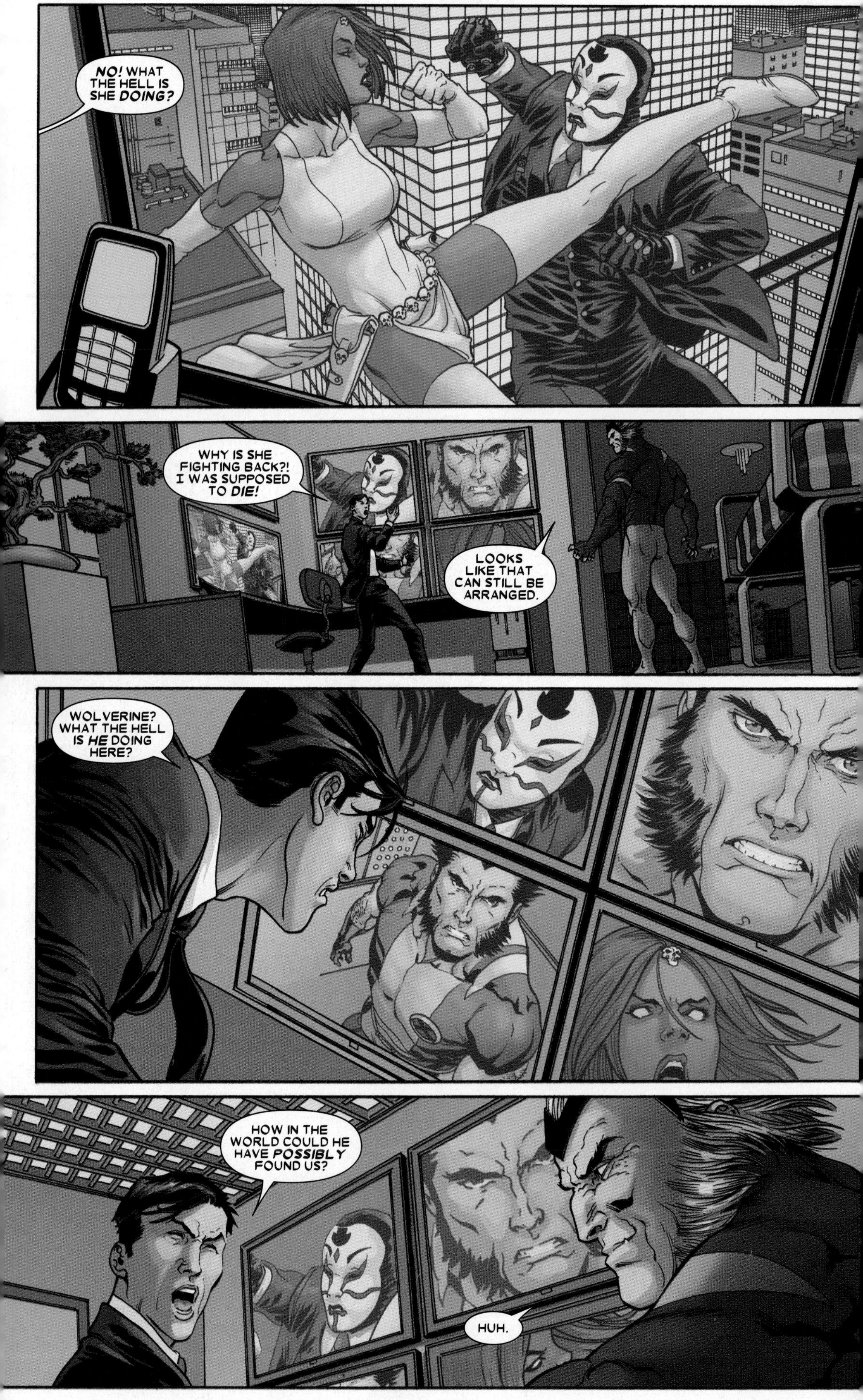
NO! WHAT THE HELL IS SHE DOING?
WHY IS SHE FIGHTING BACK?! I WAS SUPPOSED TO DIE!
LOOKS LIKE THAT CAN STILL BE ARRANGED.
WOLVERINE? WHAT THE HELL IS HE DOING HERE?
HOW IN THE WORLD COULD HE HAVE POSSIBLY FOUND US?
HUH.

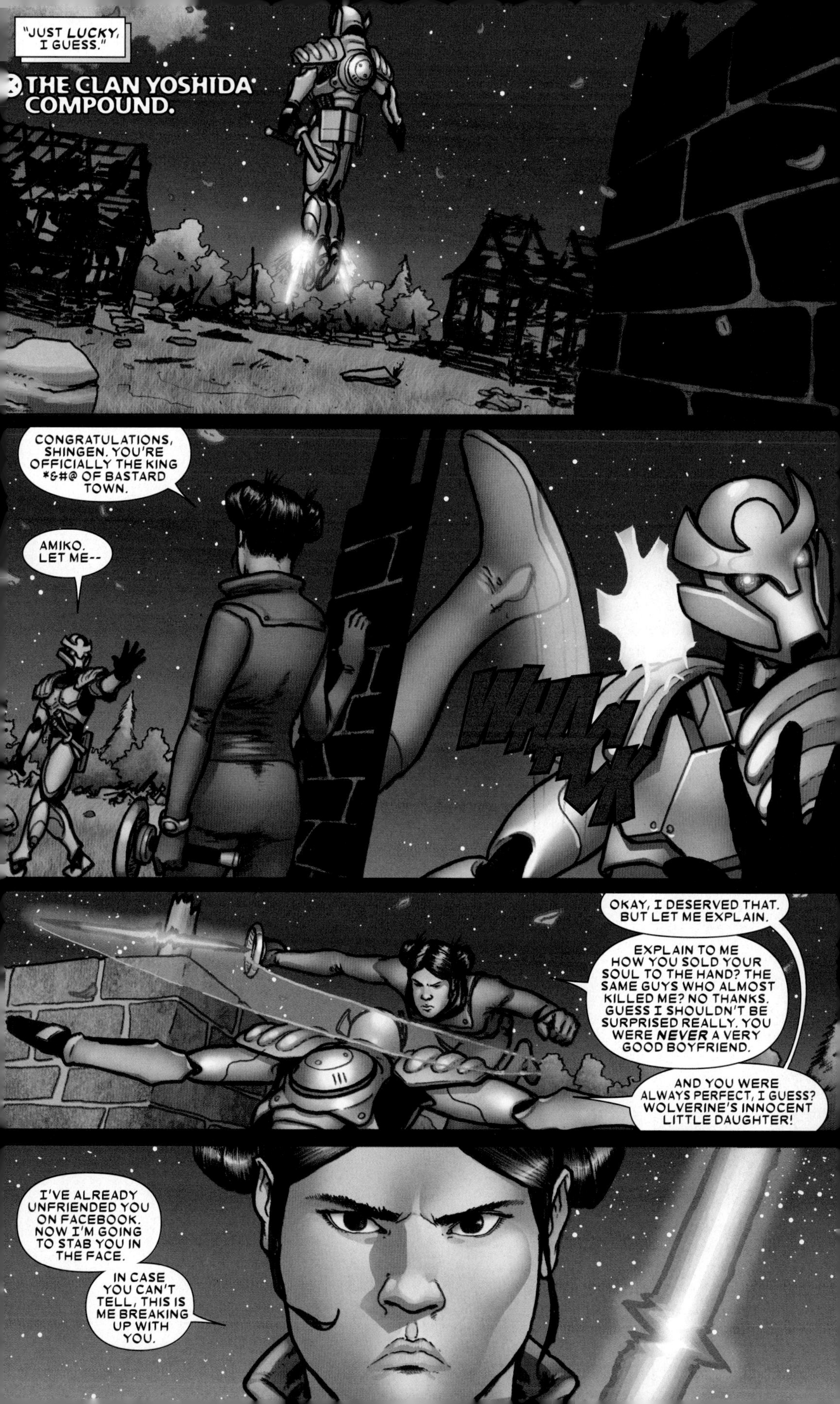
"JUST LUCKY, I GUESS."
THE CLAN YOSHIDA COMPOUND.
CONGRATULATIONS, SHINGEN. YOU'RE OFFICIALLY THE KING *&#@ OF BASTARD TOWN.
AMIKO. LET ME--
WHACK
OKAY, I DESERVED THAT. BUT LET ME EXPLAIN.
EXPLAIN TO ME HOW YOU SOLD YOUR SOUL TO THE HAND? THE SAME GUYS WHO ALMOST KILLED ME? NO THANKS. GUESS I SHOULDN'T BE SURPRISED REALLY. YOU WERE NEVER A VERY GOOD BOYFRIEND.
AND YOU WERE ALWAYS PERFECT, I GUESS? WOLVERINE'S INNOCENT LITTLE DAUGHTER!
I'VE ALREADY UNFRIENDED YOU ON FACEBOOK. NOW I'M GOING TO STAB YOU IN THE FACE.
IN CASE YOU CAN'T TELL, THIS IS ME BREAKING UP WITH YOU.

YOU! YOU DID THIS. YOU SOLD ME OUT. TO *WOLVERINE!*

THAT'S ONE WAY OF LOOKING AT IT. ANOTHER MIGHT BE TO SAY...

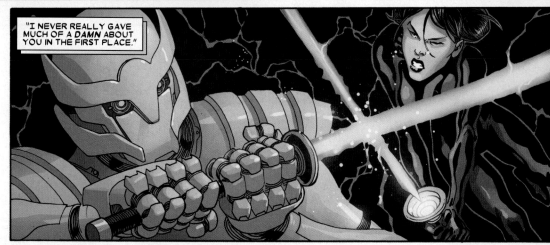

"I NEVER REALLY GAVE MUCH OF A *DAMN* ABOUT YOU IN THE FIRST PLACE."

YOU UNGRATEFUL--

GAH!

YOU HAD YOURSELF A HUMDINGER OF A PLAN. AND SO FAR IT'S BEEN RUNNING LIKE CLOCKWORK. BUT YOU WERE DEAD WRONG ABOUT JUST *TWO* LITTLE THINGS.

BEING INVISIBLE IS GOOD, YOU SEE, BUT YOU DON'T EVER WANNA BE *TOO* INVISIBLE. 'CAUSE THEN THE PEOPLE AROUND YOU MIGHT START TO FORGET...

"JUST EXACTLY WHAT THEY EVER NEEDED YOU FOR IN THE FIRST PLACE."

YOU STUPID DOG-FACED SONUVA--

THE OTHER THING YOU WERE WRONG ABOUT...WAS *ME.* I DIDN'T GO THROUGH EVERYTHING I BEEN THROUGH THESE LAST FEW MONTHS JUST TO COME BACK AS THE SAME OLD FELLA I *WAS* BEFORE. EVEN THOUGH YOU GOTTA ADMIT, THAT FELLA WAS PRETTY DOG-GONE BADASS.

I CAME BACK FOR SOMETHING BIGGER.

"A WHOLE HELLUVA LOT BIGGER."

SO I GUESS THIS IS WHERE WE PART WAYS, GŌDA. WOLVERINE'LL BE ALONG ANY MINUTE NOW TO KILL YOU.

AND JUST SO YOU KNOW, BEING STABBED WITH THEM *CLAWS* A' HIS...IT *HURTS* LIKE HOLY HELL. BUT CONGRATULATIONS, YOU WANTED TO BE INVISIBLE...

YOU DEFINITELY WILL BE NOW.

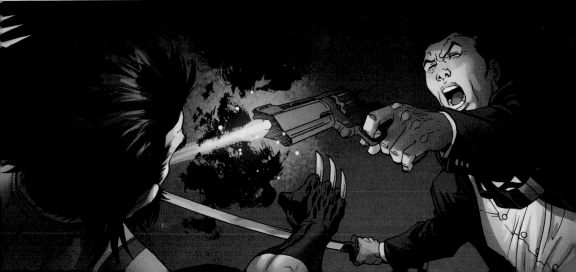

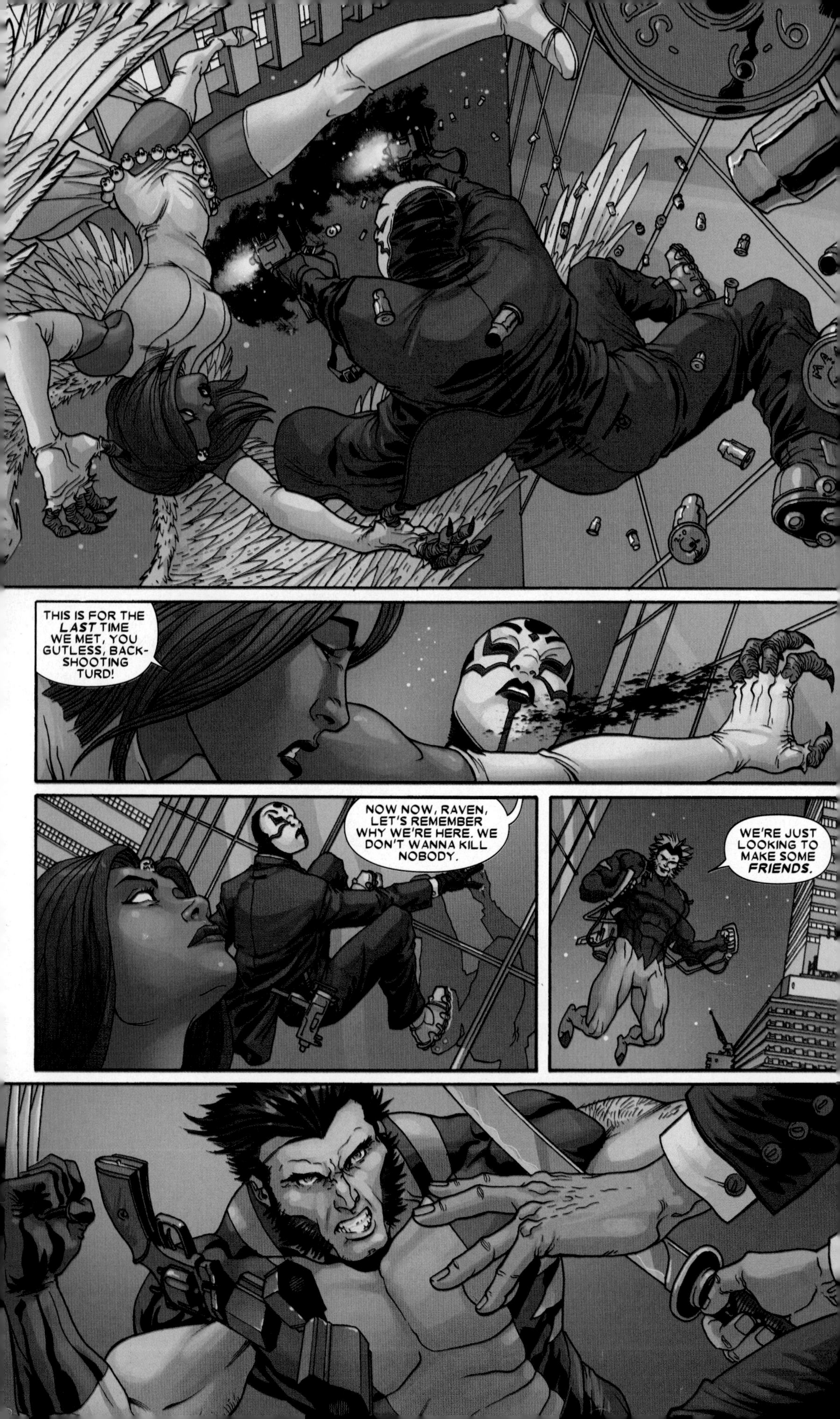
THIS IS FOR THE LAST TIME WE MET, YOU GUTLESS, BACK-SHOOTING TURD!
NOW NOW, RAVEN, LET'S REMEMBER WHY WE'RE HERE. WE DON'T WANNA KILL NOBODY.
WE'RE JUST LOOKING TO MAKE SOME FRIENDS.

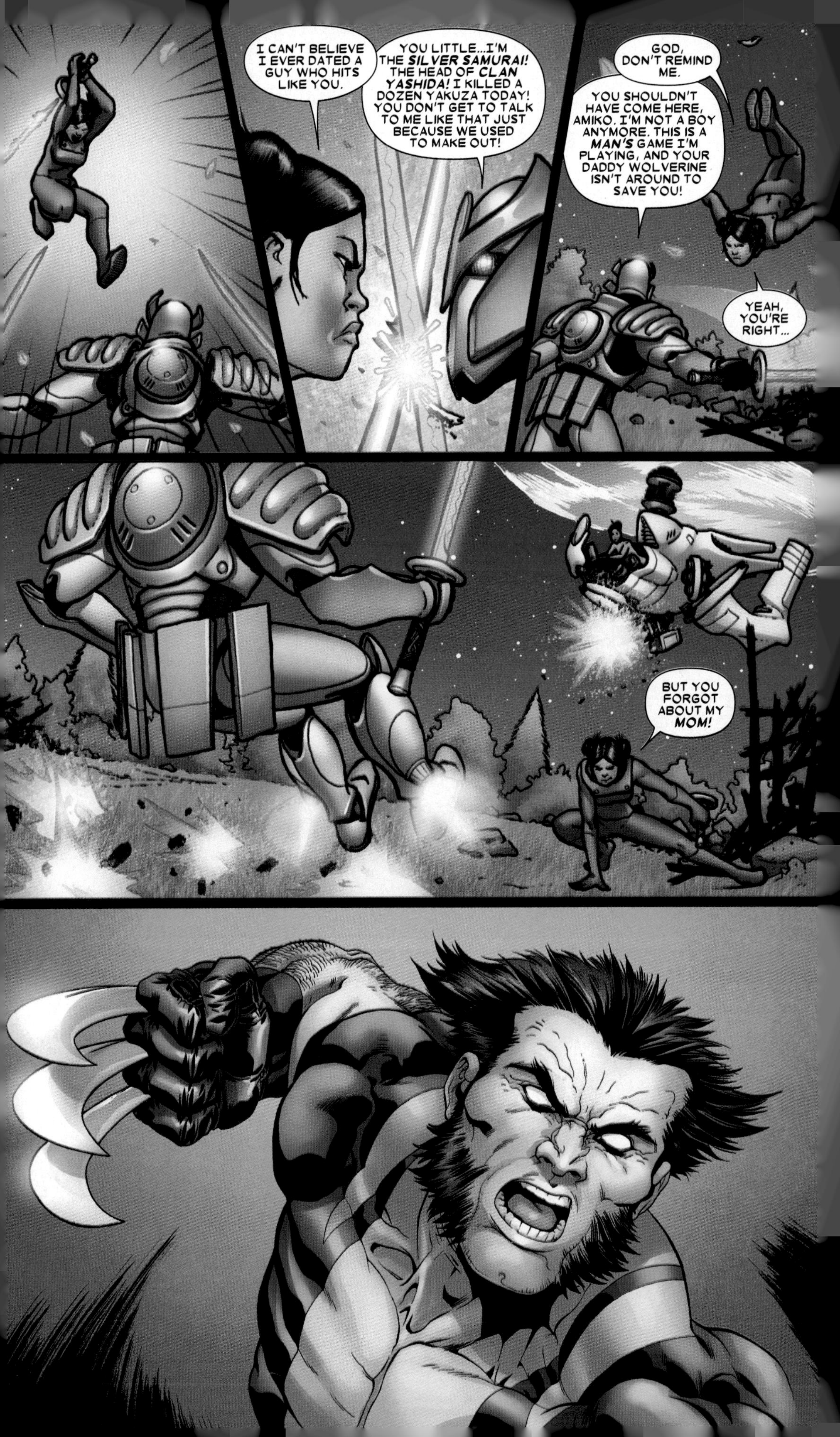
I CAN'T BELIEVE I EVER DATED A GUY WHO HITS LIKE YOU.
YOU LITTLE...I'M THE SILVER SAMURAI! THE HEAD OF CLAN YASHIDA! I KILLED A DOZEN YAKUZA TODAY! YOU DON'T GET TO TALK TO ME LIKE THAT JUST BECAUSE WE USED TO MAKE OUT!
GOD, DON'T REMIND ME.
YOU SHOULDN'T HAVE COME HERE, AMIKO. I'M NOT A BOY ANYMORE. THIS IS A MAN'S GAME I'M PLAYING, AND YOUR DADDY WOLVERINE ISN'T AROUND TO SAVE YOU!
YEAH, YOU'RE RIGHT...
BUT YOU FORGOT ABOUT MY MOM!

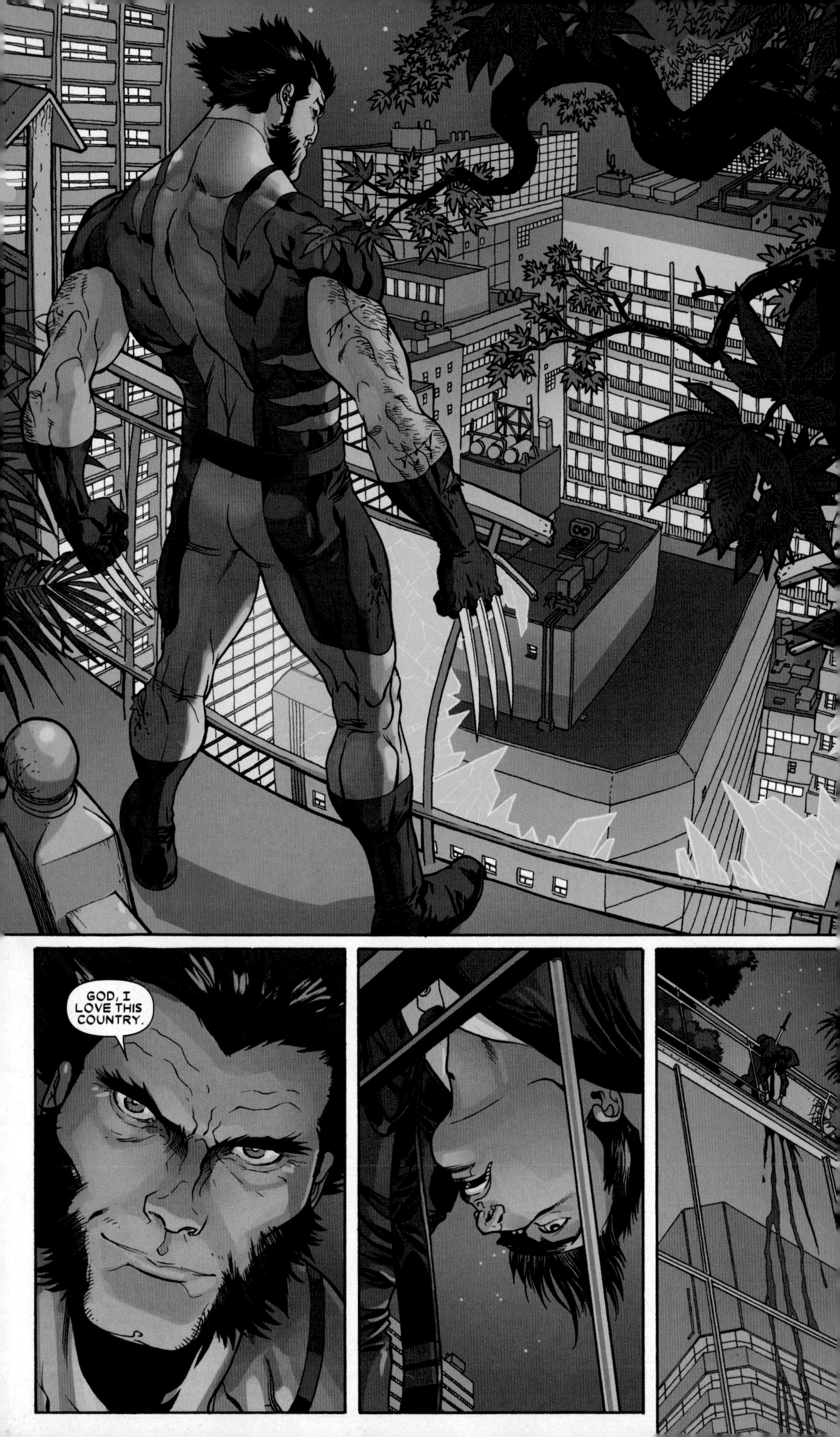
GOD, I LOVE THIS COUNTRY.

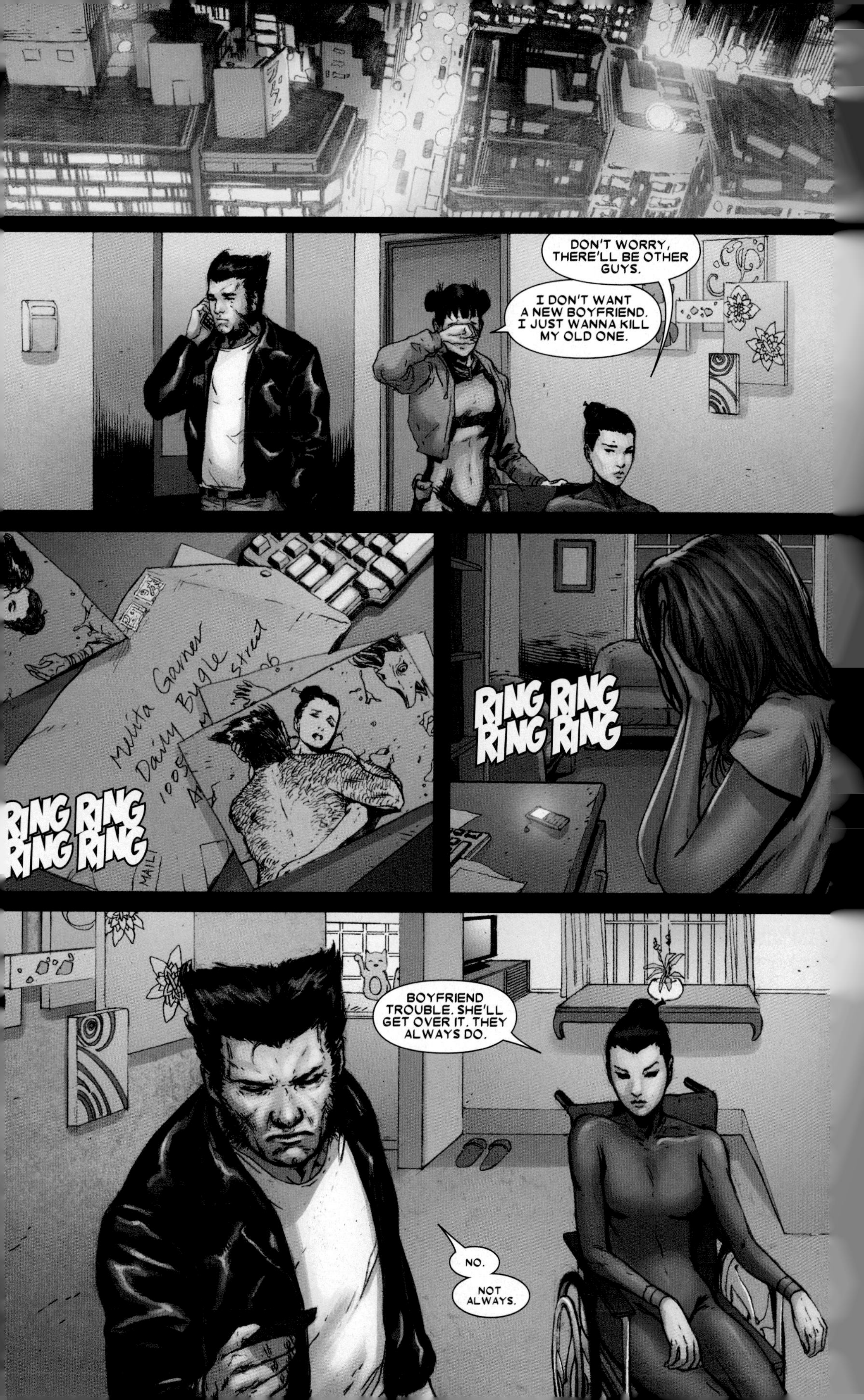
DON'T WORRY, THERE'LL BE OTHER GUYS.
I DON'T WANT A NEW BOYFRIEND. I JUST WANNA KILL MY OLD ONE.
Melita Garner
Daily Bugle
RING RING RING RING
RING RING RING RING
BOYFRIEND TROUBLE. SHE'LL GET OVER IT. THEY ALWAYS DO.
NO.
NOT ALWAYS.

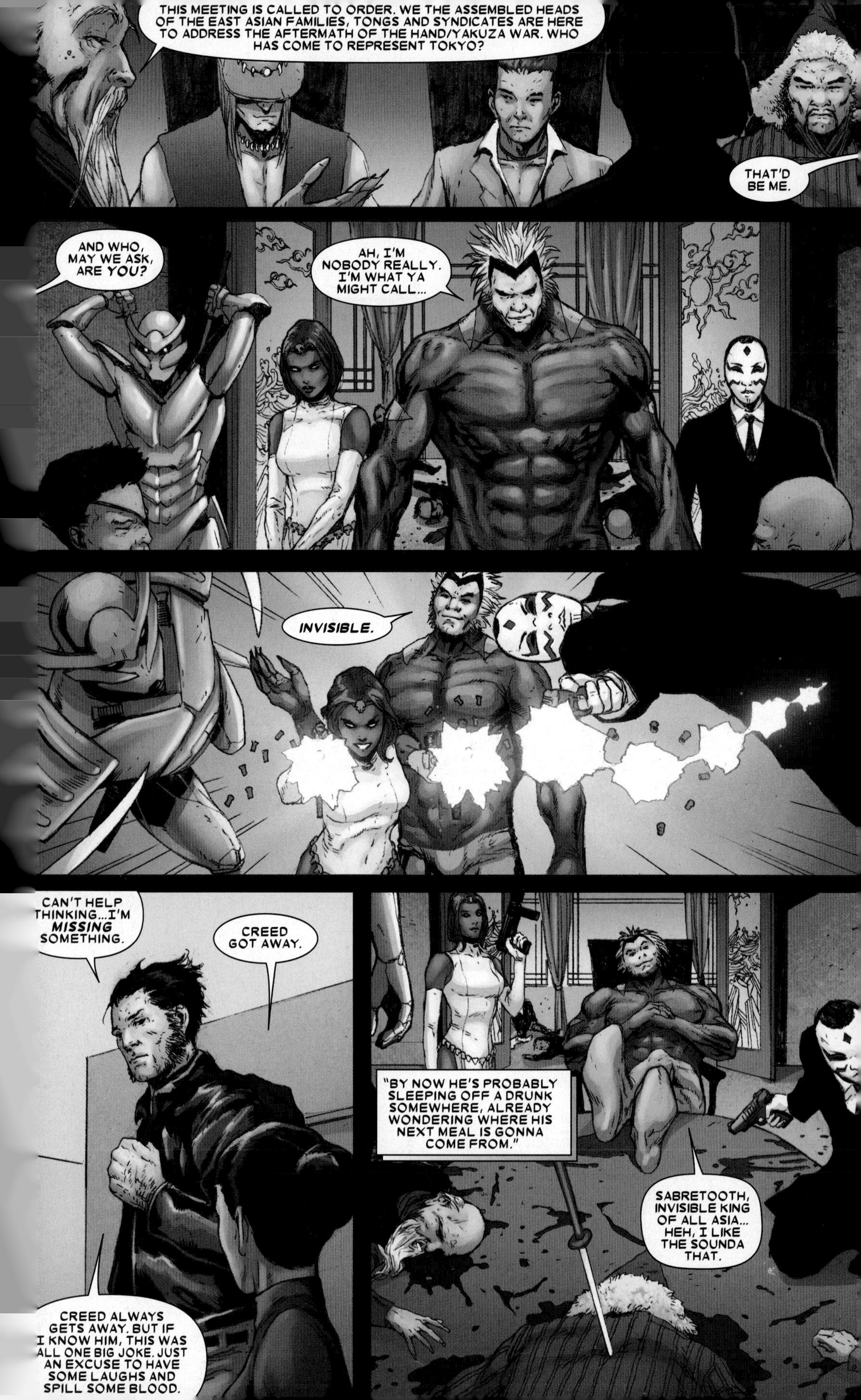
THIS MEETING IS CALLED TO ORDER. WE THE ASSEMBLED HEADS OF THE EAST ASIAN FAMILIES, TONGS AND SYNDICATES ARE HERE TO ADDRESS THE AFTERMATH OF THE HAND/YAKUZA WAR. WHO HAS COME TO REPRESENT TOKYO?
THAT'D BE ME.
AND WHO, MAY WE ASK, ARE YOU?
AH, I'M NOBODY REALLY. I'M WHAT YA MIGHT CALL...
INVISIBLE.
CAN'T HELP THINKING...I'M MISSING SOMETHING.
CREED GOT AWAY.
CREED ALWAYS GETS AWAY. BUT IF I KNOW HIM, THIS WAS ALL ONE BIG JOKE. JUST AN EXCUSE TO HAVE SOME LAUGHS AND SPILL SOME BLOOD.
"BY NOW HE'S PROBABLY SLEEPING OFF A DRUNK SOMEWHERE, ALREADY WONDERING WHERE HIS NEXT MEAL IS GONNA COME FROM."
SABRETOOTH, INVISIBLE KING OF ALL ASIA... HEH, I LIKE THE SOUNDA THAT.

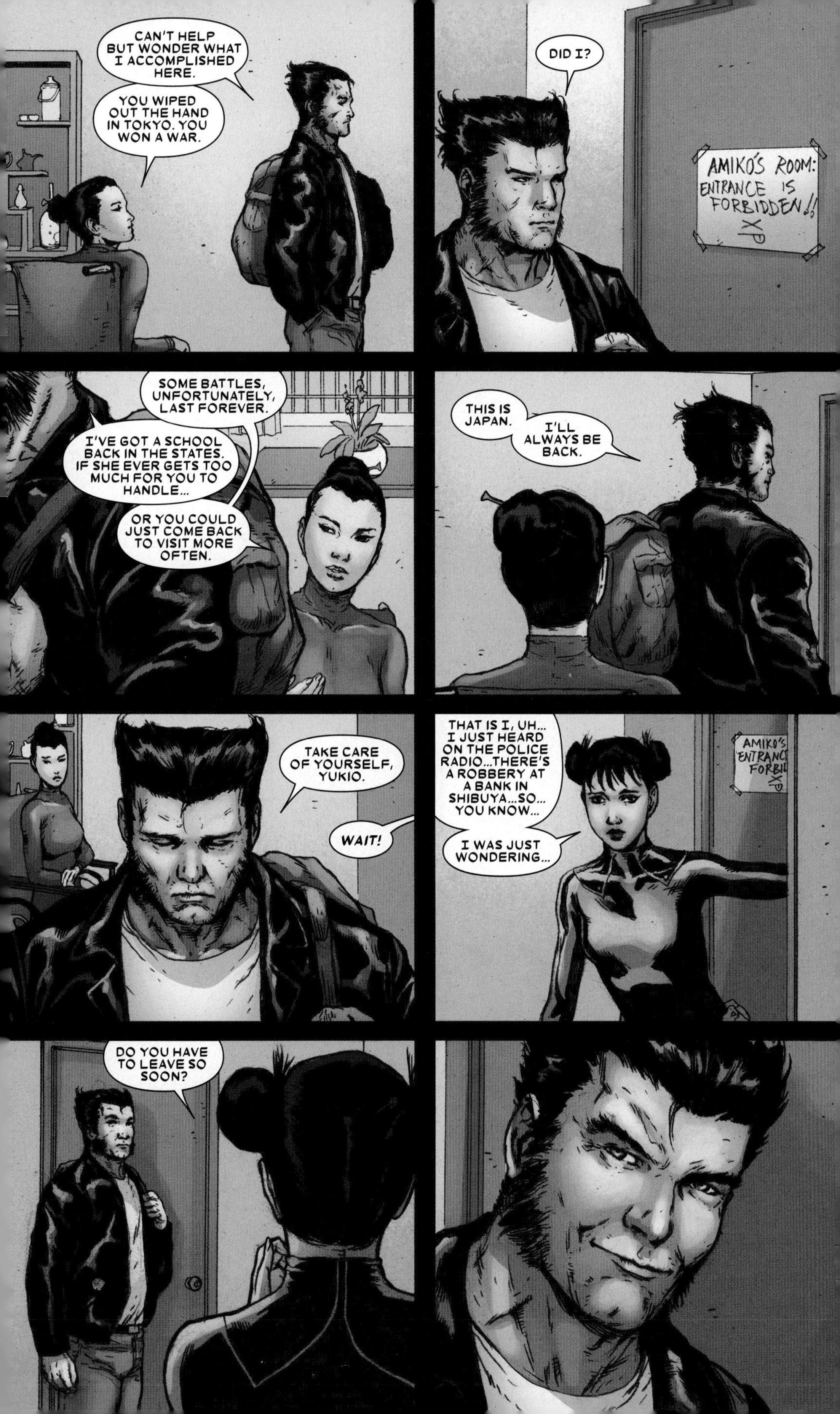

CAN'T HELP BUT WONDER WHAT I ACCOMPLISHED HERE.
YOU WIPED OUT THE HAND IN TOKYO. YOU WON A WAR.
DID I?
AMIKO'S ROOM: ENTRANCE IS FORBIDDEN!!
SOME BATTLES, UNFORTUNATELY, LAST FOREVER.
I'VE GOT A SCHOOL BACK IN THE STATES. IF SHE EVER GETS TOO MUCH FOR YOU TO HANDLE...
OR YOU COULD JUST COME BACK TO VISIT MORE OFTEN.
THIS IS JAPAN.
I'LL ALWAYS BE BACK.
TAKE CARE OF YOURSELF, YUKIO.
WAIT!
THAT IS I, UH... I JUST HEARD ON THE POLICE RADIO...THERE'S A ROBBERY AT A BANK IN SHIBUYA...SO... YOU KNOW...
I WAS JUST WONDERING...
DO YOU HAVE TO LEAVE SO SOON?

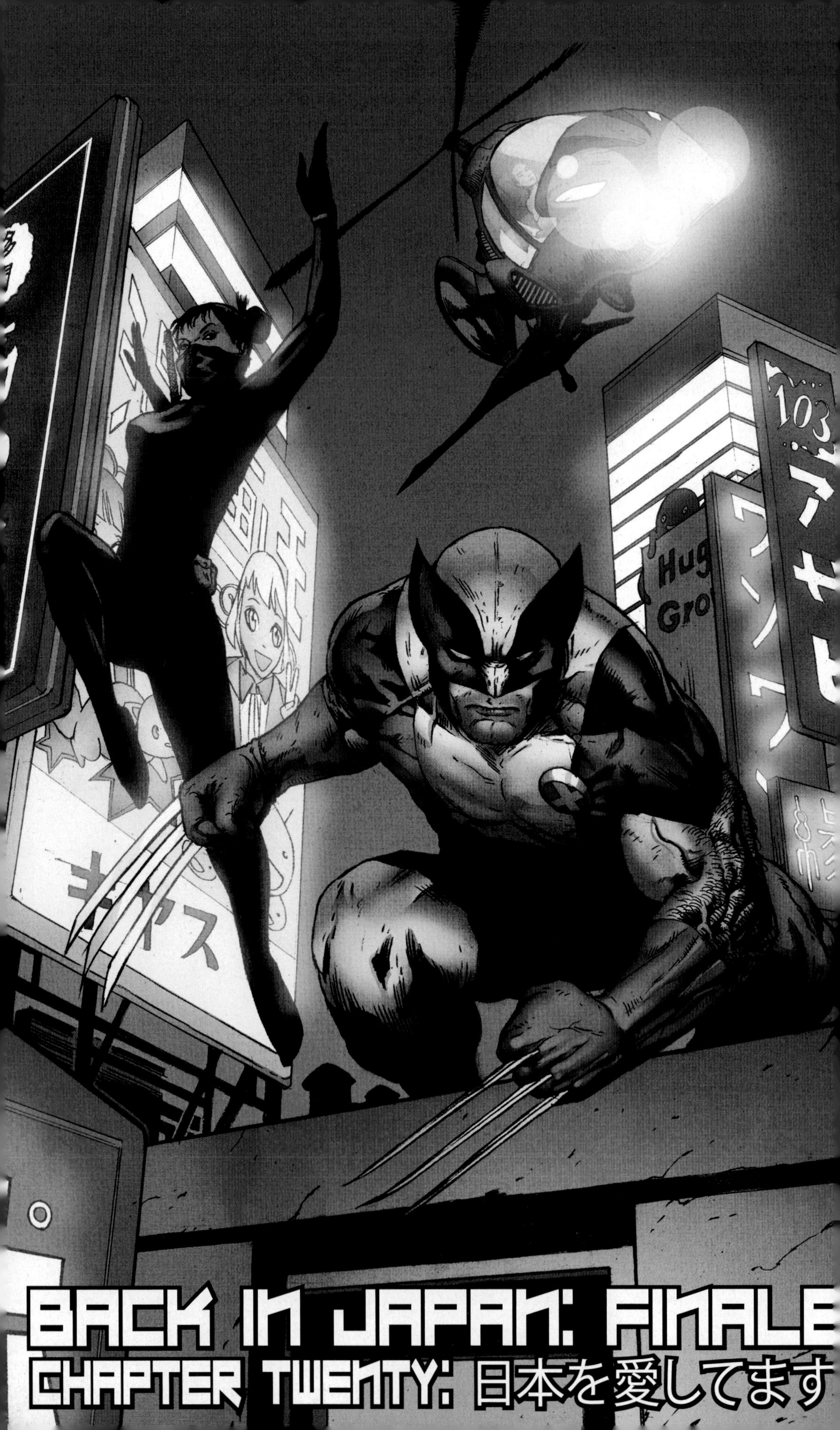
103
BACK IN JAPAN: FINALE
CHAPTER TWENTY: 日本を愛してます

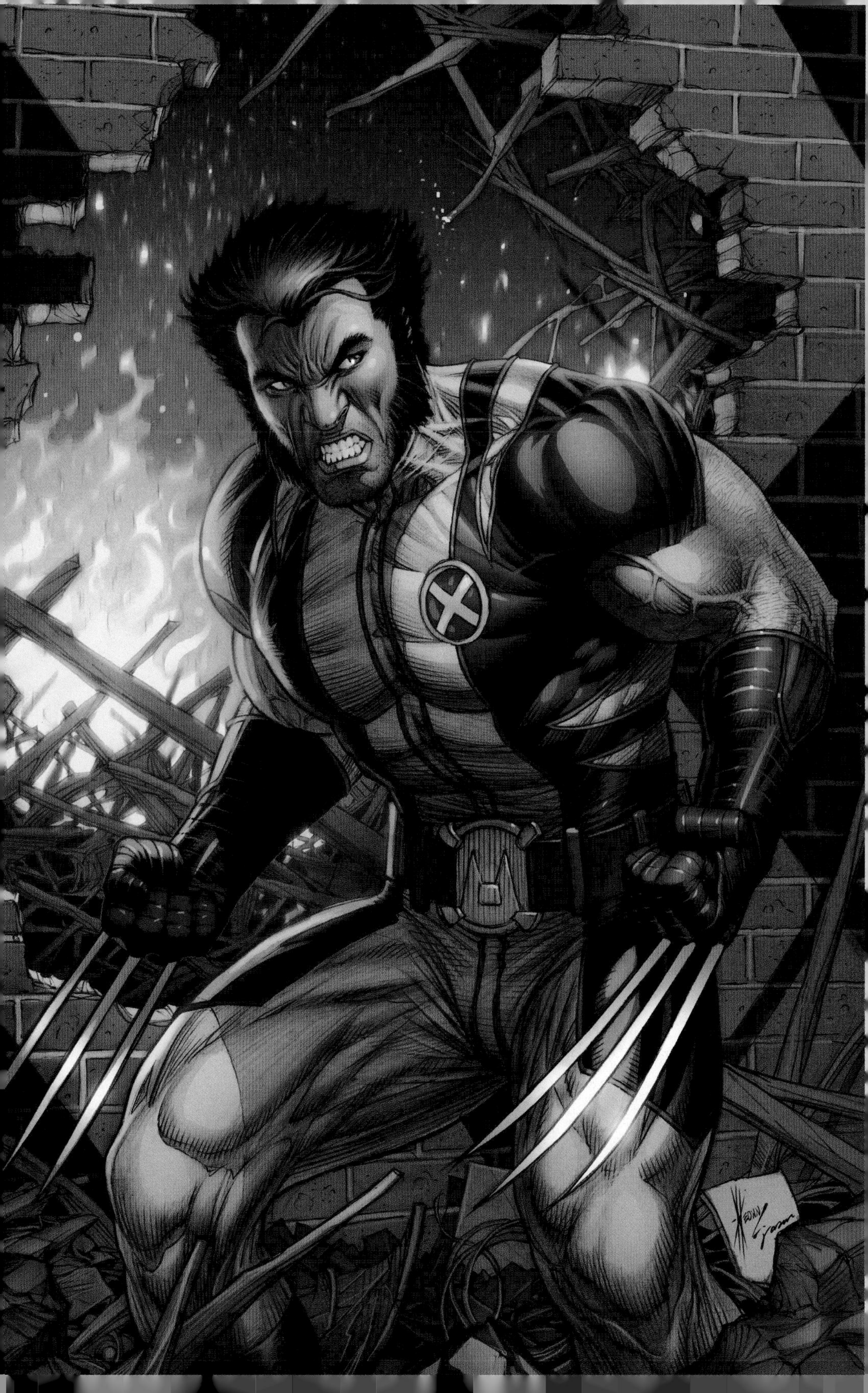

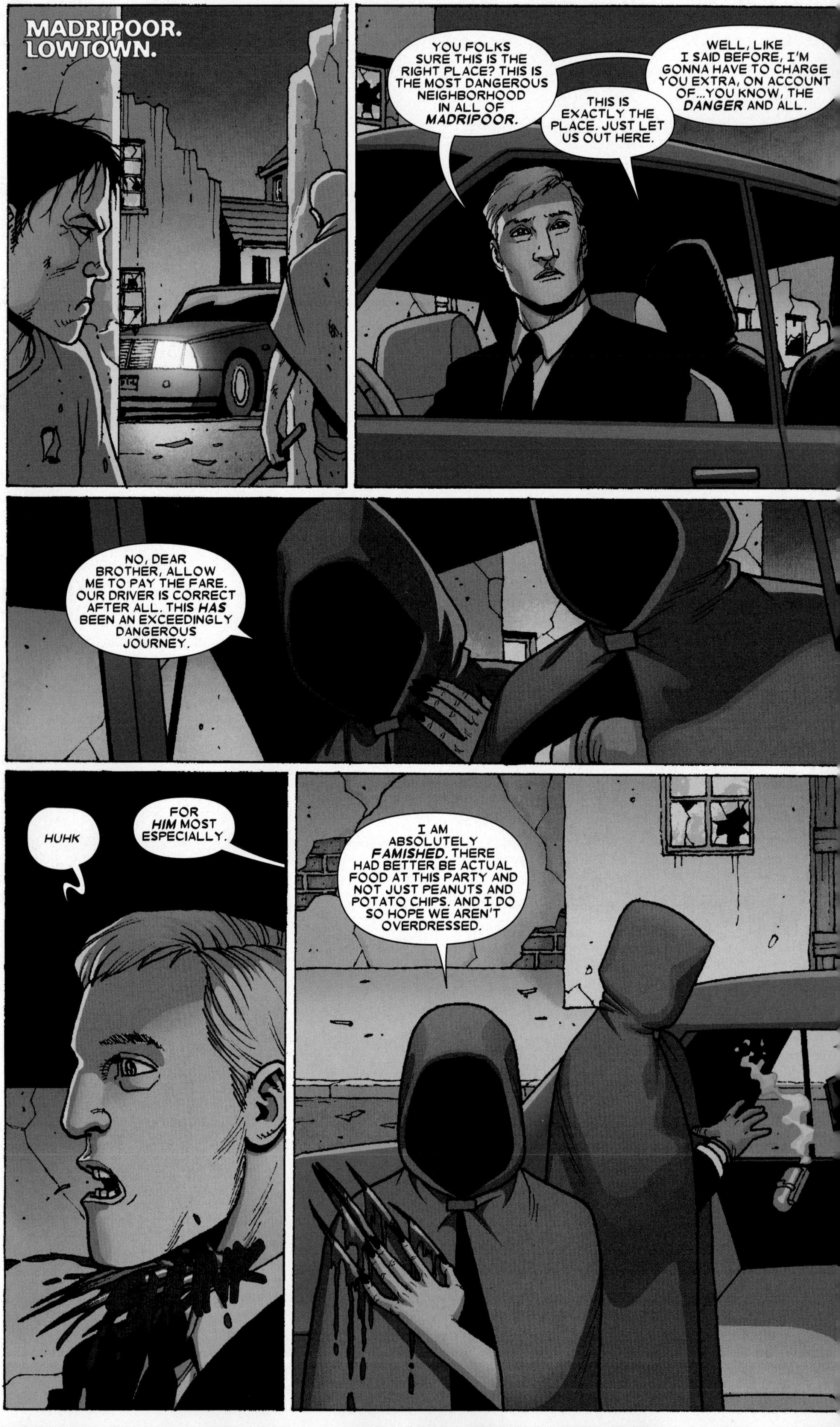
MADRIPOOR.
LOWTOWN.
YOU FOLKS SURE THIS IS THE RIGHT PLACE? THIS IS THE MOST DANGEROUS NEIGHBORHOOD IN ALL OF MADRIPOOR.
THIS IS EXACTLY THE PLACE. JUST LET US OUT HERE.
WELL, LIKE I SAID BEFORE, I'M GONNA HAVE TO CHARGE YOU EXTRA, ON ACCOUNT OF...YOU KNOW, THE DANGER AND ALL.
NO, DEAR BROTHER, ALLOW ME TO PAY THE FARE. OUR DRIVER IS CORRECT AFTER ALL. THIS HAS BEEN AN EXCEEDINGLY DANGEROUS JOURNEY.
HUHK
FOR HIM MOST ESPECIALLY.
I AM ABSOLUTELY FAMISHED. THERE HAD BETTER BE ACTUAL FOOD AT THIS PARTY AND NOT JUST PEANUTS AND POTATO CHIPS. AND I DO SO HOPE WE AREN'T OVERDRESSED.

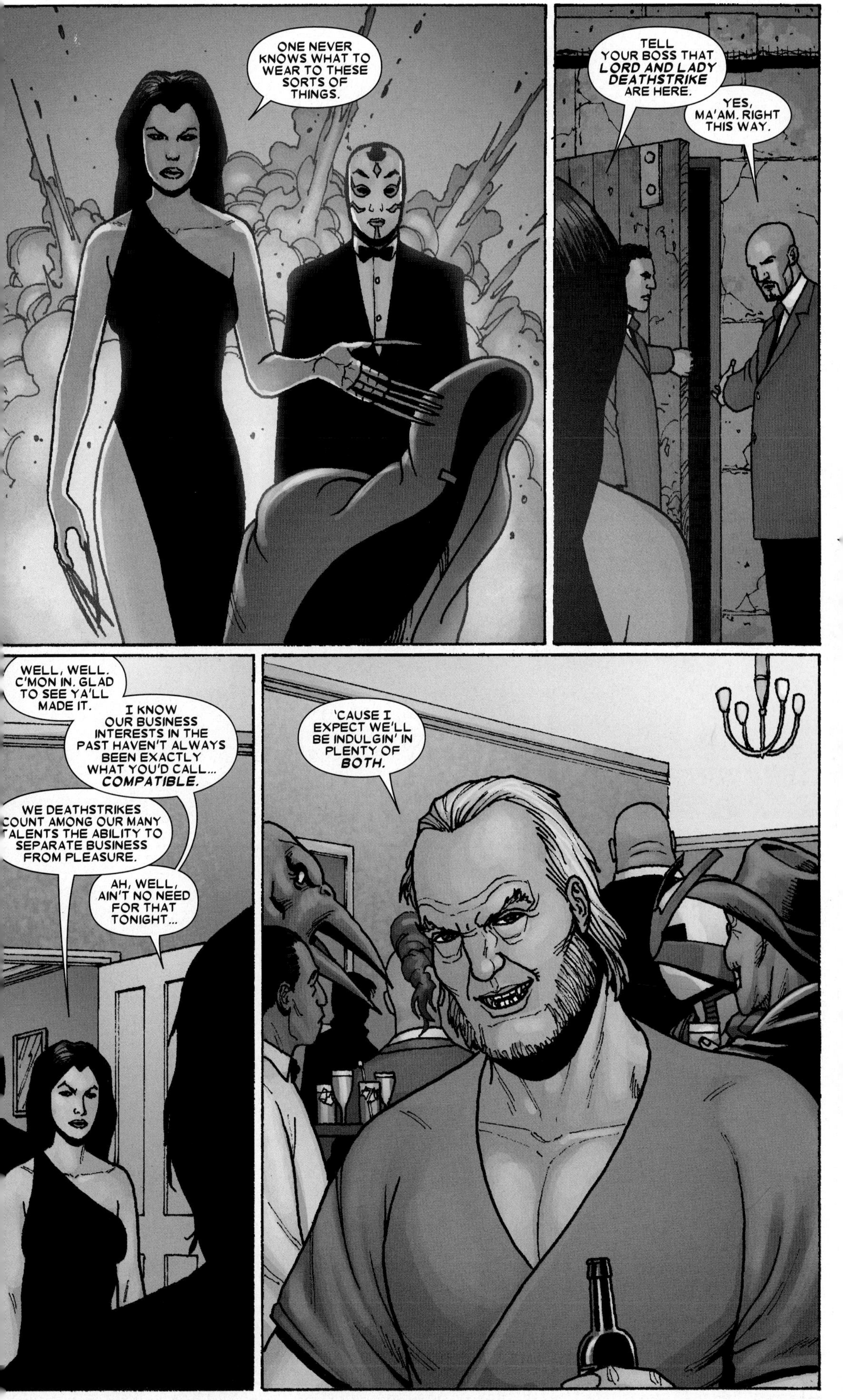
ONE NEVER KNOWS WHAT TO WEAR TO THESE SORTS OF THINGS.
TELL YOUR BOSS THAT LORD AND LADY DEATHSTRIKE ARE HERE.
YES, MA'AM. RIGHT THIS WAY.
WELL, WELL. C'MON IN. GLAD TO SEE YA'LL MADE IT.
I KNOW OUR BUSINESS INTERESTS IN THE PAST HAVEN'T ALWAYS BEEN EXACTLY WHAT YOU'D CALL... COMPATIBLE.
WE DEATHSTRIKES COUNT AMONG OUR MANY TALENTS THE ABILITY TO SEPARATE BUSINESS FROM PLEASURE.
AH, WELL, AIN'T NO NEED FOR THAT TONIGHT...
'CAUSE I EXPECT WE'LL BE INDULGIN' IN PLENTY OF BOTH.

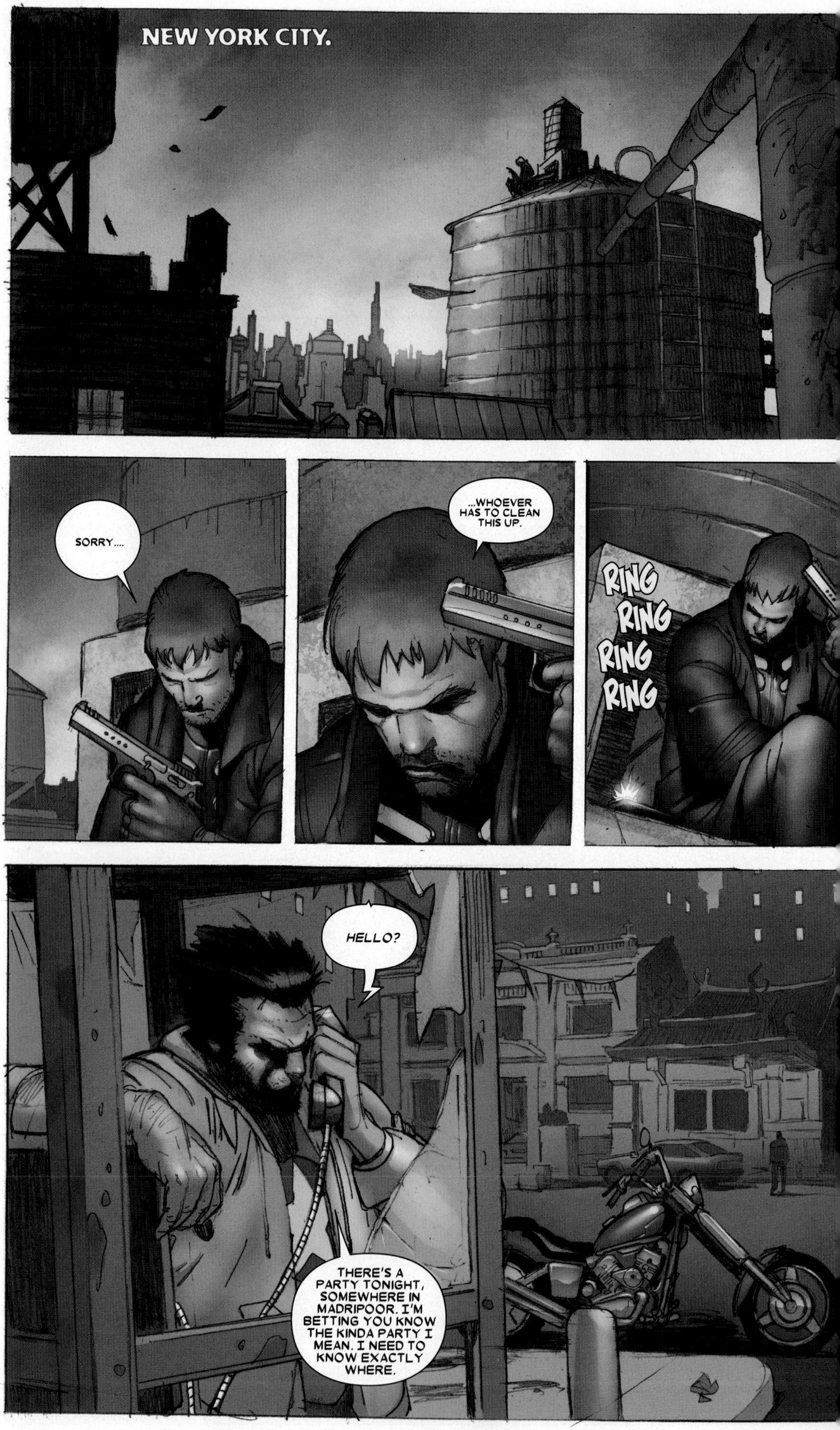
NEW YORK CITY.
SORRY....
...WHOEVER HAS TO CLEAN THIS UP.
RING RING RING RING
HELLO?
THERE'S A PARTY TONIGHT, SOMEWHERE IN MADRIPOOR. I'M BETTING YOU KNOW THE KINDA PARTY I MEAN. I NEED TO KNOW EXACTLY WHERE.

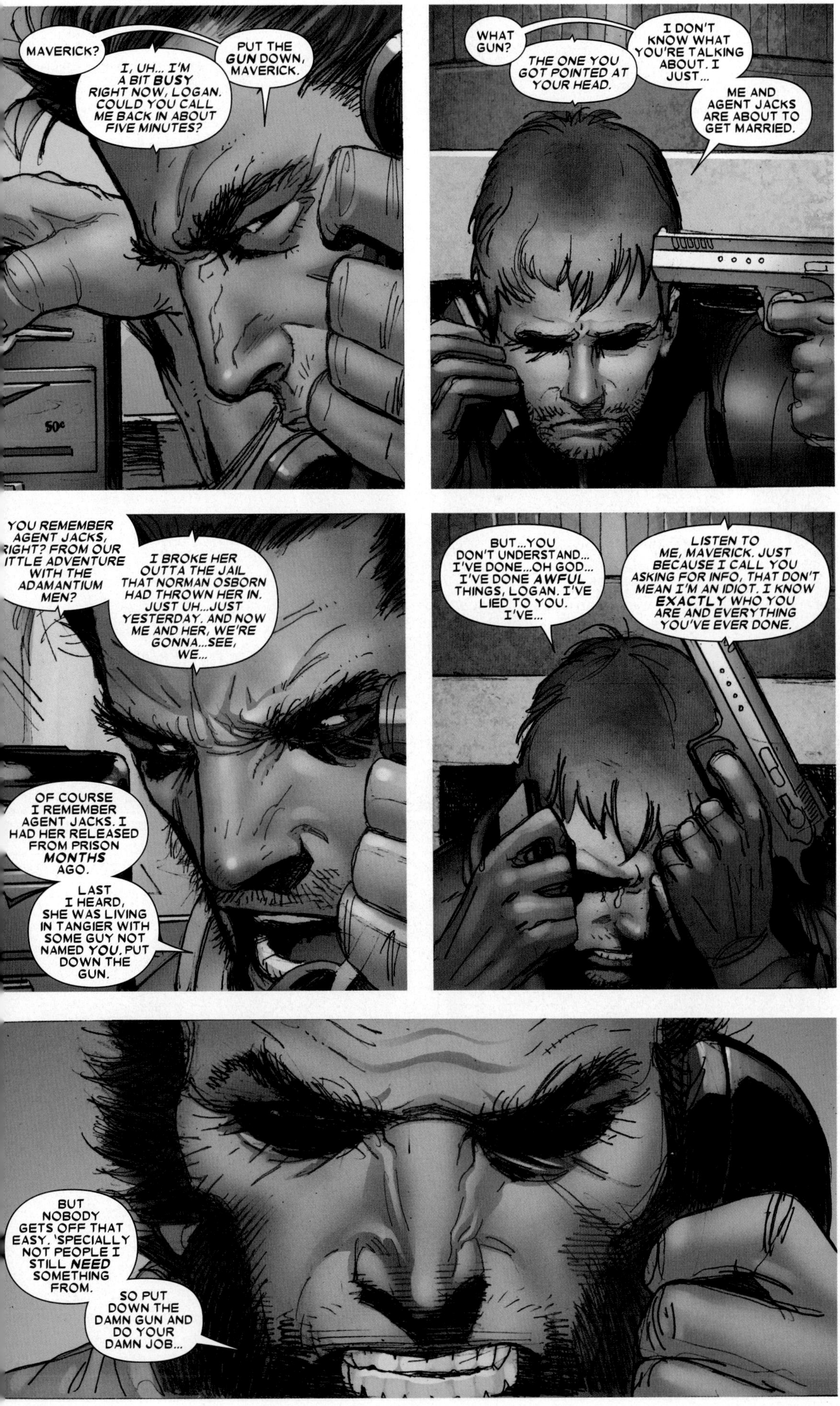
MAVERICK?
I, UH... I'M A BIT BUSY RIGHT NOW, LOGAN. COULD YOU CALL ME BACK IN ABOUT FIVE MINUTES?
PUT THE GUN DOWN, MAVERICK.
WHAT GUN?
THE ONE YOU GOT POINTED AT YOUR HEAD.
I DON'T KNOW WHAT YOU'RE TALKING ABOUT. I JUST...
ME AND AGENT JACKS ARE ABOUT TO GET MARRIED.
YOU REMEMBER AGENT JACKS, RIGHT? FROM OUR LITTLE ADVENTURE WITH THE ADAMANTIUM MEN?
I BROKE HER OUTTA THE JAIL THAT NORMAN OSBORN HAD THROWN HER IN. JUST UH...JUST YESTERDAY. AND NOW ME AND HER, WE'RE GONNA...SEE, WE...
OF COURSE I REMEMBER AGENT JACKS. I HAD HER RELEASED FROM PRISON MONTHS AGO.
LAST I HEARD, SHE WAS LIVING IN TANGIER WITH SOME GUY NOT NAMED YOU. PUT DOWN THE GUN.
BUT...YOU DON'T UNDERSTAND... I'VE DONE...OH GOD... I'VE DONE AWFUL THINGS, LOGAN. I'VE LIED TO YOU. I'VE...
LISTEN TO ME, MAVERICK. JUST BECAUSE I CALL YOU ASKING FOR INFO, THAT DON'T MEAN I'M AN IDIOT. I KNOW EXACTLY WHO YOU ARE AND EVERYTHING YOU'VE EVER DONE.
BUT NOBODY GETS OFF THAT EASY. 'SPECIALLY NOT PEOPLE I STILL NEED SOMETHING FROM.
SO PUT DOWN THE DAMN GUN AND DO YOUR DAMN JOB...

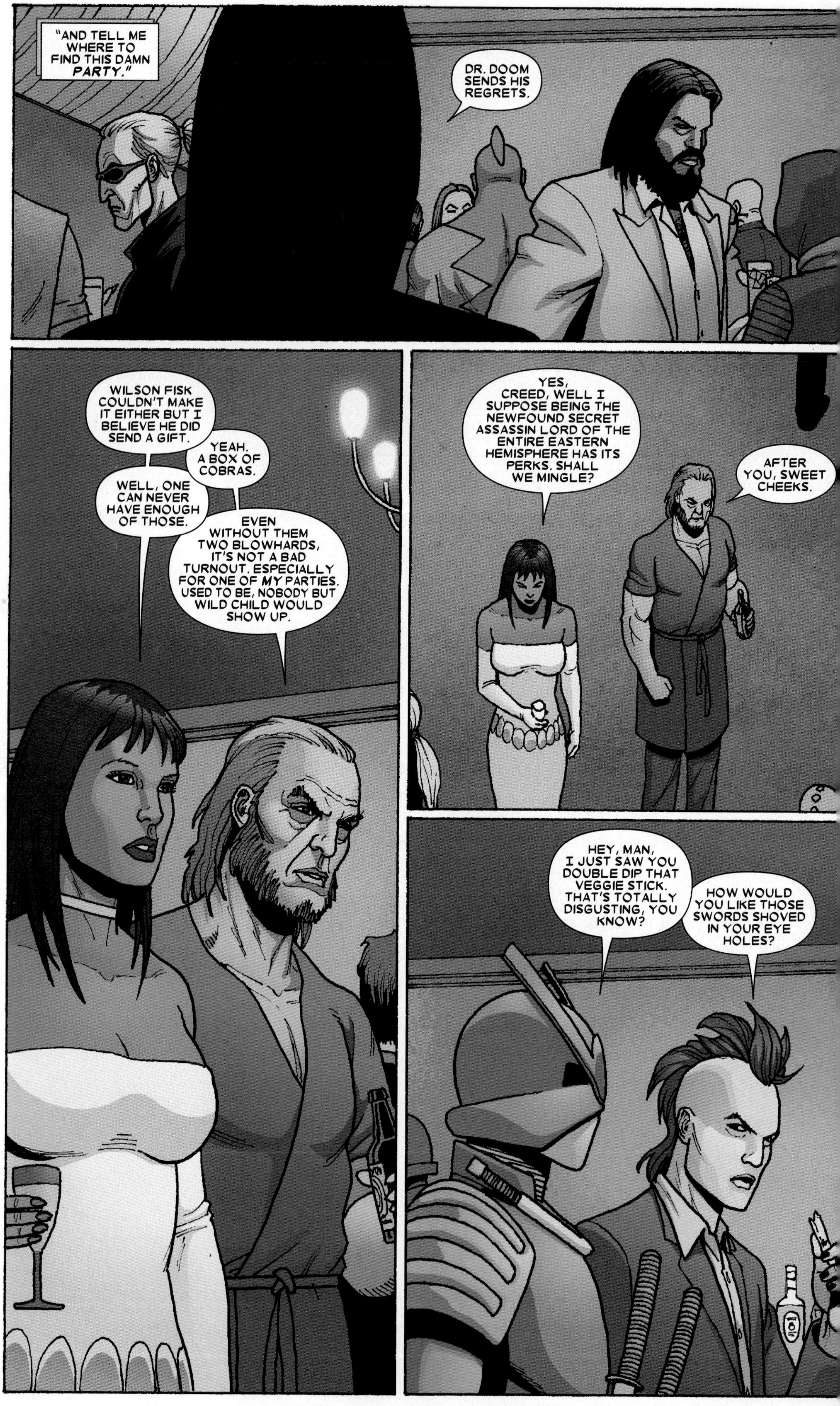
"AND TELL ME WHERE TO FIND THIS DAMN *PARTY*."
DR. DOOM SENDS HIS REGRETS.
WILSON FISK COULDN'T MAKE IT EITHER BUT I BELIEVE HE DID SEND A GIFT.
YEAH. A BOX OF COBRAS.
WELL, ONE CAN NEVER HAVE ENOUGH OF THOSE.
EVEN WITHOUT THEM TWO BLOWHARDS, IT'S NOT A BAD TURNOUT. ESPECIALLY FOR ONE OF *MY* PARTIES. USED TO BE, NOBODY BUT WILD CHILD WOULD SHOW UP.
YES, CREED, WELL I SUPPOSE BEING THE NEWFOUND SECRET ASSASSIN LORD OF THE ENTIRE EASTERN HEMISPHERE HAS ITS PERKS. SHALL WE MINGLE?
AFTER YOU, SWEET CHEEKS.
HEY, MAN, I JUST SAW YOU DOUBLE DIP THAT VEGGIE STICK. THAT'S TOTALLY DISGUSTING, YOU KNOW?
HOW WOULD YOU LIKE THOSE SWORDS SHOVED IN YOUR EYE HOLES?

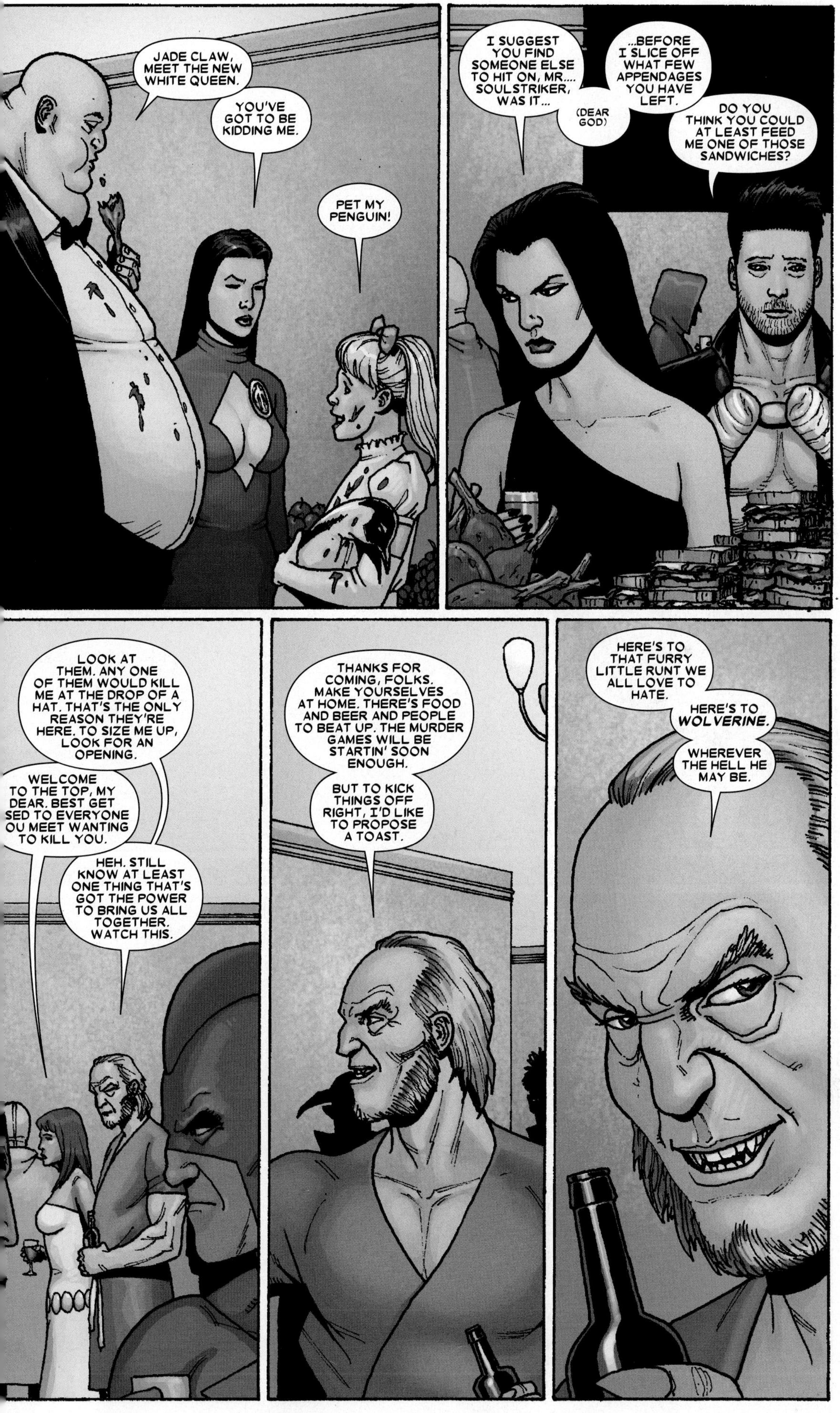

JADE CLAW, MEET THE NEW WHITE QUEEN.
YOU'VE GOT TO BE KIDDING ME.
PET MY PENGUIN!
I SUGGEST YOU FIND SOMEONE ELSE TO HIT ON, MR.... SOULSTRIKER, WAS IT...
(DEAR GOD)
...BEFORE I SLICE OFF WHAT FEW APPENDAGES YOU HAVE LEFT.
DO YOU THINK YOU COULD AT LEAST FEED ME ONE OF THOSE SANDWICHES?
LOOK AT THEM. ANY ONE OF THEM WOULD KILL ME AT THE DROP OF A HAT. THAT'S THE ONLY REASON THEY'RE HERE. TO SIZE ME UP, LOOK FOR AN OPENING.
WELCOME TO THE TOP, MY DEAR. BEST GET SED TO EVERYONE OU MEET WANTING TO KILL YOU.
HEH. STILL KNOW AT LEAST ONE THING THAT'S GOT THE POWER TO BRING US ALL TOGETHER. WATCH THIS.
THANKS FOR COMING, FOLKS. MAKE YOURSELVES AT HOME. THERE'S FOOD AND BEER AND PEOPLE TO BEAT UP. THE MURDER GAMES WILL BE STARTIN' SOON ENOUGH.
BUT TO KICK THINGS OFF RIGHT, I'D LIKE TO PROPOSE A TOAST.
HERE'S TO THAT FURRY LITTLE RUNT WE ALL LOVE TO HATE.
HERE'S TO *WOLVERINE.*
WHEREVER THE HELL HE MAY BE.

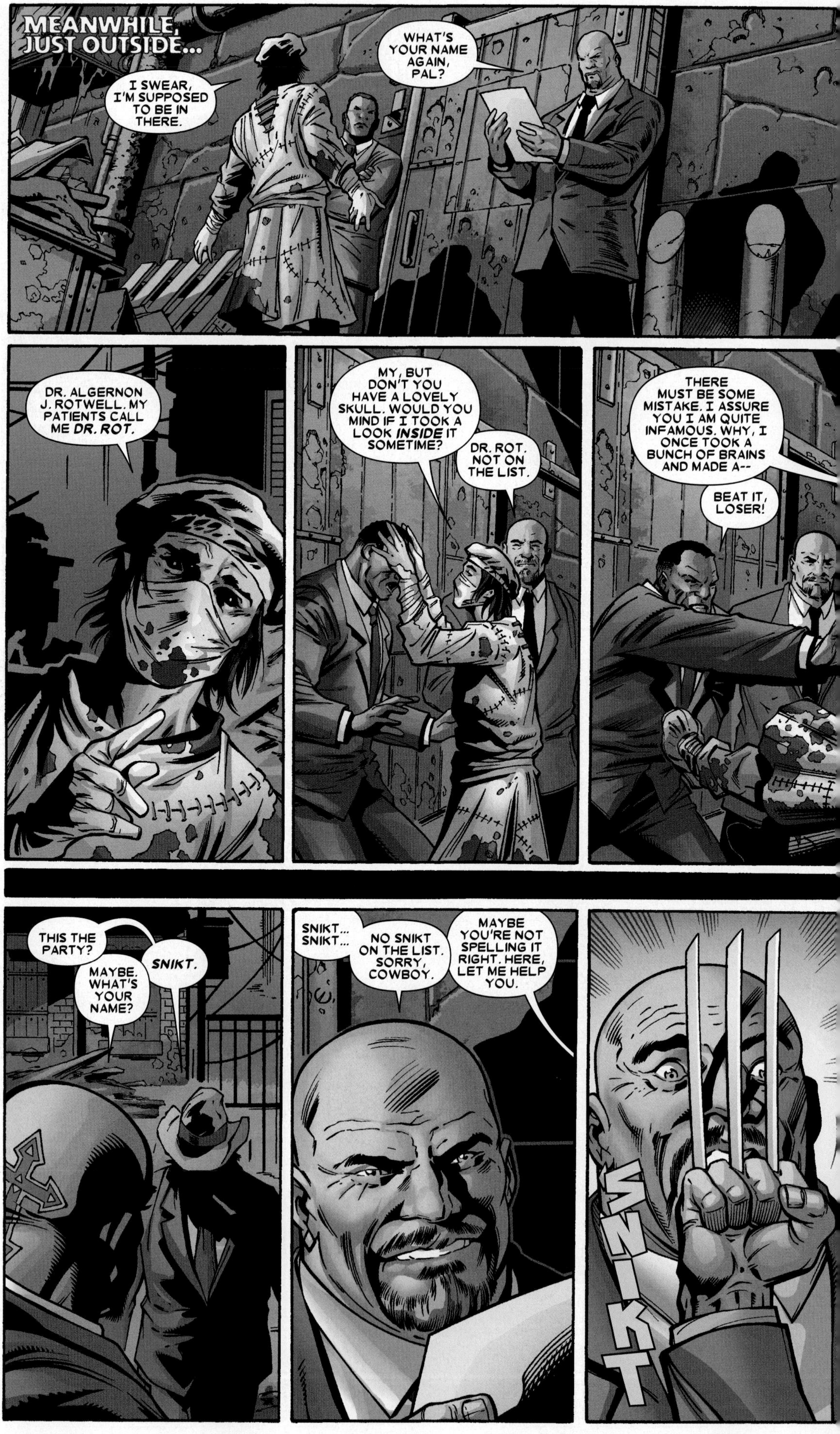

MEANWHILE, JUST OUTSIDE...
I SWEAR, I'M SUPPOSED TO BE IN THERE.
WHAT'S YOUR NAME AGAIN, PAL?
DR. ALGERNON J. ROTWELL. MY PATIENTS CALL ME DR. ROT.
MY, BUT DON'T YOU HAVE A LOVELY SKULL. WOULD YOU MIND IF I TOOK A LOOK INSIDE IT SOMETIME?
DR. ROT. NOT ON THE LIST.
THERE MUST BE SOME MISTAKE. I ASSURE YOU I AM QUITE INFAMOUS. WHY, I ONCE TOOK A BUNCH OF BRAINS AND MADE A--
BEAT IT, LOSER!
THIS THE PARTY?
MAYBE. WHAT'S YOUR NAME?
SNIKT.
SNIKT... SNIKT...
NO SNIKT ON THE LIST. SORRY, COWBOY.
MAYBE YOU'RE NOT SPELLING IT RIGHT. HERE, LET ME HELP YOU.
SNIKT

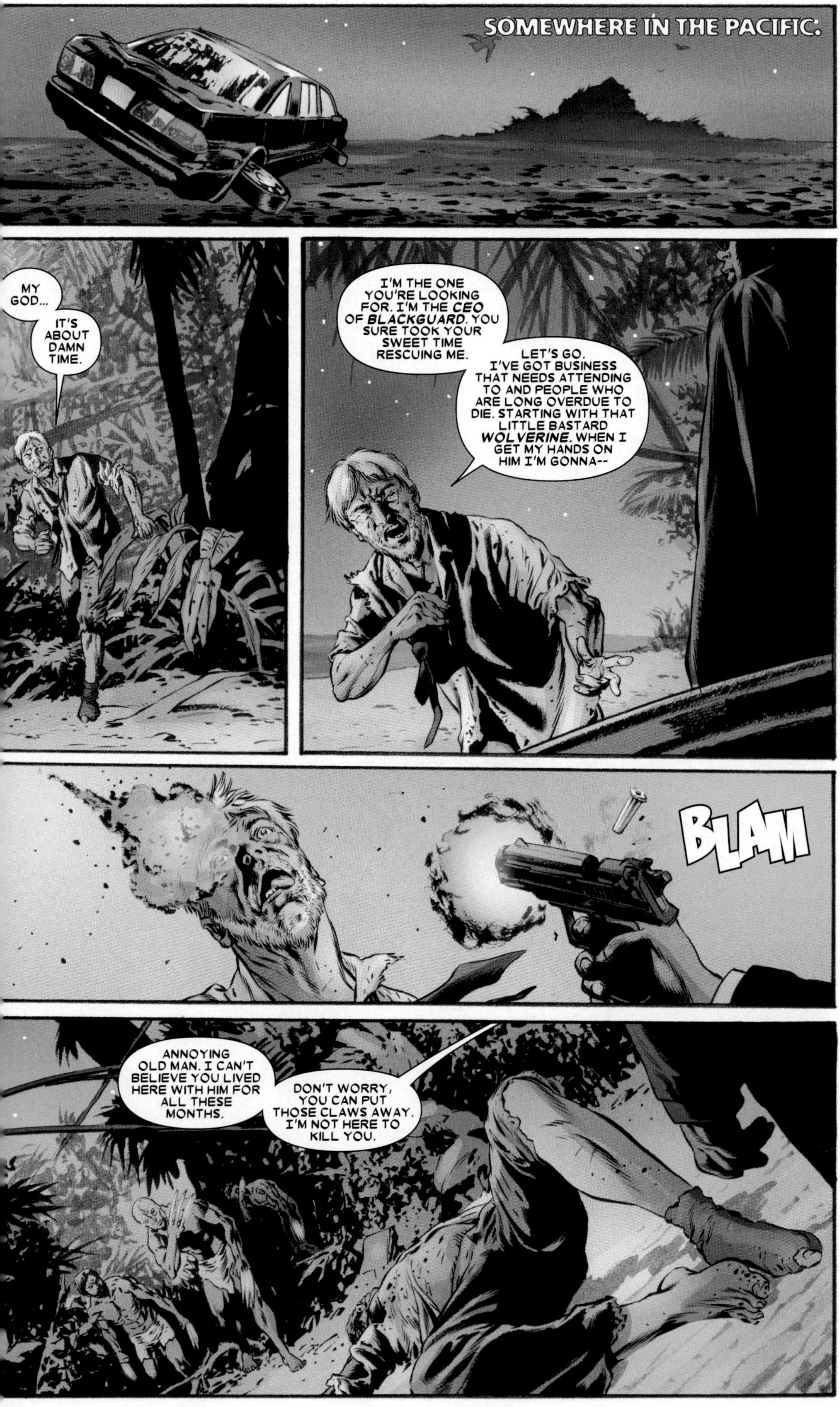
SOMEWHERE IN THE PACIFIC.
MY GOD...
IT'S ABOUT DAMN TIME.
I'M THE ONE YOU'RE LOOKING FOR. I'M THE CEO OF BLACKGUARD. YOU SURE TOOK YOUR SWEET TIME RESCUING ME.
LET'S GO. I'VE GOT BUSINESS THAT NEEDS ATTENDING TO AND PEOPLE WHO ARE LONG OVERDUE TO DIE. STARTING WITH THAT LITTLE BASTARD WOLVERINE. WHEN I GET MY HANDS ON HIM I'M GONNA--
BLAM
ANNOYING OLD MAN. I CAN'T BELIEVE YOU LIVED HERE WITH HIM FOR ALL THESE MONTHS.
DON'T WORRY, YOU CAN PUT THOSE CLAWS AWAY. I'M NOT HERE TO KILL YOU.

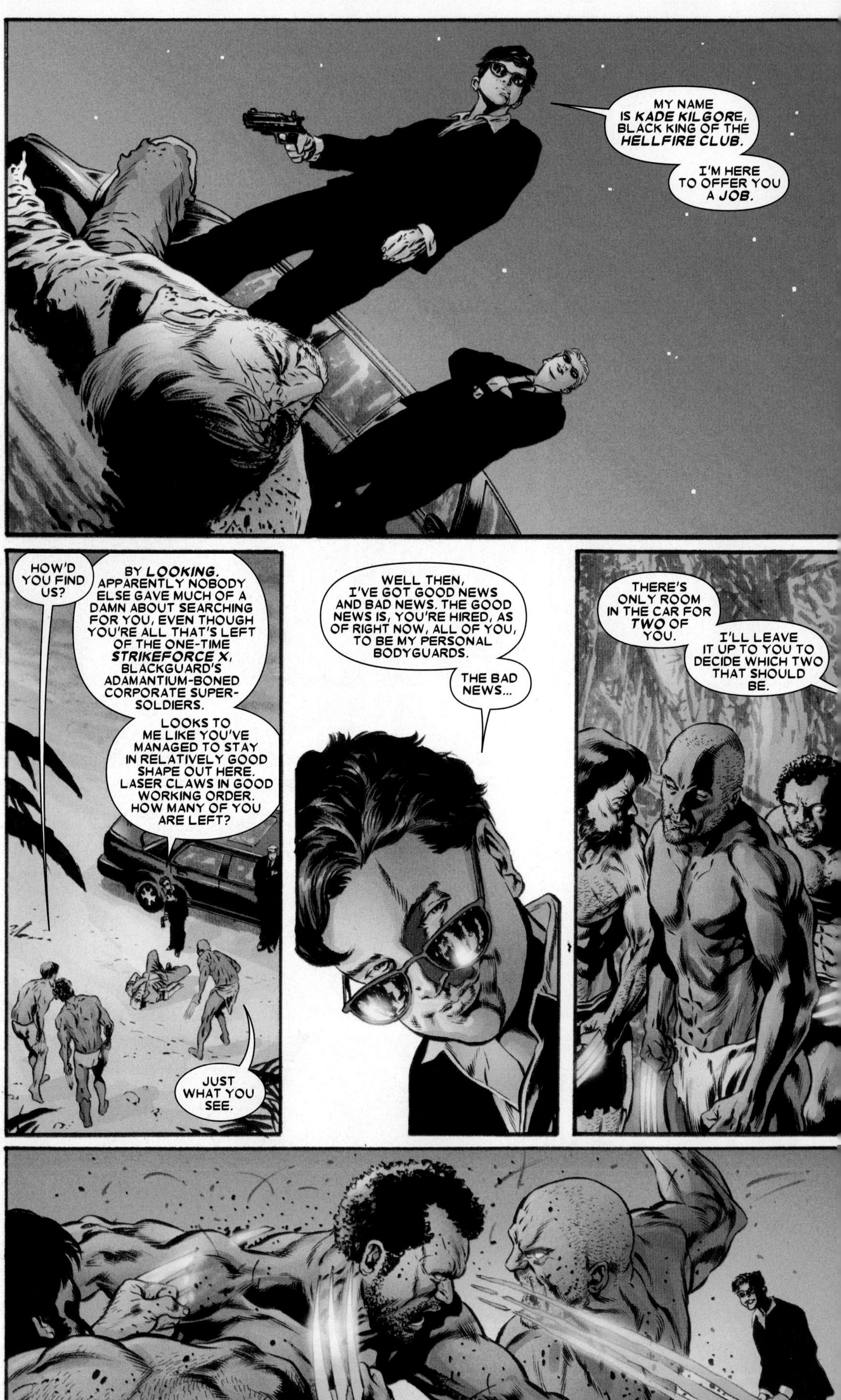

MY NAME IS KADE KILGORE, BLACK KING OF THE HELLFIRE CLUB.
I'M HERE TO OFFER YOU A JOB.
HOW'D YOU FIND US?
BY LOOKING. APPARENTLY NOBODY ELSE GAVE MUCH OF A DAMN ABOUT SEARCHING FOR YOU, EVEN THOUGH YOU'RE ALL THAT'S LEFT OF THE ONE-TIME STRIKEFORCE X, BLACKGUARD'S ADAMANTIUM-BONED CORPORATE SUPER-SOLDIERS.
LOOKS TO ME LIKE YOU'VE MANAGED TO STAY IN RELATIVELY GOOD SHAPE OUT HERE. LASER CLAWS IN GOOD WORKING ORDER. HOW MANY OF YOU ARE LEFT?
JUST WHAT YOU SEE.
WELL THEN, I'VE GOT GOOD NEWS AND BAD NEWS. THE GOOD NEWS IS, YOU'RE HIRED, AS OF RIGHT NOW, ALL OF YOU, TO BE MY PERSONAL BODYGUARDS.
THE BAD NEWS...
THERE'S ONLY ROOM IN THE CAR FOR TWO OF YOU.
I'LL LEAVE IT UP TO YOU TO DECIDE WHICH TWO THAT SHOULD BE.

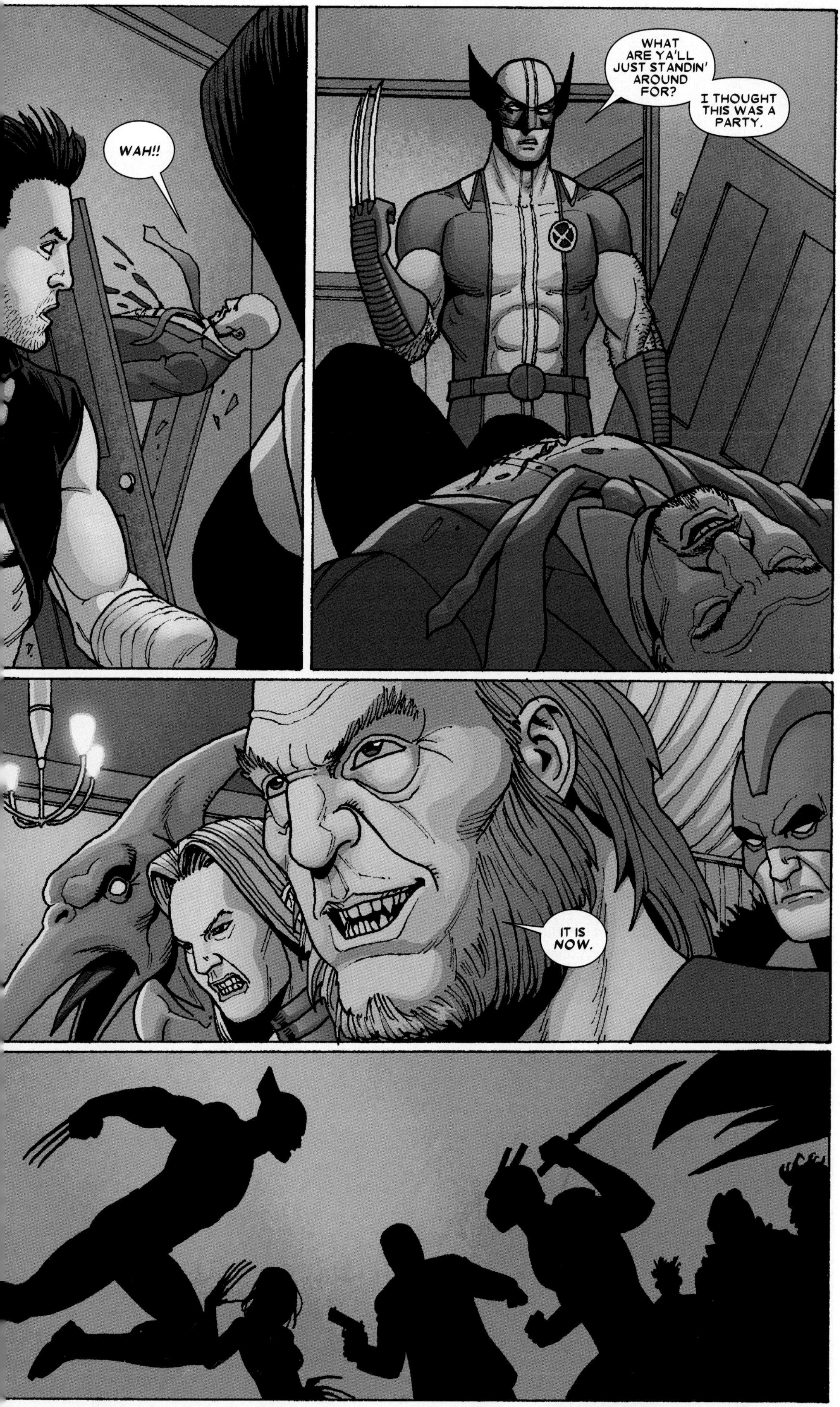
WAH!!
WHAT ARE YA'LL JUST STANDIN' AROUND FOR?
I THOUGHT THIS WAS A PARTY.
IT IS NOW.

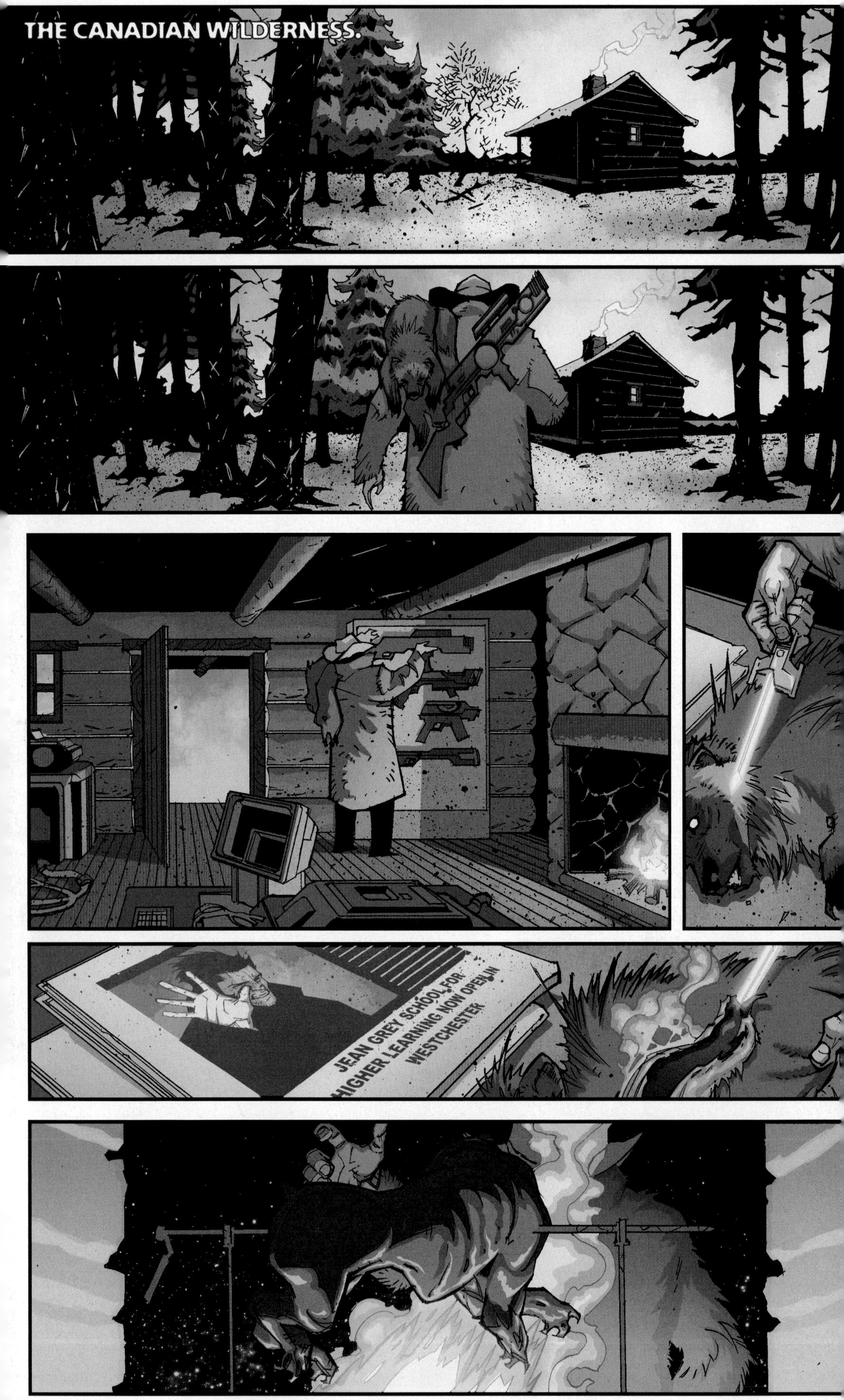
THE CANADIAN WILDERNESS.
JEAN GREY SCHOOL FOR
HIGHER LEARNING NOW OPEN IN
WESTCHESTER

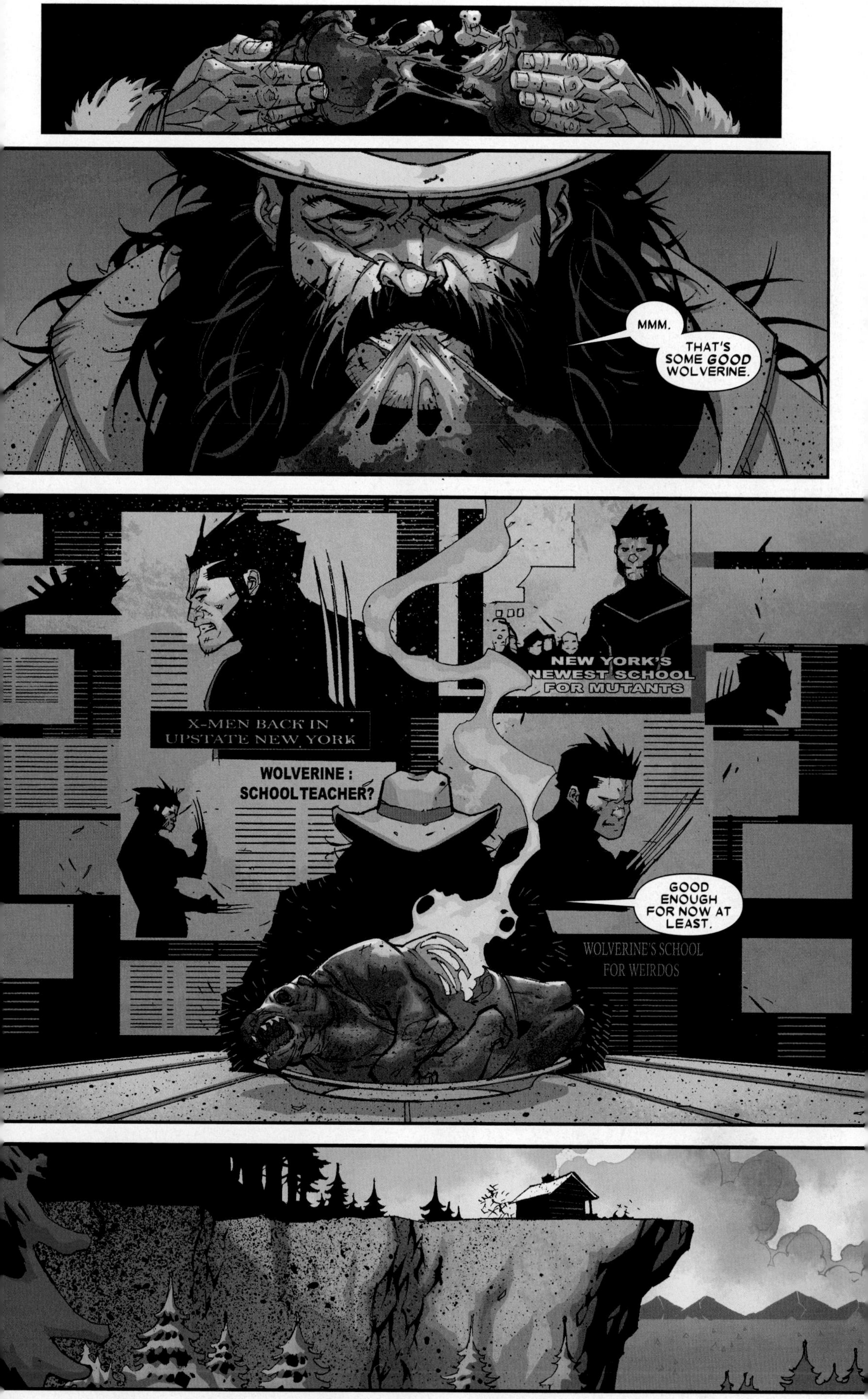
MMM.
THAT'S SOME GOOD WOLVERINE.
X-MEN BACK IN UPSTATE NEW YORK
NEW YORK'S NEWEST SCHOOL FOR MUTANTS
WOLVERINE : SCHOOLTEACHER?
GOOD ENOUGH FOR NOW AT LEAST.
WOLVERINE'S SCHOOL FOR WEIRDOS

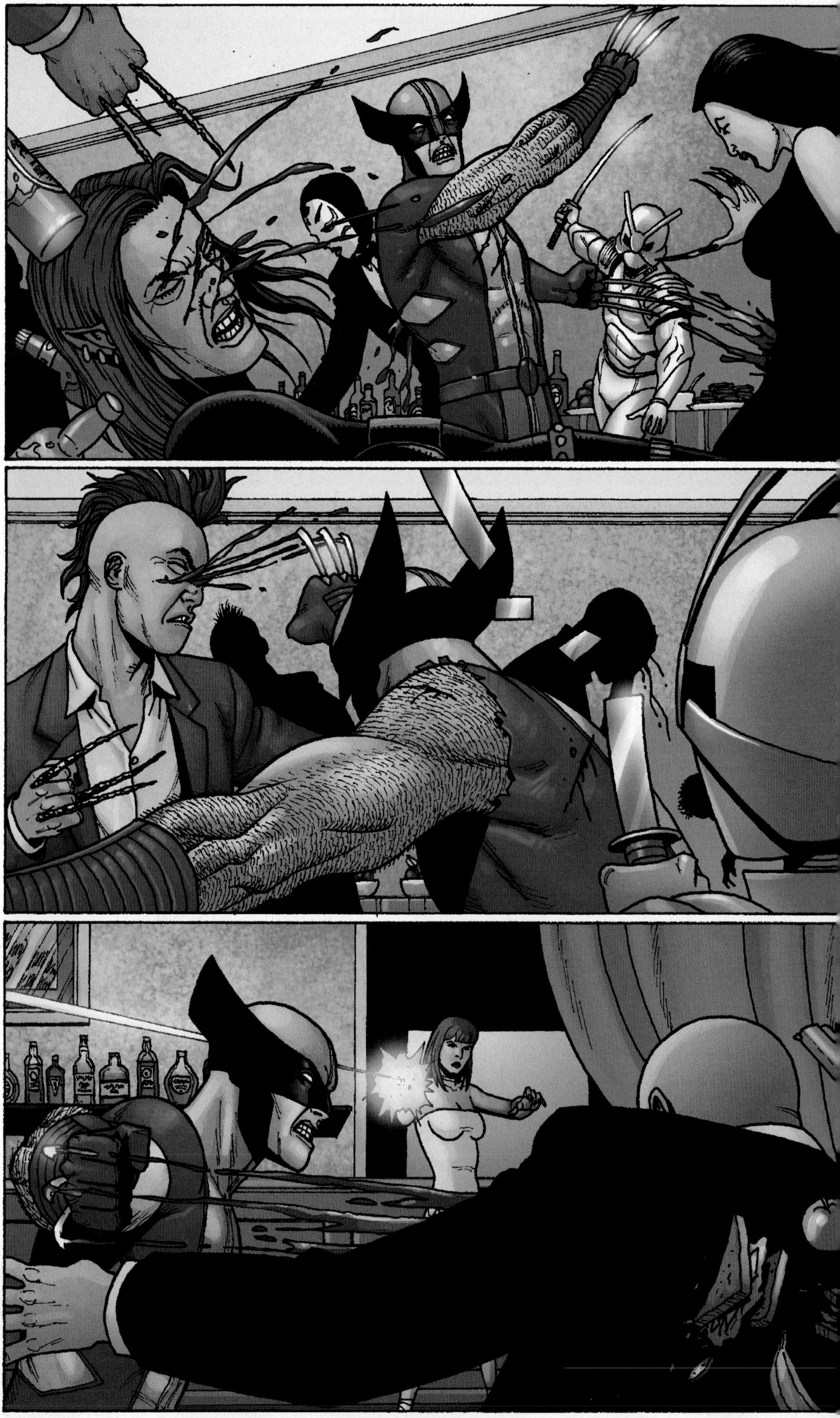

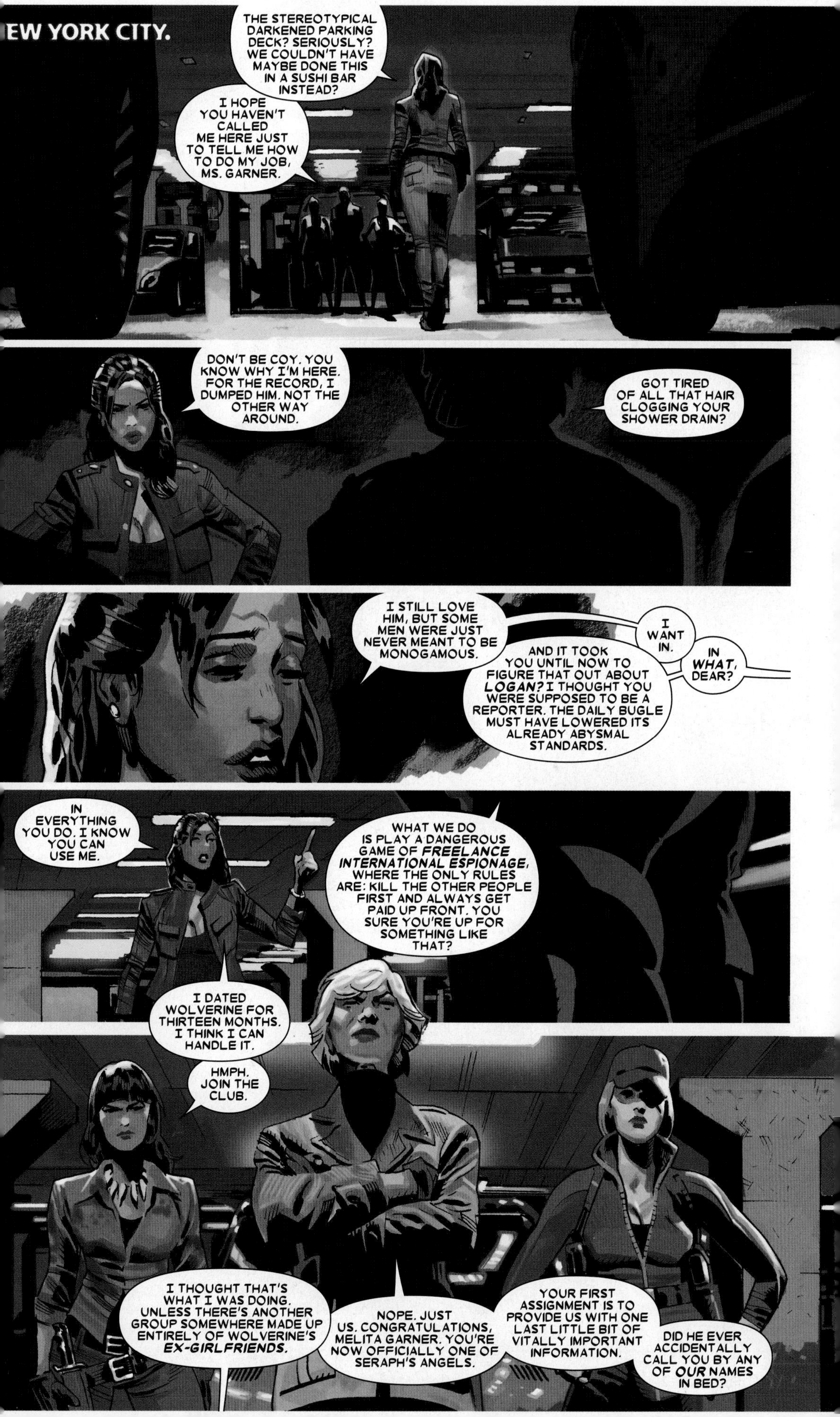

EW YORK CITY.
THE STEREOTYPICAL DARKENED PARKING DECK? SERIOUSLY? WE COULDN'T HAVE MAYBE DONE THIS IN A SUSHI BAR INSTEAD?
I HOPE YOU HAVEN'T CALLED ME HERE JUST TO TELL ME HOW TO DO MY JOB, MS. GARNER.
DON'T BE COY. YOU KNOW WHY I'M HERE. FOR THE RECORD, I DUMPED HIM. NOT THE OTHER WAY AROUND.
GOT TIRED OF ALL THAT HAIR CLOGGING YOUR SHOWER DRAIN?
I STILL LOVE HIM, BUT SOME MEN WERE JUST NEVER MEANT TO BE MONOGAMOUS.
AND IT TOOK YOU UNTIL NOW TO FIGURE THAT OUT ABOUT *LOGAN?* I THOUGHT YOU WERE SUPPOSED TO BE A REPORTER. THE DAILY BUGLE MUST HAVE LOWERED ITS ALREADY ABYSMAL STANDARDS.
I WANT IN.
IN *WHAT,* DEAR?
IN EVERYTHING YOU DO. I KNOW YOU CAN USE ME.
WHAT WE DO IS PLAY A DANGEROUS GAME OF ***FREELANCE INTERNATIONAL ESPIONAGE,*** WHERE THE ONLY RULES ARE: KILL THE OTHER PEOPLE FIRST AND ALWAYS GET PAID UP FRONT. YOU SURE YOU'RE UP FOR SOMETHING LIKE THAT?
I DATED WOLVERINE FOR THIRTEEN MONTHS. I THINK I CAN HANDLE IT.
HMPH. JOIN THE CLUB.
I THOUGHT THAT'S WHAT I WAS DOING. UNLESS THERE'S ANOTHER GROUP SOMEWHERE MADE UP ENTIRELY OF WOLVERINE'S ***EX-GIRLFRIENDS.***
NOPE. JUST US. CONGRATULATIONS, MELITA GARNER. YOU'RE NOW OFFICIALLY ONE OF SERAPH'S ANGELS.
YOUR FIRST ASSIGNMENT IS TO PROVIDE US WITH ONE LAST LITTLE BIT OF VITALLY IMPORTANT INFORMATION.
DID HE EVER ACCIDENTALLY CALL YOU BY ANY OF *OUR* NAMES IN BED?

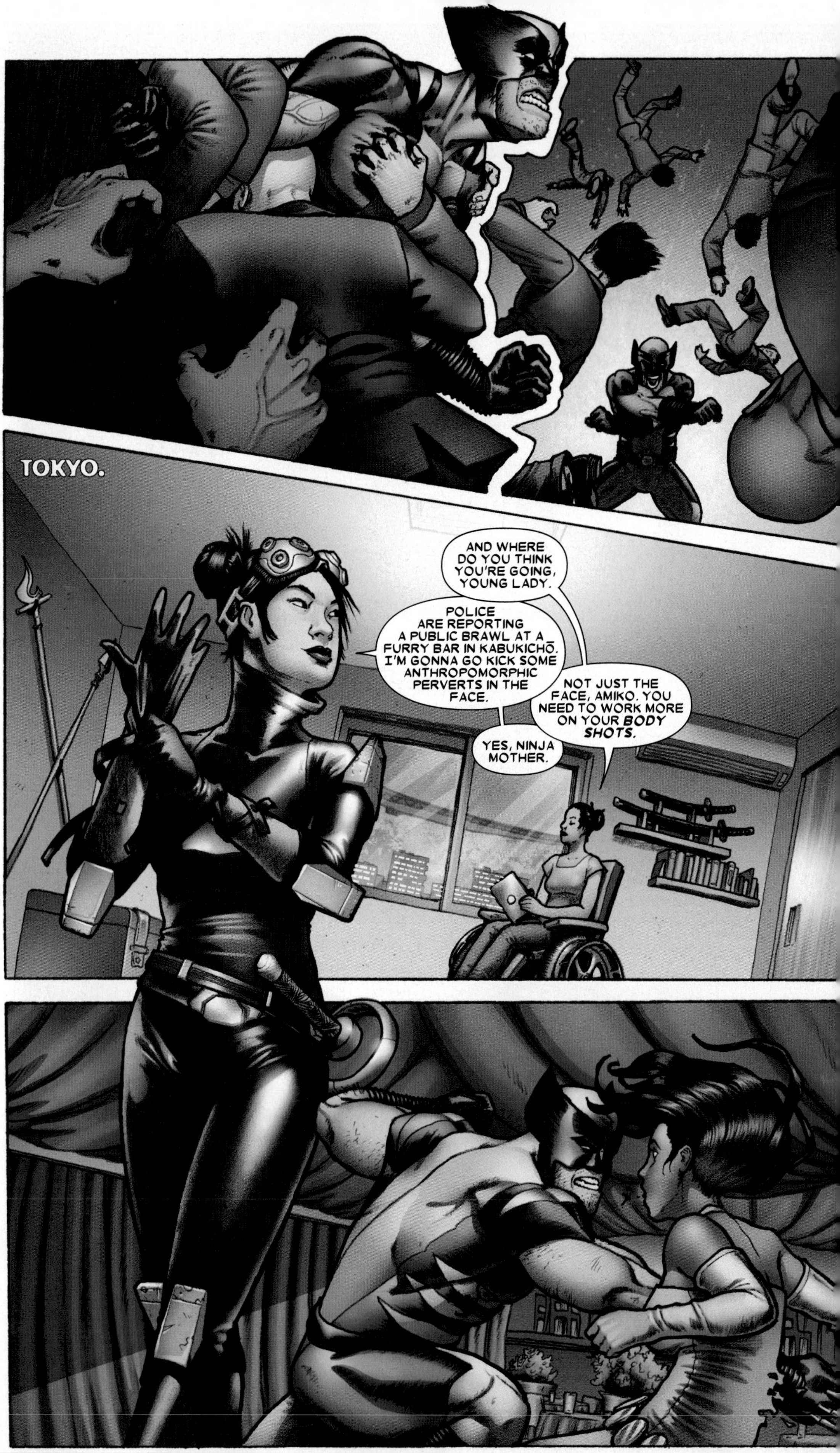
TOKYO.
AND WHERE DO YOU THINK YOU'RE GOING, YOUNG LADY.
POLICE ARE REPORTING A PUBLIC BRAWL AT A FURRY BAR IN KABUKICHŌ. I'M GONNA GO KICK SOME ANTHROPOMORPHIC PERVERTS IN THE FACE.
NOT JUST THE FACE, AMIKO. YOU NEED TO WORK MORE ON YOUR *BODY SHOTS.*
YES, NINJA MOTHER.

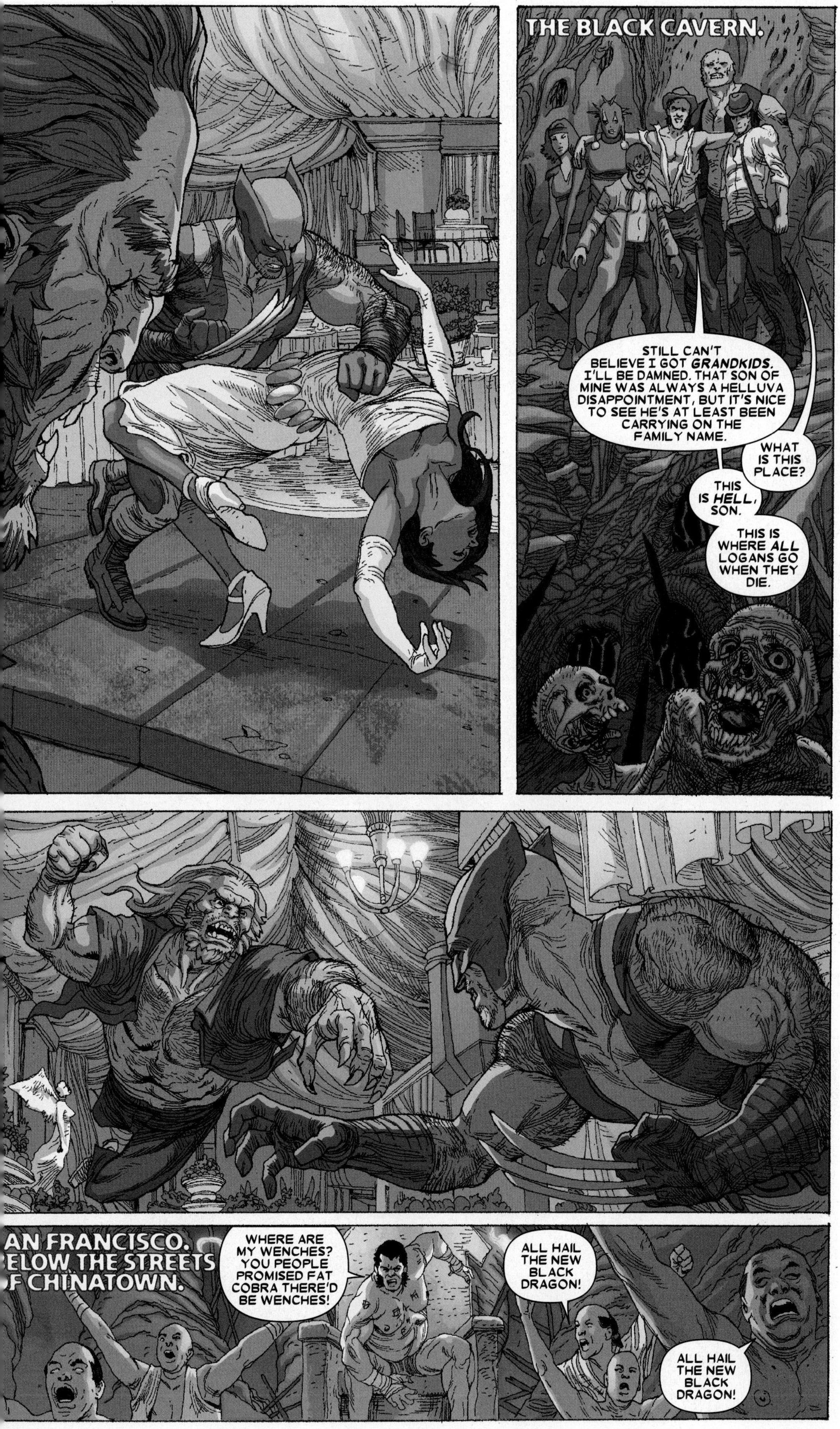
THE BLACK CAVERN.
STILL CAN'T BELIEVE I GOT GRANDKIDS. I'LL BE DAMNED. THAT SON OF MINE WAS ALWAYS A HELLUVA DISAPPOINTMENT, BUT IT'S NICE TO SEE HE'S AT LEAST BEEN CARRYING ON THE FAMILY NAME.
WHAT IS THIS PLACE?
THIS IS HELL, SON.
THIS IS WHERE ALL LOGANS GO WHEN THEY DIE.
AN FRANCISCO. ELOW THE STREETS F CHINATOWN.
WHERE ARE MY WENCHES? YOU PEOPLE PROMISED FAT COBRA THERE'D BE WENCHES!
ALL HAIL THE NEW BLACK DRAGON!
ALL HAIL THE NEW BLACK DRAGON!

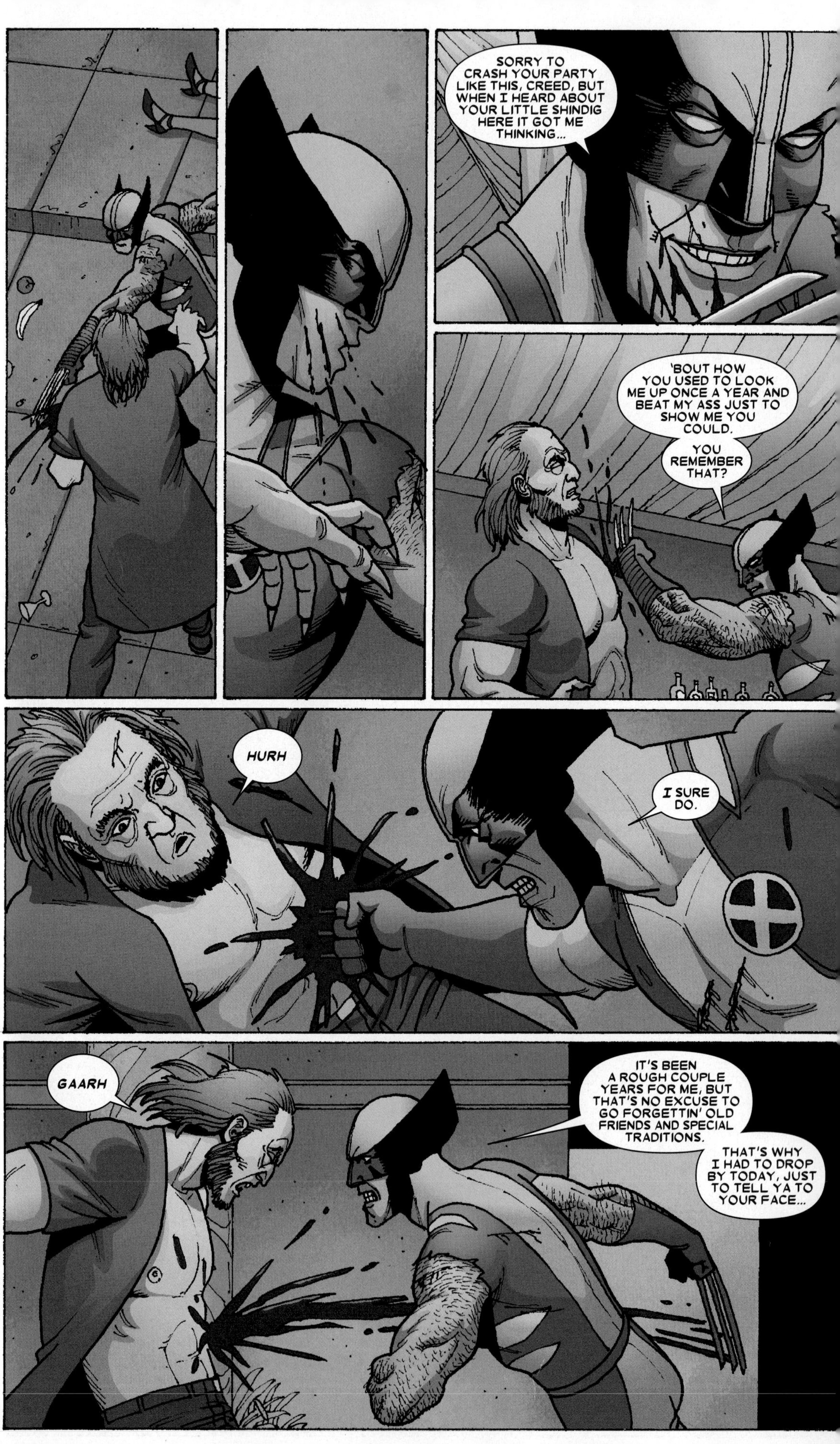
SORRY TO CRASH YOUR PARTY LIKE THIS, CREED, BUT WHEN I HEARD ABOUT YOUR LITTLE SHINDIG HERE IT GOT ME THINKING...
'BOUT HOW YOU USED TO LOOK ME UP ONCE A YEAR AND BEAT MY ASS JUST TO SHOW ME YOU COULD.
YOU REMEMBER THAT?
HURH
I SURE DO.
GAARH
IT'S BEEN A ROUGH COUPLE YEARS FOR ME, BUT THAT'S NO EXCUSE TO GO FORGETTIN' OLD FRIENDS AND SPECIAL TRADITIONS.
THAT'S WHY I HAD TO DROP BY TODAY, JUST TO TELL YA TO YOUR FACE...

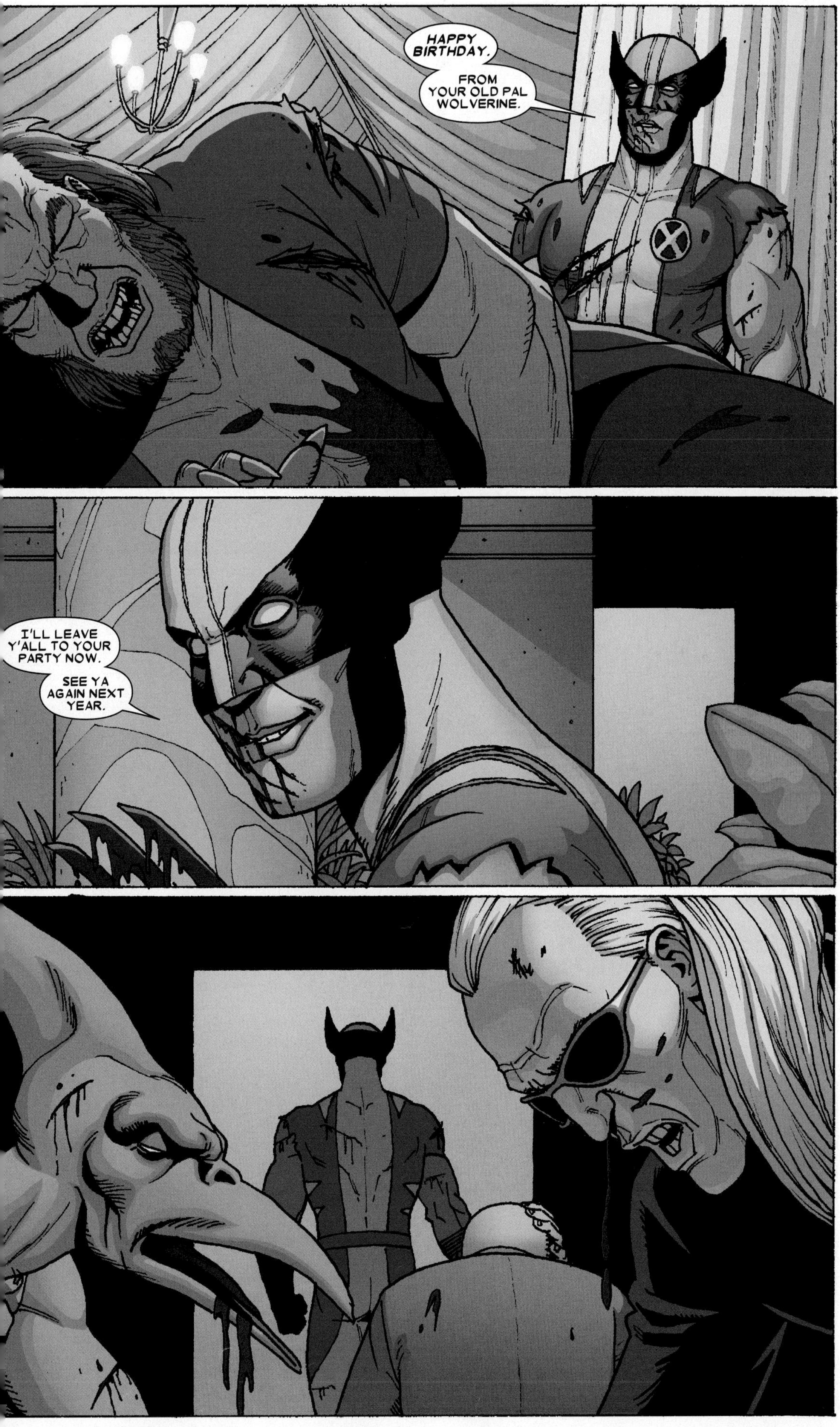
HAPPY BIRTHDAY.
FROM YOUR OLD PAL WOLVERINE.
I'LL LEAVE Y'ALL TO YOUR PARTY NOW.
SEE YA AGAIN NEXT YEAR.

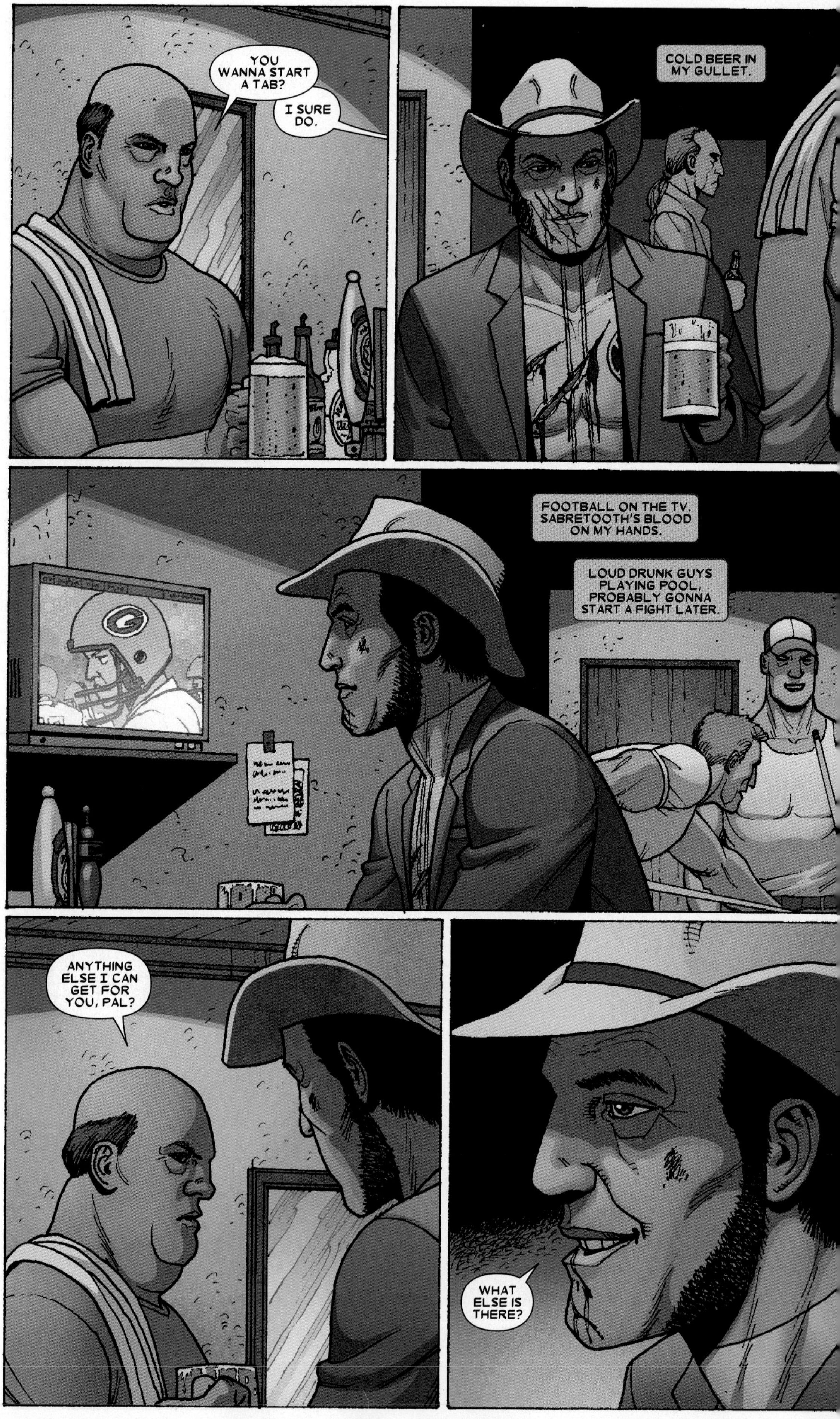
YOU WANNA START A TAB?
I SURE DO.
COLD BEER IN MY GULLET.
FOOTBALL ON THE TV. SABRETOOTH'S BLOOD ON MY HANDS.
LOUD DRUNK GUYS PLAYING POOL, PROBABLY GONNA START A FIGHT LATER.
ANYTHING ELSE I CAN GET FOR YOU, PAL?
WHAT ELSE IS THERE?

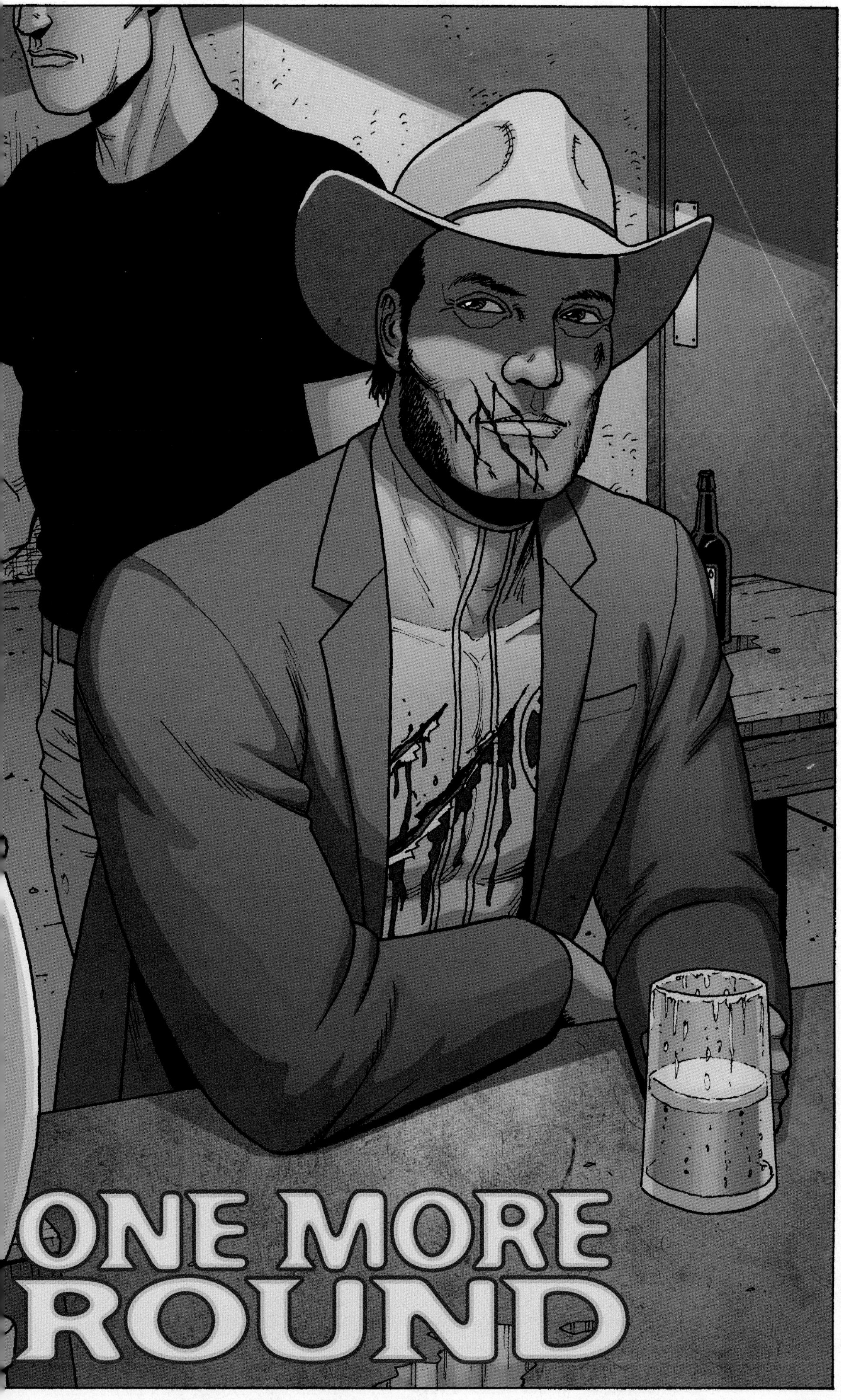
ONE MORE
ROUND

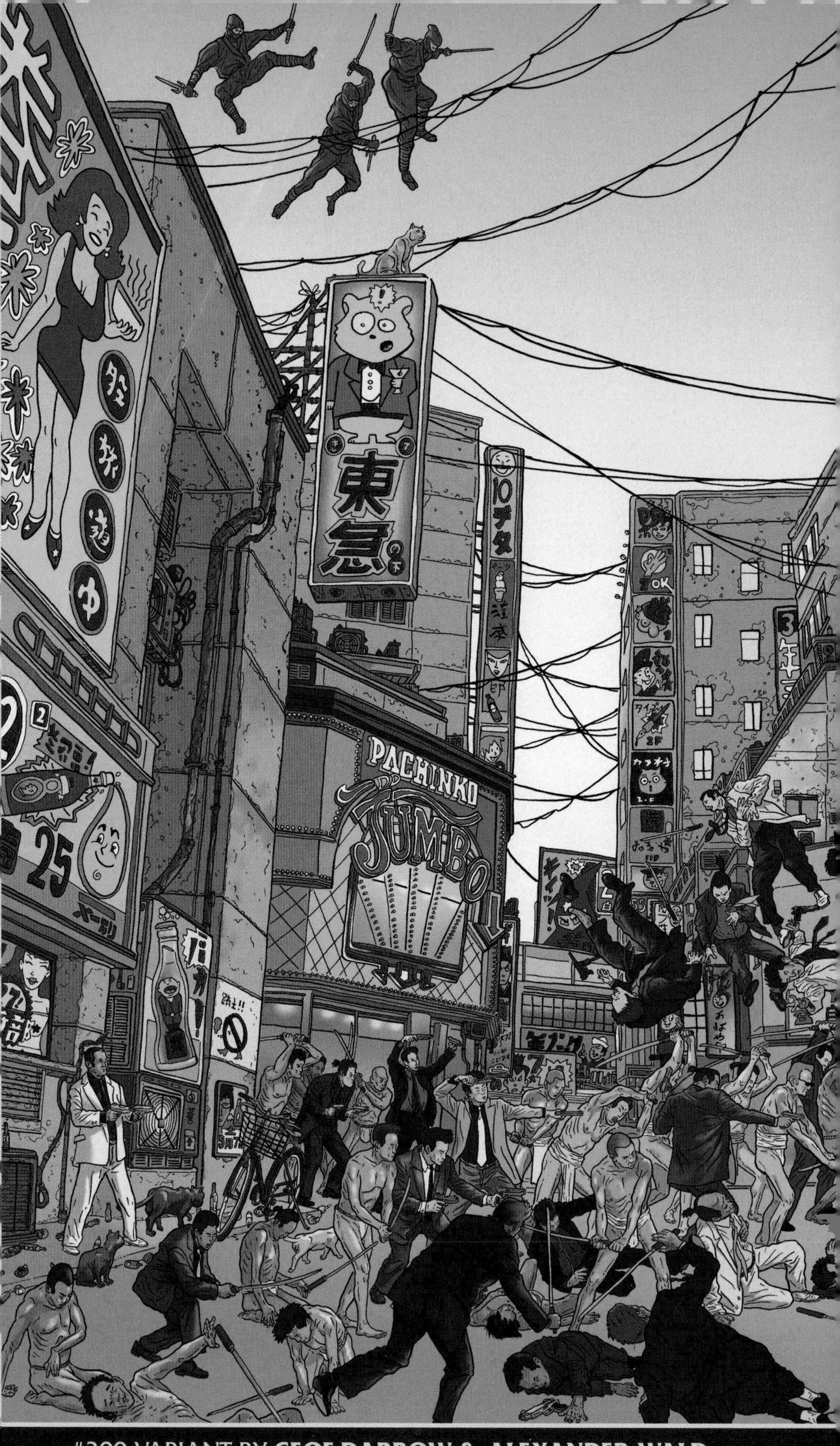
東急
PACHINKO
JUMBO
OK
25

#300 VARIANT BY **GEOF DARROW & ALEXANDER WALD**

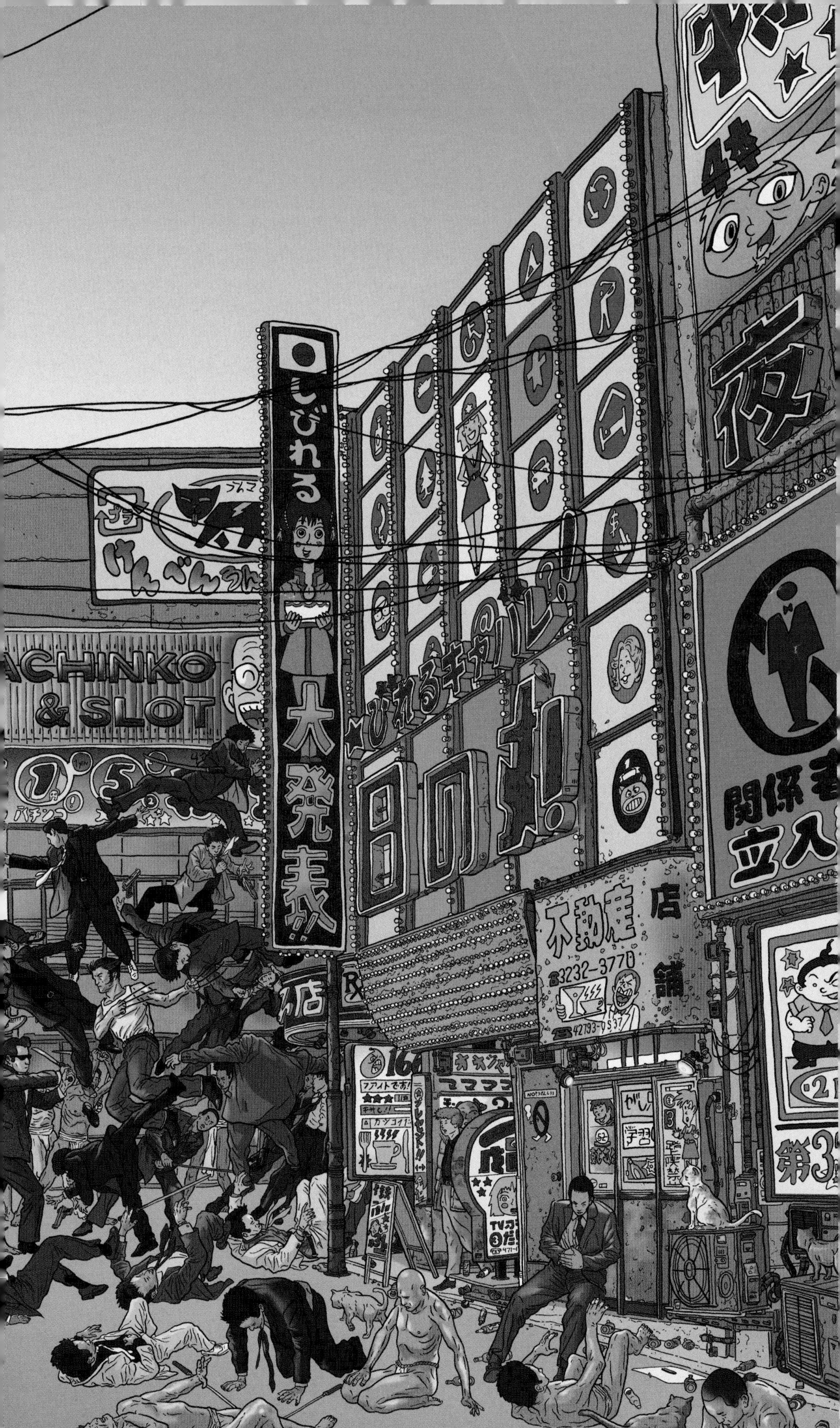
じびれる
大発表!!
ACHINKO
& SLOT
日の丸!
夜
不動産
店舗
3232-3770
4
立入

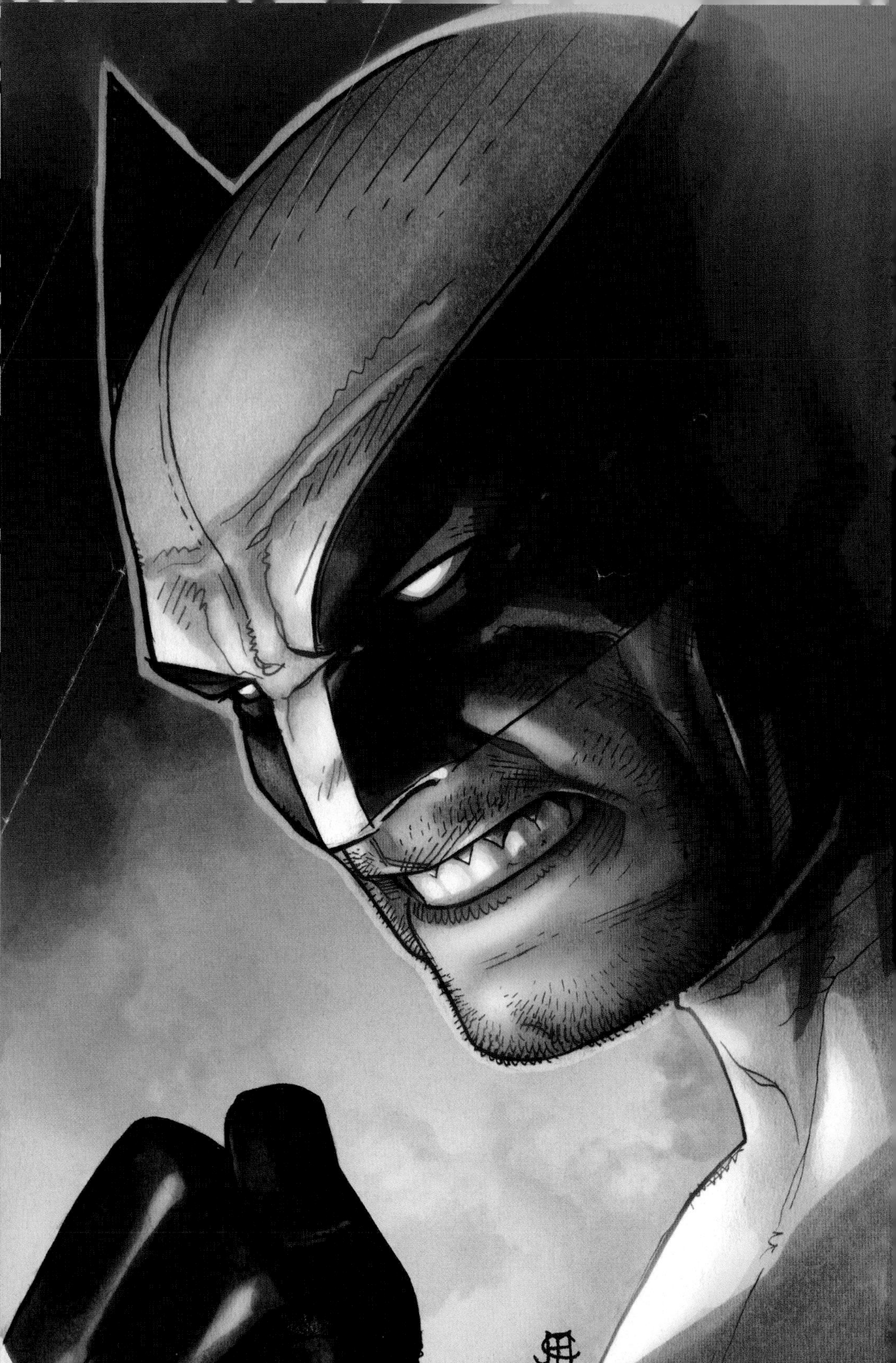

#300 VARIANT BY JIM CHEUNG & JUSTIN PONSOR

SABRETOOTH designed by Adam Kubert

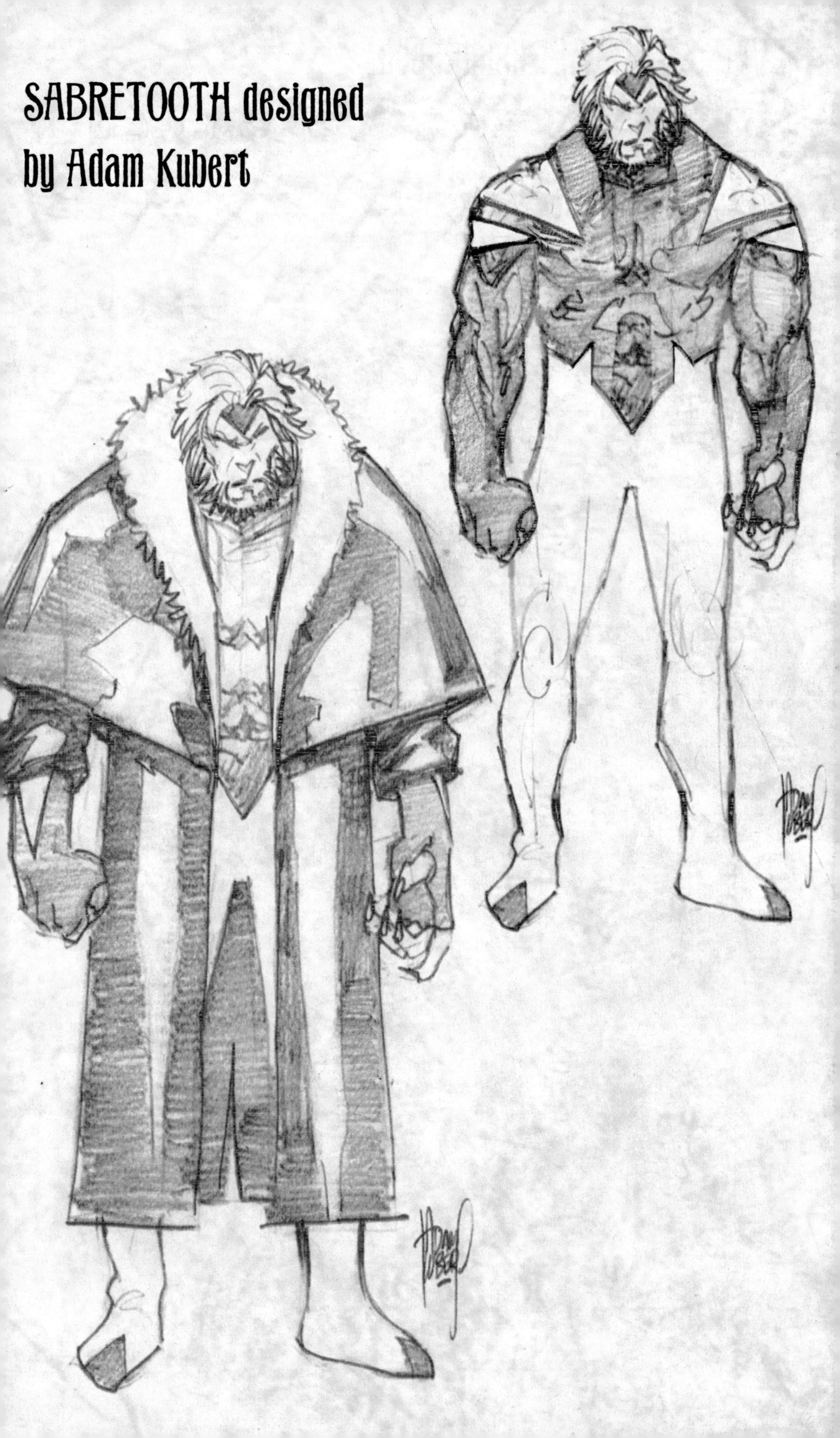

SILVER SAMURAI Design sheet.

Artist Steven Sanders: Attached is a jpeg for the final design I cranked out. Showed it to Jason today, met with approval. A suggestion was made for a flag on his back, like the samurai used to carry, with a holographic flag. Let me know what you think, and I'll be happy to make any changes or make a more polished version. Anything I have as part of the design that are not the katanas are just ideas I'm throwing out and can be rejected without hurting my feelings. But they will hurt the feelings of my cat, Mittens.

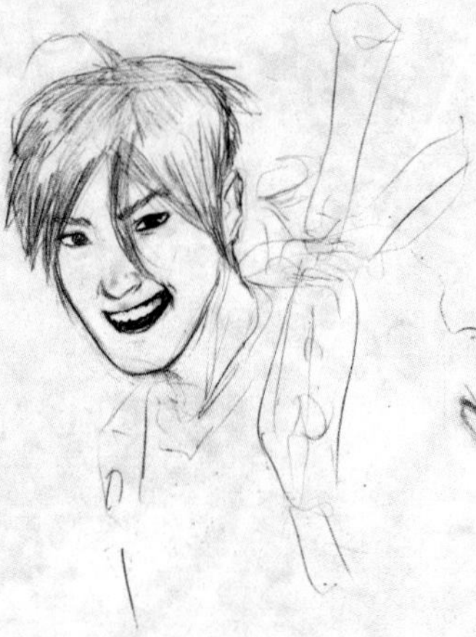

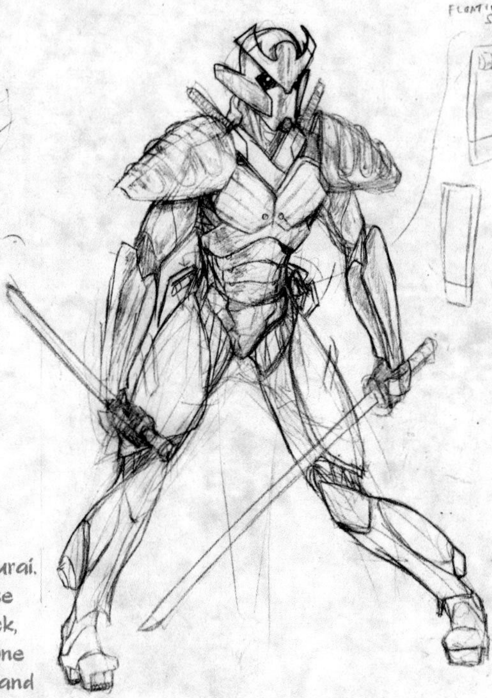

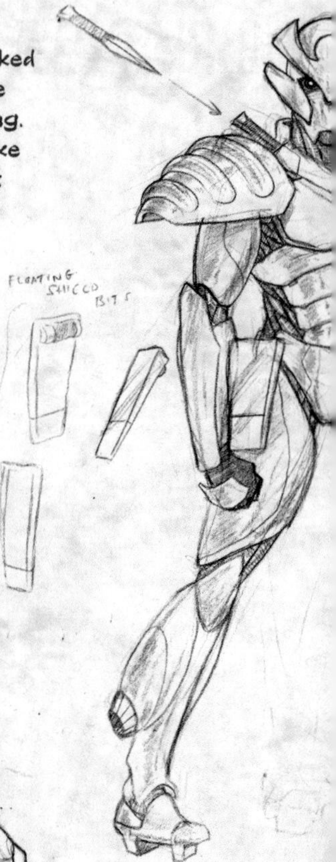

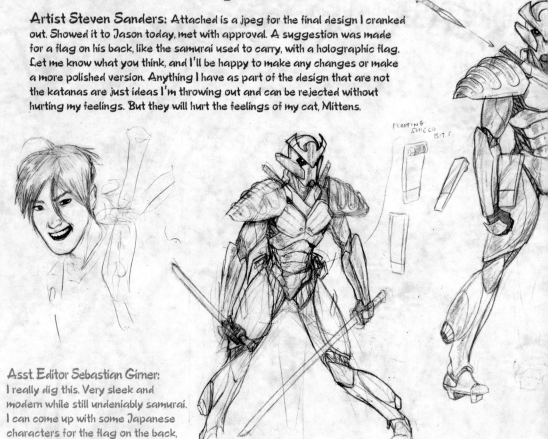

Asst. Editor Sebastian Girner:
I really dig this. Very sleek and modern while still undeniably samurai. I can come up with some Japanese characters for the flag on the back, but looking at this design I think one of those flags would be unwieldy and clutter up the character.

Also, if we need to see his face, will he take his helmet off completely or shall we have the mask part slide back to reveal his face?

S.S: Ok! Here's one way of doing a mask slide back.

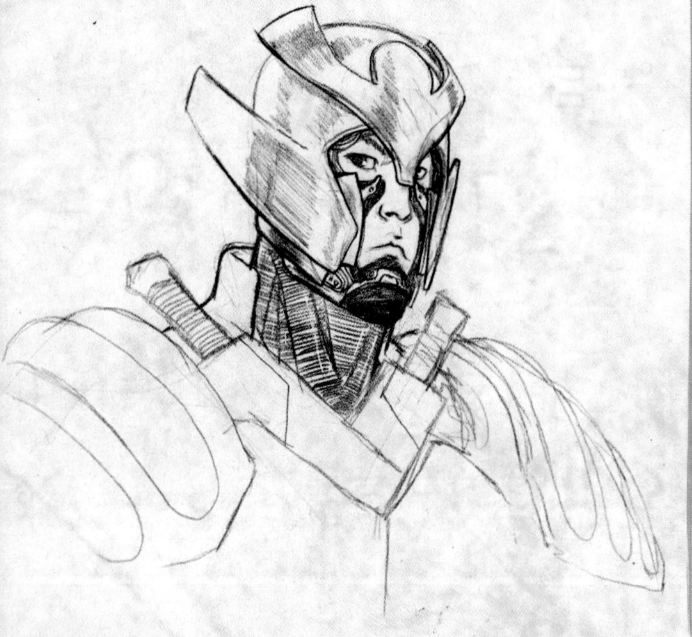

S.G: Two more small things I thought o Everyone feel free to tell me I'm nuts! Th two throwing knives on his back, I kinda think they're easy to confuse with two ti katanas, since carrying katanas on you back is something that happens a lot in comics.

What about losing the knives on his bac and instead putting a bunch of them on inside one of his sleeves OR having one the floating, detachable chassis on his armor act as a floating shuriken / throwing knife dispenser, or something similar?

Also, I dig the geta shoes he's got now. How about we keep the raised platform but also split his toes in the classic tabi-style? For some reason this kind of split-toe slipper always yells "Samurai" me.

S.S: Good point about the daggers, I the "bunch of them in the sleeves" idea, I draw up a concept and get it to you as

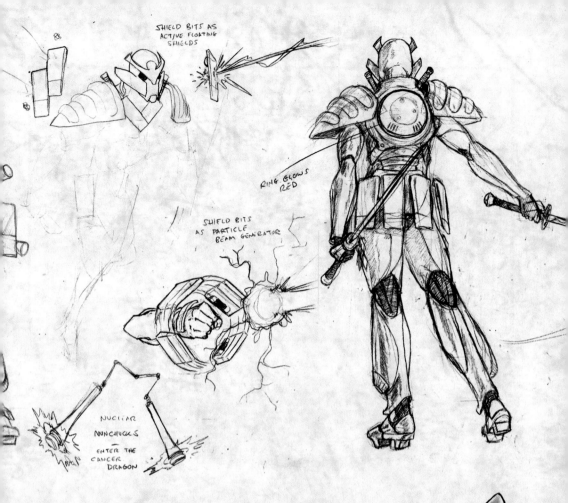

SHIELD BITS AS
ACTIVE FLOATING
SHIELDS

8.

RING GLOWS
RED

SHIELD BITS
AS PARTICLE
BEAM GENERATOR

NUCLEAR
NUNCHUCKS
—
ENTER THE
CANCER
DRAGON

...unsure if I can implement the combo geta/
... shoes without making it look awkward, but I'll
... it my best shot. I'm going to try both functional,
... the part of the geta stilts moves with the big
... and just a decorative split/wedge where the toe
... it would get.

...re's an arm dagger design, thought I'd do a full
...der on it:

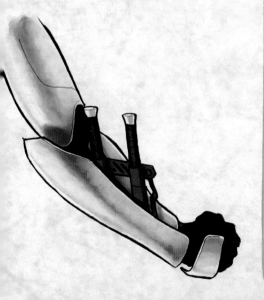

and the shoes:

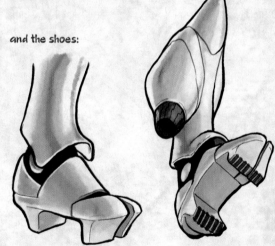

S.G: Looking at this new sketch, I know the geta clogs are historically accurate and the way you've incorporated both concepts here is really cool, but I can't shake the feeling it'll make Silver Samurai look a bit goofy. What say we keep the toe-split shoe but lose the clogs?

S.S: Ok! Hey no problem! Yeah, making them foldable/retractable was mentioned, they could pop out when needed in combat or something.

S.G: Great! Thanks a lot, Steve. I'd say we're ready to rock!

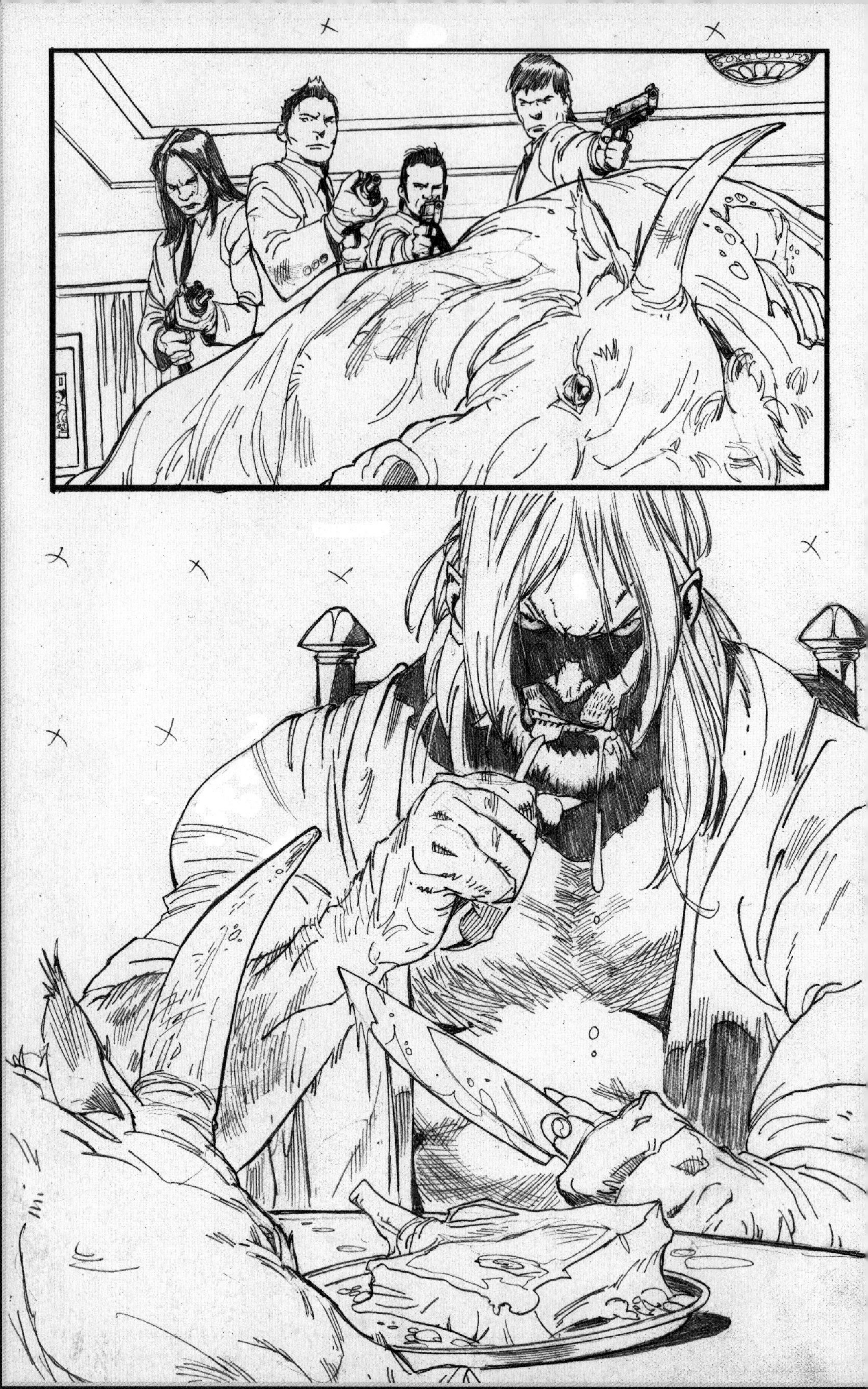

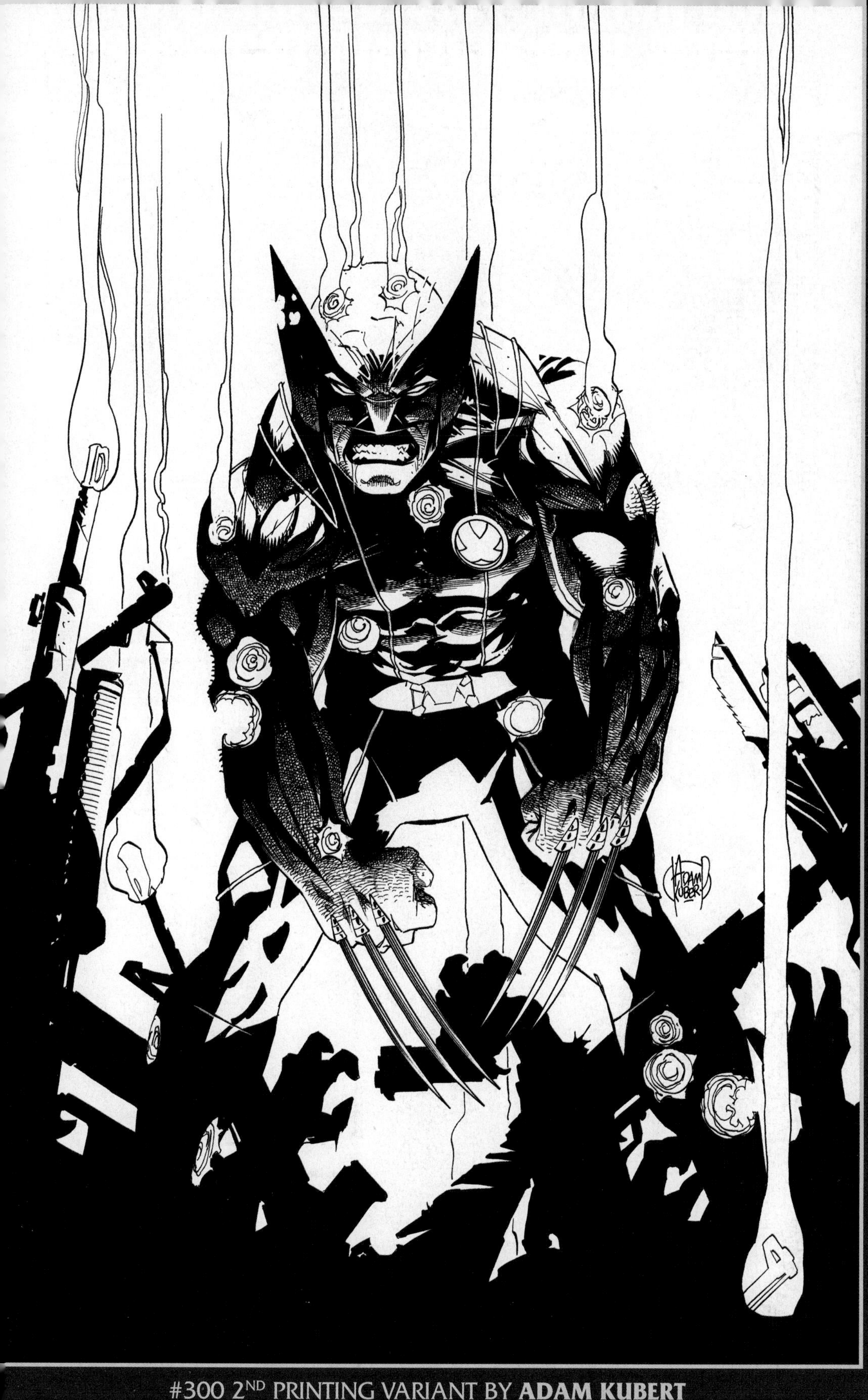
ADAM KUBERT

#300 2ND PRINTING VARIANT BY **ADAM KUBERT**

JASON AARON'S WOLVERINE IS MORE BRUTAL AND RIVETING THAN EVER!

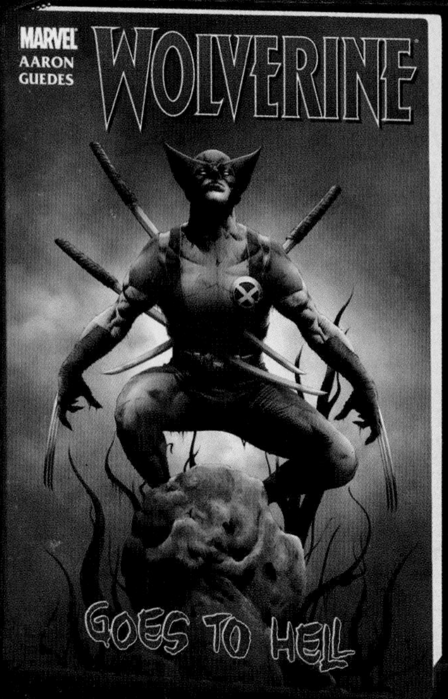
MARVEL
AARON
GUEDES
WOLVERINE
GOES TO HELL

WOLVERINE: WOLVERINE GOES TO HELL PREMIERE HC
978-0-7851-4784-8

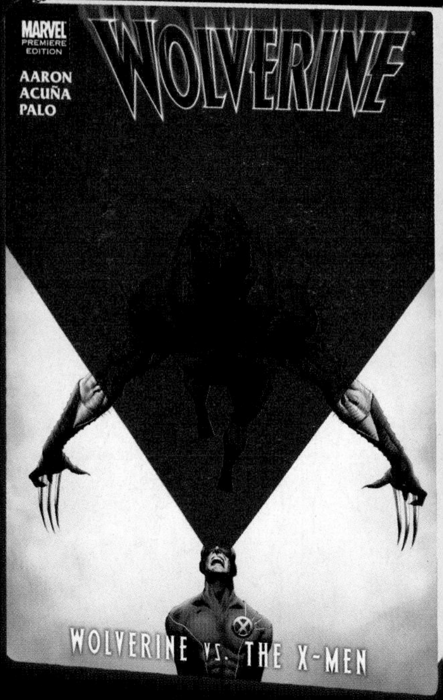
MARVEL
PREMIERE EDITION
AARON
ACUÑA
PALO
WOLVERINE
WOLVERINE VS. THE X-MEN

WOLVERINE: WOLVERINE VS. THE X-MEN PREMIERE HC
978-0-7851-4786-2

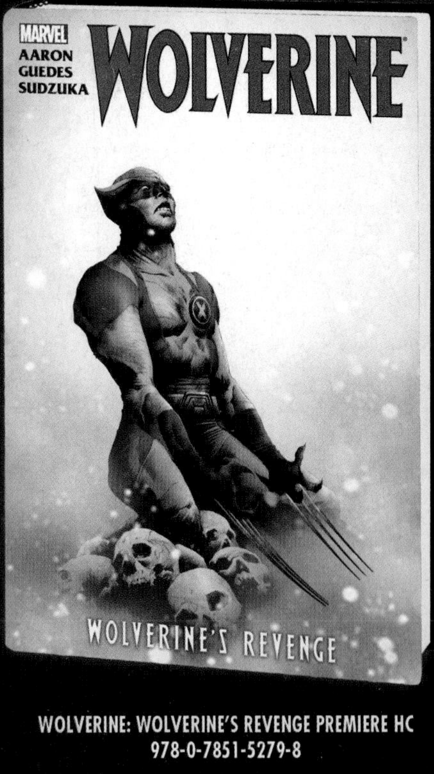
MARVEL
AARON
GUEDES
SUDZUKA
WOLVERINE
WOLVERINE'S REVENGE

WOLVERINE: WOLVERINE'S REVENGE PREMIERE HC
978-0-7851-5279-8

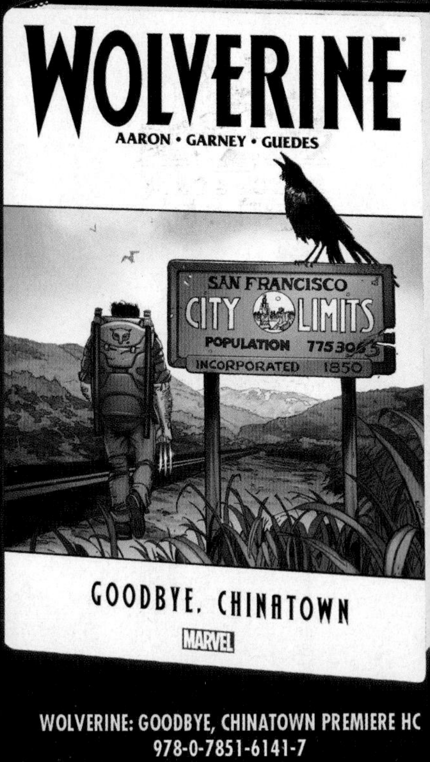
WOLVERINE
AARON • GARNEY • GUEDES
SAN FRANCISCO
CITY LIMITS
POPULATION
INCORPORATED 1850
GOODBYE, CHINATOWN
MARVEL

WOLVERINE: GOODBYE, CHINATOWN PREMIERE HC
978-0-7851-6141-7

On Sale Now

MARVEL